Conscious Contact

**Daily Meditations for the
Chemically Dependent**

Chemically Dependent Anonymous

Copyright © 2022
by

CDA COMMUNICATIONS INC.
GENERAL SERVICE OFFICE

The Twelve Steps and Twelve Traditions have been adapted with the permission of Alcoholics Anonymous World Services, Inc. (A.A.W.S).

Permission to adapt the Twelve Steps and Twelve Traditions does not mean that A.A.W.S. is affiliated with this program. A.A. is a program of recovery from alcohol only—use of A.A.'s Steps and Traditions or an adapted version of its Steps and Traditions in connection with programs and activities which are patterned after A.A., but which address other problems, or use in any other non-A.A. context, does not imply otherwise.

Library of Congress Catalog Number: 2006901776

ISBN 978-0-9778506-0-0

PRINTED IN THE UNITED STATES OF AMERICA
2006
REPRINTED 2008
THIRD PRINTING 2011
FOURTH PRINTING 2016
FIFTH PRINTING 2022

Dedication

We, as members of CDA, would like to dedicate this meditation book to all people in recovery from addiction to mood-changing and mind- altering chemicals—*past, present, and future*.

Inspired by our Higher Power, this book was written and produced exclusively by CDA members for the benefit of those who still suffer from chemical dependency, both in and out of our Fellowship.

CDA was established as an "inclusive" program of recovery rather than "exclusive." We are a bridge *between* fellowships, a 12-step approach that offers recovery to people who are addicted to any type of chemical substance. Our goal is to practice and demonstrate the spiritual principles of love, tolerance, and unity as found in our Twelve Steps and Twelve Traditions.

In Love and Service,

CDA Meditation Committee

The CDA Fellowship

Chemically Dependent Anonymous is a 12-step fellowship for anyone seeking freedom from drug and alcohol addiction. We of CDA do not make distinctions in the recovery process based on a particular substance. The basis of our program is abstinence from all mood-changing and mind-altering chemicals, including street-type drugs, alcohol and unnecessary medication.

The primary purpose of CDA as a whole is to remain clean and to help others like us gain recovery. By sharing our Experience, Strength and Hope with each other, we solve ourcommon problem and help others recover from chemical dependence which has made their lives unmanageable.

CDA is not affiliated with any political, religious, or commercial organizations or institutions.

CDA remains grateful to the co-founders and Fellowship of Alcoholics Anonymous for the Twelve Steps and Twelve Traditions which are the basis of our program.

January 1

The sky's the limit! ~In loving memory of Ron R.

Because of the *commitment* of the men and women who began our fellowship, we have seen our members overcome all types of obstacles. In CDA we consistently demonstrate the perseverance, willingness, and commitment it takes to turn around battered lives in ways we never thought possible. We become better spouses, parents, and friends; we can change or start new careers; we get out of debt; and we overcome other addictive behavioral or personal challenges. Our founders were not just *interested* in recovery; they were *committed* to it. They believed in themselves and in us. Because of this commitment we now can live fulfilling lives and see our dreams come true. Living the CDA way of life is not something we do when it's convenient. We carry CDA forward with no excuses, only results.

**With each day I make a new commitment
to our wonderful way of life.**

Through CDA, these people have been able to establish new lives for themselves, with a commitment not often found in others.
~*Chemically Dependent Anonymous* P XIV

January 2

If you judge, investigate. ~Seneca

HOW to work the Program is simple: Honesty, Open-mindedness, and Willingness to try. Yet so many of us had already made up our minds prior to attending even our first meeting that this program was not for us because_____(fill in the blank). We had not investigated CDA—we just knew it wasn't any good. We had *contempt* before we knew what we were talking about. Maybe we based our contempt on what others had said. Maybe we "knew" better because we had been to another 12-step program. That is not the HOW of recovery. Sadly, after we get to CDA, we may still fail to investigate people, places, and things before judging. How about that meeting we "know" we won't like? Or talking to that guy who is such a blowhard? By learning to be honest, open-minded, and willing, we allow ourselves to investigate options before snapping our mind shut. This simple concept is what keeps us growing each day the CDA way.

**I know HOW to approach this day:
Honestly, Open-mindedly, and Willingly.**

Honesty, Open-mindedness, and Willingness to Try. This is H.O.W. the Program works. With these qualities, we are on our way to recovery.
~Chemically Dependent Anonymous P 103

January 3

We faced three disturbing realizations: 1. We are powerless over our addiction and our lives are unmanageable; 2. Although we are not responsible for our disease, we are responsible for our recovery; 3. We can no longer blame people, places, and things for our addiction.
~Narcotics Anonymous P 15

Yikes, *WE* are the addicts! *WE* are responsible for our recovery, NOT the people we blamed for our addiction. We can blame them no longer. Yes, these are disturbing realizations. Who wants to look at themselves as the source of their problems when blaming the other guy means *that guy* must do something about it, not us? Yet, we learn that our recovery must be based on personal responsibility. The good news is we don't have to assume full responsibility forever—just for today. Taking responsibility for today is all that is required of us. At some point, these disturbing realizations are no longer disturbing.

**I am responsible for the actions
that support my recovery.**

My disease didn't arise out of a lack of parental love {...}. They helped give me something to return to when everything else around me had deteriorated.
~*Chemically Dependent Anonymous* P 204-205

January 4

Alcoholism comes to a person; a person doesn't go looking for it. ~Sister Maurice

It's a pretty safe bet that none of us woke up one fine morning and announced, "I think I'll become an addict today! I want to make my parents proud and impress my friends. Why don't I swing by the liquor store and pick up a 12-pack and then on the way home stop by the crack house and give them any money I have left?" Just like a heat-seeking missile, chemical dependency hunts us down, and we usually are not aware of just when the disease goes off inside us. But just because we didn't ask for this disease doesn't mean we get to pity ourselves. Who asks for cancer, diabetes, or multiple sclerosis? Unlike most other diseases, we actually have a choice in our recovery! Wow, what a blessing! So, instead of feeling sorry that this "terrible" disease found us, we ought to give thanks that such a glorious recovery hasfound us!

I turn my "dis-ease" to a sense of ease by giving thanks that recovery found me.

We believe that, for one reason or another, a force of a positive nature that we call our Higher Power guidedus here to CDA.
~*Chemically Dependent Anonymous* P 14

January 5

Excellence is an art won by training and habituation. We do not act rightly because we have virtue or excellence, but we rather have those because we have acted rightly. We are what we repeatedly do. Excellence, then, is not an act but a habit. ~Aristotle

The Steps don't know or care who works them. The Steps don't know or care how many times they are worked. Step Three doesn't discern, "Oh, this guy is special, he doesn't need me." Just as Step Four doesn't say, "This gal has got a great mind. She doesn't need to write down an inventory. Keeping it in her head will be fine." Members of CDA have learned that if you work the Steps, they *will* work. The only time they do not work is when you do not work them. So, we get into the habit of working our Steps by doing them in the manner suggested by our sponsors. *We are what we repeatedly do!* We ask ourselves, "What am I doing today that defines who I am?"

I work the Steps so they can work on me.

As we work the Steps, our spirits begin to heal and we develop a relationship with a higher power.
~*Chemically Dependent Anonymous* P 31

January 6

We can change our negative beliefs about life and whether we have the power to stop our pain and take care of ourselves. ~Melody Beattie

They tell us there are no victims, only volunteers. Yet, why does it so often *feel* like we are being victimized? This is because we have not yet learned to take responsibility for our own choices in recovery. When using, our disease chose for us. In early recovery our sponsor may have chosen for us. Today, we must choose for ourselves. If someone is being abusive with us, we have not yet chosen to take personal responsibility for how we allow others to treat us. If we always sit home alone, we have not yet chosen to be of service in the Program. If we suffer from feelings of depravation in our lives, it is because we have not yet chosen to let our Higher Power become our Employer. Our choices reflect our beliefs. Whether they are negative or positive is up to us.

**The choices I make today will
affect my tomorrows.**

{...} I used to think that a negative attitude would be there forever and that I had no way out of my depression or my moods. I know better now.
~Chemically Dependent Anonymous P 112

January 7

Happiness is produced not so much by great pieces of good fortune that seldom happen as by little advantages that occur every day.
~Benjamin Franklin

Happiness is not by chance, good luck, or dropped in our lap by winning the lotto. It is the by-product of an attitude coupled with action. This attitude comes because of our willingness to learn from the Fellowship, and the action comes when we apply what we learn. The attitude that creates happiness is expressed in the Prayer of Saint Francis. We seek to give ... not to receive, to serve ... not to be served, and to care ... not to be cared for. The actions that create those "little advantages" that produce happiness are reaching out to give, serving within the Fellowship, and caring for newcomers as they enter the rooms. When practicing the right attitude, coupled with the right action, we find that happiness is that certain something acquired while we're too busy to be miserable.

I seek to give rather than receive, to serve rather than be served, and to care for rather than be cared for.

What I've learned through all that's happened to me is that if I'm not spiritually fulfilled, I won't be happy.
~Chemically Dependent Anonymous P 227

January 8

Listen to guidance and follow the guidance given to your heart. Expect guidance to come in many forms; in dreams, in times of quiet solitude and in the words and deeds of wise elders and friends.
~The Sacred Tree

Many of us come into the rooms with a chip on our shoulders about God and especially about organized religion. Advice we hear includes borrow our God, use a doorknob, use the group, or wait and see; don't look for God—let God find you. As alcoholics and addicts, we have well-established track records of being untrustworthy and unreliable. However, in the matter of choosing a Higher Power that works for us, only we are trusted with that precious and awesome responsibility. We are not told to whom to pray, whose path to follow, or to what religion to subscribe. The freedom to choose a Higher Power that works for us is that vital act of accepting trust that frees us from the bonds of active addiction.

I am grateful for the gift of choice that gave me the God of my understanding.

As long as we remain willing and teachable, we will be able to accept this new way of living and our growth and success will be limited only by our imaginations.
~Chemically Dependent Anonymous P 93

January 9

Our whole attitude and outlook on life will change. ~Barbara S. Cole

The essence of all growth in CDA is a willingness to change for the better. We attain this willingness for change by working through the Steps which enables us to see our attitude and our perception on life transform. Newcomers ask us, "When does it get better?" We tell them, "It gets better when your behavior changes." Gradually, what newcomers *need* to do becomes what they *want* to do, and change becomes simple. In the new lives we create, we slowly shed the fear of the past and fear of the unknown while eagerly grasping the freedom that this program so generously offers. Our negative thoughts and ideas are replaced with positive ones. As a result of this, *we transform,* attaining the spiritual awakening that is needed to become the people we are meant to be.

My new outlook on life is mirrored, as I slowly become the person I always pretended to be.

Having had a spiritual awakening as a result of these Steps, we tried to carry this message to other chemically dependent persons and to practice these principles in all our affairs.
***~Chemically Dependent Anonymous* P 22**

January 10

Always be a first rate version of yourself, instead of a second-rate version of somebody else.
~Judy Garland

Each of us is an individual and there are as many ways to work the Program as there are those of us in recovery. It is one of the great gifts of our fellowship that we all suffer from the same disease, escape that disease following the same path, and yet retain our individuality with no leaders and no "laws." Each of us can recover *in the Fellowship* yet retain our own uniqueness. But we do not allow the uniqueness of our personal recovery to become so elaborate that it becomes our companion and ally, fostering the feeling that no one understands the complexity of *our* recovery. This wouldn't leave room for the healing powers of a caring sponsor and a safe circle of friends. We need them in our lives so that we *can find* our own path in recovery—through the unique experiences that others willingly share with us.

The special people who help me be a first-rate version of myself are easy to find. They are right in front of me; my Higher Power puts them there.

But even as our diversity makes us unique, our addiction makes us all one and the same.
~Chemically Dependent Anonymous **P 11**

January 11

Tain't worthwhile to wear a day all out before it comes. ~Sarah Orns Jewett

In recovery we often hear that we must clear away the wreckage of our past. A caveat to this in CDA is that we are told *not to* clear away the wreckage of our future! Why are we told to deal with the wreckage of our past but leave the future to itself? As addicts, we tend to worry needlessly when planning events because we're usually attempting to project the outcome as well. Projection of every possible negative result is living in the "wreckage" of that future. The "wreckage" we create in our minds is our imaginary future. The funny thing is, we can never live in that future, for it is always the present. Those who have not learned to stay in today make themselves sick over possible results that seldom come to be. When we remain in today and trust in the process, we can draw on our current strength and guidance. It is always now and always today. We barely have control over the time called "now." So, let's try and enjoy it!

I must be present to win.

As far back as I can remember, I always looked for a way to avoid the reality of living in the present moment. Life was scary and unpredictable and there was nothing solid to hang on to or believe in.
~Chemically Dependent Anonymous **P 273**

January 12

My Higher Power gives the best to me when I give my choice to Him. ~The Pocket Sponsor

We spiritually wake up to a bright shining light, delivered from past despair and darkness. We learn, through our Eleventh Step, to reach for our Higher Power and communicate *at the deepest level*. This becomes our shining light. In this communication (one of sharing and listening), we are guided through another day of recovery. We know that if we give our best to spirituality, His grace, love, and tolerance is given to us. But giving our best to God does not mean "thinking" about it, mouthing the words, or simply reading this meditation. Giving our best means asking for direction and then actually *taking that direction*. Giving our best is not a theory, it is an action. So, we ask ourselves this question, "Am I ready and willing to accept God's illuminated path by doing the footwork? Or am I still shining that tiny flashlight of self-will through the darkness?"

God gave me self-will and I choose to *will* that back to God.

And there are those who are conscious of a powerful or subtle spiritual experience. The light is let into the dark places within and the presence of God is felt.
~Chemically Dependent Anonymous P 43-44

January 13

When we do the best we can, we never know what miracle is wrought in our life, or in the life of another. ~Helen Keller

We want to learn to live our lives in such a way that when we die people will be sad, not relieved. As we practice the principles and do the next right thing, we may change lives in ways that we will never understand. We touch people without knowing who we have helped. And most of all, we help ourselves. Many people falter because they ask, "How do I know what my best is?" Our answer: "WWBBD. What Would Bob and Bill Do?" This is a powerful question. Bob and Bill worked the 12-step A.A. Program to the best of their ability on a daily basis. If we attend meetings, use a sponsor, and read our 12-step texts, we *will* know what they would do. If we are confused about something thrown our way, then we can use this question to determine what our spiritual answer would be: "WWBBD"

In confusing situations, I ask myself, "What would Bill and Bob do?" Then I do it.

Faith without works is dead. Working the Steps to the best of my ability is a major challenge.
***~Chemically Dependent Anonymous* P 247**

January 14

If you hate a person, you hate something in him that is part of yourself. What isn't part of ourselves doesn't disturb us. ~Hermann Hesse

Ah, yes! How many times have we come across someone who really rubs us the wrong way? We may even want to confront that person on their irritating traits—in the name of honesty, of course. Our arrogance tells us that a few well-chosen words *from us* will set them straight. Hopefully, we are reminded by our sponsor that we may want to discuss it with the person in the mirror before confronting the one who is rubbing us the wrong way. Frustrating as it may seem at the time, what bugs us the most in another so often reflects our own stuff. Once we examine the situation more carefully inside and out (theuncomfortableness *inside* us triggered by traits coming *out* in them), we may see our own character traits getting rubbed out.

I do not worry about rubbing out their character defects. I learn to rub out my own.

The image in the mirror slowly shakes its head. Yes, there has been change but surely it is not enough. Surely there could be more sincerity, greater risk-taking, deeper belief and less indulgence in character defects.
~Chemically Dependent Anonymous P 44

January 15

We can feel ourselves soften when we move our attention from self-defeating thoughts into our hearts, where love lives. ~Ruth Fishel

Sometimes it appears as if our thoughts were on the warpath, determined to attack us as if they were attempting to win some unnamed battle. Sometimes thoughts attack us when we wake in the middle of the night, unable to fall back asleep due to the war dance going on in our head. Our thoughts attack us when we hurl retorts back and forth rehearsing imaginary battles. We think, "If he says that, I'll say this ..." and "Next time, I'll say this to her ...." When the mind attacks our peace, a good way to defuse the energy is to focus on our hearts where love abides. Practicing this on a regular basis makes it easier to find peace when stress and conflict creep into our minds. The more often we practice the easier it becomes. Staying in negative thoughts creates unpleasant emotions. Moving into our hearts creates peace and, yes, we do deserve to feel peaceful!

When stress attacks, I become aware of my self-talk and move my focus to my heart instead.

After practicing meditation for some time, I came to the realization that my mind had begun to calm down.
~*Chemically Dependent Anonymous P 60*prendre

January 16

When many hundreds of people are able to say that the consciousness of the presence of God today is the most important fact of their lives, they present a powerful reason why one should have faith. ~Twenty-Four Hours a Day

As we go through the day, there are always littlethings reminding us of God's presence: a bird landing on a nearby branch to sing; the contented 'ribbit' of a happy frog; the smile of a stranger; a delicate flower drawing our attention in an otherwise busy landscape;the smell of a grove of pine trees; the clouds against abright blue sky drawing us away from the cares of the moment. The details we notice are an exclamation point to the wonders of God's world. When noticing them, we acknowledge how important a divinepresence is for us and we establish a conscious contact. What might we miss had we not discovered sobriety and the importance of spirituality in all that we see and do?

I establish contact with God by appreciating the divine details of sober living.

I'm beginning to notice things that I never paid attention to before. I see flowers blooming, I noticethe change in seasons, I realize that there's snow on the ground- all the things I've ignored all these years.
~Chemically Dependent Anonymous P 193

January 17

Many people are walking around wounded, caught up in the past and unable to make the changes that are needed to move forward.
~Rosemarie Rosetti

Many of us could be described as the walking wounded. Our pasts hold some mighty harsh realities that can appear to be deal breakers for a happy future. Some of us have killed others accidentally or by design; we have broken the hearts of our mothers; some of us abandoned our children or abused them. We have been the curse and cause of much pain in our families, and we have used and abused those closest to us. Yet, in the Program, we hear that "we will not regret the past nor wish to shut the door on it." How can this be? We are also told that to hide our past and lock it away is "self-centered and in direct conflict with our new way of living." When we work with others, we share our story with all the harsh realities that once made us the walking wounded. We are the walking warriors, using our past to save others. Let's not regret a past that can save lives!

**I do not regret my past, and thus,
I'm free to claim my future.**

Some of us look at Step Four with dread, believing it is that fateful time when we reveal all the ugliness in our past to someone else.
~Chemically Dependent Anonymous P 35

January 18

Life says yes to me now. ~Iyanla Vanzant

Eventually life says "yes" to all who dedicate themselves to our way of life in Chemically Dependent Anonymous. When we began this program as newcomers, the old-timers had many wise anecdotes and bits of advice for us. One of the things they told us was to imagine how good our life could ever get. "Get clean and sober," they told us, "and your life will get even better than what you just imagined." That might have been good enough for us, but they continued, "*Stay* clean and sober and it will get a hundred times better than that! But, on the otherhand," the old-timer's warned, "Imagine the very worst your life could be. Start drinking and drugging again and it will get *worse* than that and, before long, it will get even worse than that!" Whether life says "yes" to us now or "no" to us now is entirely based on our commitment to recovery.

**My actions today define the increase
above anything I can imagine.**

People who have more time than I in CDA say, "Keep coming back. It keeps getting better." But I can't imagine that my life could be any better than it is now.
~Chemically Dependent Anonymous P 194

January 19

Happiness is getting what we want, but success is wanting what we get. ~Ron R.

The challenge in our new way of life can be to remember that we were saved from our addictions by God and other people, not by intellect, muscle, or self-will. We are called to "give back" to our fellowship— not "race" to acquire creature comforts, status, and prestige. We must keep in mind that a symptom of our disease is one of imbalance, and that our newfound acquisitions can affect our priority system. Without the proper priorities we cannot be the successful people we have come to expect in recovery. Acquiring creature comforts and status must never take priority over our responsibilities to give back to the Fellowship. The good news is that we have a sponsor and home group that expect some accountability fromus. They help keep our priorities in balance. This way,when we do get the things we want, we will not only be happy, but we will be successful as well!

**My recovery is God's gift to me and
what I do with it is my gift to God.**

For instance, when a relationship or a job takes top priority, we can lose focus on what we've learnedabout honesty or humility. When that happens, we tend to slide into old behaviors.
***~Chemically Dependent Anonymous* P 64-65**

January 20

Masquerading as a normal person day after day is exhausting. ~Anonymous

When practicing our addictions, we went day after day acting as if we were fine and the world around us was crazy. Even though many of us worked each day, had families, and may have appeared as if we were pillars of our community, we still abused our drug of choice with abandon. We never realized we were only fooling ourselves by denying our shame and dependenceand acting "as if" all was well. Once we discovered recovery, we realized that our take on "normal" behavior was utterly abnormal. The masquerade we called "living" was actually a disease. The Second Step sets us free with its words, "Came to believe thata Power greater than ourselves could restore us to sanity." Working this Step each morning keeps us free from the bondage of addiction masquerading as our life.

Today I believe that a Power greater than me is my link to living in a sane and rational world.

{W}e came to believe that a Power greater than ourselves could restore us to sanity.
~*Chemically Dependent Anonymous* P 31

January 21

Where does the spirit live?
Inside or outside
Things remembered, made things,
Things unmade. ~Seamus Heaney

We pray in the morning to turn our will over to the God of our understanding. But if we take our will back, where can the Spirit of God live? We need to align our will to that of our Higher Power's, that is, the Spirit of God manifested within us. When we take back control of our will, the Spirit has no place to express Itself. Our sponsors tell us to pray and meditate in order to hear the voice of the Spirit that dwells within. We cannot take for granted that our Higher Power is working within us if we do not ask each day for that to happen. When we search for God, we turn to where the Spirit lives, and come to know that it lives *within* and works *throughout* us.

I allow the Spirit of God,
as I understand the Spirit, to
manifest in and through me.

...{W}e are developing a habit of self-examination, meditation and prayer that allows us to continue to grow in recovery and trusting God. Our spirit is awakened to the reality of God's abiding presence.
~Chemically Dependent Anonymous P 62

January 22

The past is but the beginning of a beginning, and all that is and has been, is but the twilight of the dawn. ~H.G. Wells

Each day is the beginning of our new life as we practice living it without the use of mind-affecting chemicals. We often hear, "Each day is a new beginning," and "Today is the first day of the rest of your life." Does this mean that we forget the past andit counts for naught? Maybe being chemically dependent and walking through a living hell was not the past we wanted to base our new beginning on each day, but our past was and continues to be the beginning of this beginning. Without our past, we could not embark on today in this way. It took every single bit of our past to turn us into the strong, dedicated people we are today. For most of us, most of the time we are pretty much in love with our new clean and sober beginnings.

Anytime I choose, I can begin today over again, making any past the beginning of a new beginning.

I recognize that my past is why I'm here today. Iaccept that I can't change the things I did because they were meant to be. Those past events brought medown so I could look inside.
~Chemically Dependent Anonymous P 197

January 23

Whenever a mind is simple, it is able to receive divine wisdom. ~Ralph Waldo Emerson

Many 12-step slogans and acronyms are not very politically correct like KISS—Keep It Simple Stupid. This can offend newcomers because they think they are being called "stupid." At a time when experts are frantic to build our self-esteem, this sounds inappropriate. But our recovery is based on facts, not pop psychology, and we find that the slogans are often wisdom written in shorthand. After all, how *smart* is it to analyze, justify, and rationalize ourselves into paralysis? That is just what happens when we get so smart that we begin to read between the lines, looking for what is *really* meant, rather than the simple words on the page. The politically correct can tweak the KISS acronym to: "Keep It Simple Smarty" or "Sweetheart" or "Keep It *Super* Simple." Yet, no matter how we say it, if we are not keeping it simple, then we *are* pretty stupid!

I keep it simple and surrender.

It was pop psychology time and I didn't have the foggiest notion of what was going on. I was dazed and confused, a walking contradiction —"partly truth and partly fiction," as I think a songwriter once wrote.
~*Chemically Dependent Anonymous* P 329

January 24

I don't think happiness is a remedy for unhappiness, like there, that was unhappy, now this is happy! ~Nigella Lawson

Our society emphasizes that we ought to be happy overall as a whole. Happiness is presented as the only "healthy" state of being. *You must be happy and that's it!* Life is not happy or unhappy in such a black and white manner. If we're not happy, society often insists that something must be wrong. Yet, unhappiness is not a symptom of sickness. Instead, being unhappy is an expression of life—a natural reaction to situations we don't like. It is a natural reaction to frustration, disappointments, unrequited love, and the bumps along the highway of life. It is *healthy* to be unhappy when life throws us curves. We mustn't take in the message to be unhappy about being unhappy. Only chronic and unexplained unhappiness needs to be viewed as if "something is wrong."

**When unhappy, I live with only
one unhappiness, not two. I refuse to be
unhappy about being unhappy.**

Throughout my using days I would always say, "I just want to be happy."
~*Chemically Dependent Anonymous* P 165

January 25

We too need to get over the questions that focus on the past and on the pain—"Why did this happen to me'" —and ask instead the question which opens doors to the future: "Now that this has happened, what shall I do about it?"
~Harold S. Kushner

Why him or her, why me, why now, why this way? "Why, why, why" is the loser's chant. The question "why" keeps us focused on explanations, not resolutions. Once we stop analyzing *why*, we can ask the question that carries the solution within itself. "What do I do now?" This question places our focus in the present so we can reclaim our life, not simply lament it. We have found that if the addict within can get us asking the wrong questions, it won't have to worry about our recovery-oriented answers! We learn to drop the questions that focus on blame and the past and to ask questions that contain the answers within the question such as, "What do I …?" and "How can I …?" We do not receive the right answer when we ask the wrong question.

I ask not "why" this or that has happened, but "how" to deal with it now.

We ask three questions: Am I paying attention to my spiritual needs? Am I passing on what I've received? Am I living the principles I've come to hold so dear?
***~Chemically Dependent Anonymous* P 68**

January 26

Just for today I shall be unafraid. Particularly, I shall be unafraid to be happy, to enjoy what is good, what is beautiful, and what is lovely in life.
~Father John Doe

In the 12-step programs, we learn that joy, peace, love, and happiness rightfully belong to us. Only fear stands between us and what is rightfully ours. If we work our Steps as directed, we *must* face our fears. Yet, we don't have to face them alone because we have a new Employer. And our Employer has a really good employee assistance program that we can take advantage of. It's called Chemically Dependent Anonymous. One of the greatest benefits of CDA is that no fear will be faced alone. Thus, we see that the Power behind us is far greater than the fear ahead of us. Additional fringe benefits of working for this new Employer are joy, peace, love, and happiness.

**I open myself up to
God's way of doing business.**

If we ask for help, and let God's plan, timing and will be ours, we can let go of our old ideas. Fear of the future will leave us.
~Chemically Dependent Anonymous P 96

January 27

Can I control my use of any form of mind or mood altering chemicals? Most addicts will see that control is impossible the moment it is suggested.
~Narcotics Anonymous P 19

In CDA we acknowledge our weakness regarding not just our drug of choice, but to all mind-altering and mood-changing chemicals. We have learned that, for us, abusing prescribed medications or the use of any other chemical is considered a relapse. At one time, we were all delusional about our ability to control the use of any mind-altering or mood-changing chemical. Often, coming into recovery, we try to maintain that delusion to some degree. Maybe we think we can join another program that only specifies one chemical so we can keep using others. Maybe we keep our physician in the dark about our addiction so he might prescribe something if we should decide we need it. Fortunately, CDA is our safe haven. CDA is a place where we can explore the delusion that we might be able to use something at some time for some reason.

"Recovery is recovery is recovery" can only be understood if I know a "drug is a drug is a drug."

{I} stopped taking any mood-altering substance, except for coffee. My "clean time" has just recently entered a phase which I dare call recovery.
~Chemically Dependent Anonymous P 167

January 28

You can either be a host of God or a hostage of your Ego. ~Wayne Dyer

Eventually we come to find out that we are three people:
- The person we want to be
- The person we don't want to be
- The person we are

Accepting ourselves for who we are isn't always easy. Sometimes, we are the person we imagine ourselves to be such as some spiritual guru that people in the Program are very impressed by. Sometimes, we act like the person we don't want to be such as some self-absorbed "me-me-me" character. Either way, we are the hostage of our ego that Dyer speaks of. It is only when we are simply and purely the person we are that we can be a host of God.

**Allowing myself to just be me,
I create the space for God to
work through me.**

I accept whatever you have to give me knowing that it will be what is best for me. Your guidance, your power and your love will meet my every need and will work through me to help others.
~Chemically Dependent Anonymous P 34

January 29

If you judge people, you have no time to love them. ~Mother Teresa

There are times when we hear people share in meetings and we don't agree with their ideas, or we believe they are misunderstanding the Program. Maybe they have "rules" about what sponsors are supposed to do. Maybe they think the Program tells us how and when we are allowed to date in recovery. Maybe they present their opinions as program "facts." When we hear things we don't think are program, we learn how not to judge them. We learn that the best form of correction is to become a living program by showing them through the power of example. When judging others, we block our thought process to love. Mother Teresa did not judge the poor, she fed them. CDA has taught us that we do not judge the poor in spirit, we nourish them.

I may be the best or only example of the CDA Program that a newcomer ever sees.

We are not judges. God is the only one who has a right to judge for He alone knows the workings of our minds.
~Chemically Dependent Anonymous P 73

January 30

Our troubles, we think are basically of our own making. ~Alcoholics Anonymous P 62

Sometimes it's just easier to make the world seem crazy than it is to just admit to our own insanity or character defects. It's the snide look on the cashier's face, not our own impatience. It's the slow waitress, not the fact that we didn't give ourselves enough time. It's the stupid county code, not the fact that we didn't bring our dog's pooper scooper to the park. We have a propensity for saying, "My mistake, *your* craziness," excusing our own actions while accusing others of the same type of behavior. Unfortunately, we do have the ability to make the world seem unbelievably crazy. We do this because we don't want to see that it is our own failings that are usually at the base of our annoyances and irritations.

I work Step Ten when things don't seem to go right. That way, I don't go in the wrong direction for too long.

As I grew increasingly more aware in my recovery—it was around the nine-month mark—I realized that there was a pattern in my life that was the source of my troubles.
~Chemically Dependent Anonymous P 36-37

January 31

Why am I so sad? Why am I so upset? I should put my hope in God ... ~ Psalm 43:5

Many of us came into the rooms of CDA carrying a heart full of lifelong pain. We may have sought therapy to relieve the suffering, religion to quiet our spirit, or a relationship to fix us and make the pain go away. These things didn't seem to work for long, if at all. We continued to drown our sorrows or self-medicate away the misery. It seldom occurred to us that the use of alcohol and drugs *might be the cause of the pain*, not the cure. It surely didn't occur to us that therapy, religion, or relationships were hopeless in our lives so long as we were using. We learn in Step Two that a God of our understanding is the solution and the hope that we seek. Chemicals themselves were the barrier between us and our Higher Power, and if they didn't actually start the pain, they surely prolonged it.

Mind-affecting, mood-altering chemicals and unnecessary medications are not the solution to my problems. They *are* the problems.

The pain that tore at our souls is transformed into a message of serenity, courage and wisdom.
~*Chemically Dependent Anonymous* P 68

February 1

Laugh and the Fellowship laughs with you. Cry and the Fellowship won't let you cry alone.
~Shelly M.

When we were using, by default, we ruled ourselves out of so many possibilities. Our options became fewer and fewer. Playfulness and laughter practically vanished from our lives. At first, mind-affecting chemicals made us laugh; although they quickly robbed us of the very joy we sought by taking them. In coming to CDA, we began to get well, and we enjoyed a giggle here and a chuckle there. Sometimes people tell their stories and the whole audience laughs in glee at the silly antics of what we did while in the grips of the disease or have done even in active recovery. In A.A., they tell us that "cheerfulness and laughter make for usefulness" (*Alcoholics Anonymous* P 132). Laughter does become part of the equation again. The Program and the Fellowship have given us the ability to laugh again. So, give back to the Fellowship by allowing your laughter to arise from deep within.

**The Fellowship tells me,
"Laugh like you mean it," and I do.**

When people were at the meetings, they were laughing from their hearts. I liked that.
~Chemically Dependent Anonymous P 346

February 2

People are lonely because they build walls instead of bridges. ~Joseph Fort Newton

Lonely and alone are not the same thing. You can be alone without being lonely, and you can be lonely in a crowd of people. We come to trust in the Fellowship. We learn that none of us need ever be lonely again— so long as *we choose not to be*. The old-timers tell us that we get lonely when we build walls instead of doorways, or barricades instead of bridges. Building walls and barricades *is a choice*; therefore, loneliness is a choice. In times of trouble, and in times of stress, we can choose to open ourselves up or we can choose to erect a barrier. "Opening the door" and "building the bridge" means we needn't be lonely, even when alone. Opening doors and building bridges involves allowing ourselves to be vulnerable by attending meetings, introducing ourselves to people, picking up the phone, working with our sponsor, doing service work, and praying to our Higher Power.

Being alone does not mean that I am lonely.

You can get through anything just as I did. And you'll never have to do any of it alone.
~Chemically Dependent Anonymous P 311

February 3

We're all unique in our ability to share love with one another. ~Mike R.

Many times, an individual neglects the responsibility of service and sponsorship in helping a new member solely because they are not an attractive personality. The newcomer, having arrived from skid row, may act obnoxiously, dress poorly, or smell badly. More often, however, the newcomer's religious, financial, or social status is simply incongruous with our own. Love, on the other hand, would dictate that we give to all, irrespective of such circumstances. We come into the Program as irresponsible people, and we do not become responsible overnight. We strive for the perfect objective—that of loving the skid-row bum, the pimply-faced adolescent with attitude, and the woman with infected needle marks on her arms—but we often fall short. Even when we can't muster loving feelings, we reach out anyway and claim progress. We continue our quest for unconditional love by accepting our responsibility to the newcomer.

I reach out to every newcomer, not just the socially acceptable newcomers.

I must do for the newcomer what was done for me when I came in.
~Chemically Dependent Anonymous P 151-152

February 4

We shall not cease from exploration
And the end of all our exploring
Will be to arrive where we started
And know the place for the first time. ~T.S. Elliot

Vigilance is the catalyst that fuels recovery. It creates the ability to observe and keep moving forward even when we aren't sure where the path leads. We must be watchful of the actions of others and follow their example when it works. We must also be alert to avoid the pitfalls that have impeded our fellow travelers. We must be aware of our inner guidance and turn to it when our intuition beckons. We must explore our new life with intent. For this is being vigilant. It pushes us to do our recovery work when inattention and negligence might otherwise hinder our growth. Vigilance is the driving force behind our exploration in recovery, so that every day we may know recovery for the first time.

**My recovery is not a destination.
It is a vigilant journey.**

I'm new at it but I think this is the most exciting adventure I've ever been on.
~*Chemically Dependent Anonymous* P 339

February 5

It ain't what they call you; it's what you answer to.
~W.C. Fields

We all know about the SASTOs *(Some Are Sicker Than Others)* and the SAWTOs *(Some Are Weller Than Others)* in the Program. The problem is that we aren't smart enough to predict which is which. It's been said, "Never bet on a drunk either way: to achieve sobriety or fail to grasp it." Seeing a newcomer, we might smirk, "Oh, she's just here to flirt with the guys. She'll never make it." Thirty years later, however, that same woman may be leading a spiritual retreat that we are attending. Perhaps because we are in such awe of how "spiritual" a man seems, we put him on a pedestal next to Bob S., Bill W., or Ron R., only to be 12-stepping him next month. Our job is not to predict who are the SASTOs or the SAWTOs. Our job is to be here whenever anyone, anywhere reaches out for help.

Anyone in the Program may call me a SASTO, just as long as I answer as a SAWTO.

Who would ever have believed that anyone as sick as I was at that time would become part of something so beautiful, an organization that has helped so many people?
~Chemically Dependent Anonymous P 308

February 6

Freedom from fear comes through love; may the beloved's blessing reign with all hearts!
~Nan C. Merrill

Most of us arrive at the doors of Chemically Dependent Anonymous full of fear and anxiety. We felt like we were in the darkroom where negatives were developed. How wonderful it is to be given the tools of recovery that enable us to stand in the sunlight of the Spirit, face our fears, and turn them into something positive. The love we discover in the Fellowship and from our Higher Power is the key to facing our fears. Yet, we don't go automatically from "full of fear" to "full of love." It is a process through which we allow others to be filled with love. We practice the principles of the Program and feel love. We do service for our home group, and we feel greater love. We work with others, and the love overflows. Who of us can live in fear when our lives are overflowing with love?

**When I am full of love, there is
no room for fear to develop.**

I have everything I need now and almost everything I want. I have peace of mind. I have love. I care about all of <u>you</u>.
~Chemically Dependent Anonymous P 271

February 7

*Stop judging others and you will not be judged.
For others will treat you as you treat them.*
~Matthew 7:1-2

We cannot afford the luxury of resentments, this we know. But one of the things that we fail to recognize is that resentments are created because we *judge* someone or something to be wrong. Without judging another to be wrong, we would not have resentments! We are told in Chemically Dependent Anonymous to stay focused on our side of the street and avoid attempts at correcting and judging the wrongs of others. After all, are we such great students of human relations that we can honestly assess situations that are causing us emotional upset? When we judge and resent, then sadly, we will treat the ones we resent accordingly—and it isn't with loving kindness! If we don't want to be judged or resented by others, and then treated badly, we need to *not* do it ourselves. We need to remember that breaking the cycle starts with us.

**I change the way I treat others before
I question the way God treats me.**

{W}e have the opportunity to let go of blame, examine our own emotions and attitudes, and take responsibility for our part.
~Chemically Dependent Anonymous P 40

February 8

Almost always, if I measure my decision carefully by the yardsticks of absolute honesty, absolute unselfishness, absolute purity, and absolute love, and it checks up pretty well with those four, then my answer can't be very far out of the way.
~Dr. Bob

The Twelve Steps and Twelve Traditions werefounded on the Four Absolutes. These Absolutes are the principles taught in the Oxford Movement (an early Christian group attended by the A.A. founders). A good spiritual exercise is to meditate on them and consider how they add to our decisions:

1. <u>Absolute Honesty</u>: Both with ourselves and with others, in word, deed, and thought;
2. <u>Absolute Unselfishness</u>: To be willing wherever possible to help others in need;
3. <u>Absolute Love</u>: To love God with our whole heart, mind, and soul, and to love our neighbors as ourselves; and,
4. <u>Absolute Purity</u>: Integrity and clarity of mind, of body, and of purpose.

I memorize the four absolutes and measure my decisions against their wisdom.

So we obey the spiritual principles of our program in both our personal and group lives.
~Chemically Dependent Anonymous P 81

February 9

There is nothing we can't handle together, you, me and God. ~Margo T.

One striking thing about the Twelve Steps is that they begin with the word "we." It's neither "you," nor "I," not even "they." It is *we,* for *we* do this program together. How wonderful a feeling it is to know that we are not alone any longer. What a beautiful concept to be in a fellowship where we work together as equals. We are not preached to by someone pointing a finger and saying, "You have to do thus and such." Nor are we left to our own devices by having to determine for ourselves, "I must do thus and such." The joy of the Fellowship is that *we* work together, hand in hand with one another and with a Higher Power of our own understanding. Let us always remember, there is nothing that you, I, and God cannot handle with the power of *we*.

I alone can do it, but I can't do it alone.

We've been there and we know the pain and suffering caused by this disease.
~*Chemically Dependent Anonymous* P 97

February 10

Some days you're the windshield, some days you're the bug. ~Mary Chapin Carpenter

Having the option to make different choices, when meeting the situations in our daily lives, is what makes recovery interesting. Some days we are on top of everything that rears its ugly head, feeling cheered on by our Higher Power. Other days, we are under the covers unable to peek into the light of day. Some days we are the shining ones who inspire others and, at times, it is others who must drag us out of our misery and to a meeting. No matter what the situation though, if we face it honestly, incorporating what we have learned from our home group, from literature, and from our sponsor, we can progress to a greater understanding of ourselves and others. From this, we can appreciate that we are neither the windshield nor the bug, but the guy with the squeegee.

Being my best self enables me to clean the bugs off the windshield. It is the reward for all the "work" I do.

I've come to love life and to face it daily, however difficult, non-chemically. Isn't that great?
~Chemically Dependent Anonymous P 338

February 11

Don't compromise yourself. You are all you've got. ~Janice Joplin

At a 12-step conference a speaker got a good laugh with this line, "You no longer need to punish, deceive, or compromise yourself, unless you want to stay employed." We laugh, but for some of us this may still be true. However, part of the integrity that we learn in CDA is that we no longer need to compromise ourselves for anything. Not for a job, not for a partner, not for approval. Addiction robbed us of our true selves. It hijacked our integrity and made us do things that deep down we didn't believe were right. Recovery halts the necessity of negotiating our values in order to keep going. Why? Because the God of our understanding has values that we live by. If we compromise *our values*, by default we are compromising *God's*. That is not what the Great Reality wants for us in our life. If something demands we compromise our morals and values, then God hasn't guided us there. We must find another way.

I need not compromise myself because where God guides ... He provides.

Our ability to deal with life on a daily basis was compromised.
~*Chemically Dependent Anonymous* P 25

February 12

I'm trying to free your mind, Neo. I can only open the door. You're the one who has to walk through it. ~Morpheus, The Matrix

In the midst of our addiction, we told ourselves, "This time it will be different." But every time it was predictably the same. We thought we could beat our addiction like Wiley Coyote always thought he could catch the Roadrunner. We tried every manner of idiotic behavior to control our use and deny our powerlessness, but we found ourselves getting beaten down like a cartoon character and scrambling back for more. Our minds were closed to the truth. It wasn't until we "freed our mind" and surrendered to our addiction that we had any chance of catching the Roadrunner in our life. No matter how long we stay substance free, our Wiley Coyote of denial lurks just around the corner. That is, unless we keep the door to CDA open and "walk through it."

The more I walk through the CDA door, the fewer Roadrunners I try to catch.

However difficult this admission, it opens the door to a new way of life.
~Chemically Dependent Anonymous P 26

February 13

If your life ended tomorrow, what would you regret not doing? If this were the last day of your life, would you spend it the way you're spending today? ~Oprah Winfrey

Once we stop creating trauma and drama in our lives, which is a direct result of practicing principles, our daily life can take on an air of calmness that may seem dull. We sometimes arrive at a point in recovery where we feel stagnant. We strove for so long to get chemical free, which is now the basis and pivotal point of our lives. In the beginning, getting and staying clean was traumatic, dramatic, and took a great deal of our energy. Once we don't have be on high alert at all times, we may find ourselves asking, "Is this all there is?" The answer is, "No, it's not." At our own pace, we add unfamiliar activities, face different challenges, make additional friends, and take new directions without letting go of our principles. We decide what the regrets would be if we died tomorrow, and we add them to our activities list today.

I do not forget to really enjoy myself because this moment is about to be over.

Recovery has more to offer me than simply being chemical free. This spiritual path gives my life meaning, purpose and joy.
~Chemically Dependent Anonymous P 60

February 14

The Supreme act of forgiveness is when you can forgive yourself for all the wounds you've created in your own life. Forgiveness is an act of self-love. When you forgive yourself, self-acceptance begins and self-love grows. ~Don Miquel Ruiz

During our active addiction we did not know self-forgiveness. We lived in guilt, shame, and denial—all of which prevented us from truly loving ourselves or anyone around us. When we come into recovery most of us are feeling hopeless, helpless, and ready to give up. Then we find love, support, and friendship here in the rooms. If we continue to attend meetings, share our thoughts and feelings (both good and bad), and pray to our Higher Power, in addition to having found a sponsor and begun working the Steps, we gradually learn to forgive ourselves for our behavior during active addiction. By forgiving ourselves we begin to love ourselves. The world then becomes a more beautiful place in which to live.

I accept the Fellowship loving me as I begin forgiving and thoroughly loving myself.

We are acting out of the love our Higher Power gives us, not beating ourselves up.
~Chemically Dependent Anonymous P 36

February 15

Opportunity is missed by most people because it is dressed in overalls and looks like work.
~Thomas A. Edison

Everybody, Somebody, Anybody, and Nobody. There was a meeting that needed to be opened on Monday nights. Everybody thought Somebody would do it. Anybody could have done it, but Nobody did it. Somebody got angry because it was Everybody's responsibility. Everybody said Anybody could do it, but Nobody realized Everybody wouldn't do it. It ended up that Everybody blamed Somebody when Nobody opened the meeting, even though Everybody knew that Anybody could have done it. The newcomer wondered where Everybody was, because Somebody told him that Anybody at the meeting would talk to him, except Nobody was there.

I take every opportunity to serve so that when anyone, anywhere reaches out for help, someone will be there.

Each CDA group has a set of elected officers. These individuals are trusted servants of the members. They carry out the groups' responsibilities.
~Chemically Dependent Anonymous P 72

February 16

Unless I accept life completely on life's terms, I cannot be happy. I need to concentrate not so much on what needs to be changed in this world, as to what needs to be changed in me and my attitudes. ~Dr. Paul O.

Our relationships with husbands, wives, and children; our extended family and friends; and our employers, employees, and co-workers are those that cause us the most pain in the world. Why? Because we want them to do things *our way*, live according to *our standards*, and do what *we think is right*. Rather than accept that others might have their own way of doing things, their own standards, and live by what they think is right, we judge them as being wrong if they don't do what we have in mind. Many a sponsor has seen a sponsee struggling with the inability to accept what is going on in their life. One of the first questions they ask is, "Who is not doing things your way today?"

By accepting life on life's terms, I can accept the people in my life on *their* terms, and find happiness.

Am I willing to accept my mistakes and the mistakes of others as part of being human?
~Chemically Dependent Anonymous P 38

February 17

Surrender means saying, "Okay, God I'll do whatever you want." Faith in the God of our recovery means we trust that, eventually, we'll like doing that. ~Melody Beattie

We surrender to win, not to whine. Beginners often find that "God's will" is not exactly how they thought they wanted to live. In the beginning, many of us were only doing God's will because we *had to,* not because *we wanted to*. Who wanted to put away chairs after a meeting when they could be in the parking lot flirting? Who wanted to 12-step someone at three in the morning when they had to get up early for work? Who wanted to pay back large sums of money when the victim might never find us? The wonderful thing about CDA, though, is that eventually we surrender to God's will because *we want to*! And let us always remember that the quality of our recovery is proportional to the quality of our surrender.

**I *must do* God's will until I
want to do God's will.**

The next step forward is to surrender ourselves to that power. However, most of us find control difficult to surrender.
~*Chemically Dependent Anonymous* P 31

February 18

Be the change you want to see in the world.
~Mahatma Gandhi

How often have we participated in lengthy debates about the evils of our society? Liberals bash conservatives about being "greedy," and conservatives bash liberals about "crippling" productive citizens. In recovery, the same type of discussion continues, with NA debating the usefulness of terms like "sobriety," A.A. debating exactly how much one can mention the word drugs in a meeting, and CDA deliberating about how open "open" should be. In the meantime, life goes on despite the "evils" of society, and people recover despite the language used in meetings. This is because the answers don't come through discussion, they come through experience. What works, stays; and what doesn't, goes. So, the answers to the great debates will only come as we become the answers we want to see in our world.

**I do not demand that others change to suit me.
I become the change I want to see.**

He started calling me all the time to tell me what was happening with his life and I saw a miraculous change take place in him.
~Chemically Dependent Anonymous P 263

February 19

No person is your friend who demands your silence, or denies your right to grow.
~Alice Walker

Friendship has an uncanny way of reflecting back to us who and what we really are. Our friends become a window into our character by which we can see ourselves through the eyes of others. Hopefully, we surround ourselves with those who reflect love, compassion, and honesty. When we don't, we must take stock of who we allow into our lives. This may include letting go of people who were important to us at one time. Do our friends challenge our image of ourselves? Do they make us take an honest look at who we are and how we are growing? Does their character reflect the character we want to see in ourselves? Or do they let us get complacent in our recovery by remaining silent? We need *to hear* our friends when they lovingly tell us we are straying off the path. They also need to *hear us* when we do the same.

I honor myself and my friends when I allow myself to see myself through their eyes. I "listen" to their reflection of me.

But he {my friend} said something to me that really caused me to hit my emotional bottom that night. "You know something?" he told me. "You think you're better than everybody else."
~Chemically Dependent Anonymous P 265

February 20

Both read the Bible day and night,
But thou read's black where I read white.
~William Blake

The old-timers' experiences have left us a great legacy in recovery. They told us the Twelve Steps are a simple program for complicated people. It's a simple program because the instructions are clear and concise. We're complicated people because we have a peculiar knack for reading between the lines and viewing ourselves as the exception to these simple suggestions. Because of this tendency, old-timers gave us these four questions by which we can learn to be true to our higher self:

1. Is it true or false?
2. How will it affect the other person?
3. Will it be part of the solution or part of the problem?
4. Is it right or wrong?

I make my CDA program really simple.
I take the book out and *read the black parts*.

It's very simple—so simple that I almost didn't make it. But I had, and still have, today, a desire for a new way of life.
~Chemically Dependent Anonymous P 130

February 21

As human beings, our greatness lays not so much in being able to remake the world ... as in being able to remake ourselves.
~Mahatma Gandhi

Our duty in living a clean, sober lifestyle is self-improvement. This can be attained by doing meritorious and moral actions as exemplified in the Twelve Steps. Most people seek to remake themselves in a material sense: increasing bank accounts, gaining social status, seeking fame, and improving appearances. In recovery, however, we have little interest in self-improvement regarding our socioeconomic condition. We strive instead for a spiritual self-improvement. The irony of this is that when we improve our spirit and live a meritorious and moral life, we receive material compensation in great measure! Remaking ourselves is not only a blessing to us, it also becomes a blessing to our families and communities as well.

I don't worry about remaking the world, my community, or my family. I remake myself.

{S}taying clean and sober, becoming honest and clear, having strong relationships, contributing to the community—they are simply manifestations of this powerful, life giving process of transformation.
***~Chemically Dependent Anonymous* P 63-64**

February 22

Before spiritual awakening ... work Steps, make coffee, carry the message. After spiritual awakening ... keep working Steps, keep making coffee, keep carrying the message.
~Zen for the Twelve Steps

Some spiritual experiences are the profound, "white-light, Bill W." type, but more commonly, people in the 12-step programs experience a gentler, gradual awakening. If we have the more common gradual awakening, how will we know if and when we've had the spiritual experience spoken of in the Twelfth Step? Our members report these types of indicators as hallmarks of the spiritual experience: a newfound ability to live and let live coupled with frequent attacks of smiling; a new awareness of being connected with others, nature, and a Higher Power coupled with unexpected episodes of deep appreciation; anger is no longer our first response; we lose interest in taking the inventory of those around us; and we also find ourselves loving others without any hidden agenda.

**I woke up this morning clean and sober.
That's my spiritual awakening.**

This experience was the beginning of my spiritual awakening. I finally became ready to start admitting that I had a problem with alcohol and drugs.
~Chemically Dependent Anonymous P 336

February 23

Being defeated is often a temporary condition. Giving up is what makes it permanent.
~Marilyn vos Savant

When we have a goal, we have a reason to get out of bed in the morning and to perform activities. When we fail to reach our goals, we may want to throw the blankets over our head and hide. When our goals are unrealistic (*I can sponsor twenty-five people at a time*), self-serving (*I want to be a famous circuit speaker*) or keep-up-with-the-Jones' type (*I'll host a retreat in my back yard*), those goals will probably end in failure and then we feel defeated. Defeat, however, isn't forever. We learn to reevaluate and bring our goals in line with our reality and our principles. Our newfound, Higher-Powered intuition can tell us what to do, what not to do, when to proceed, and what goals fit the principles by which we now live. We don't give up: we reevaluate.

Have I changed my goals to meet my principles or my principles to meet my goals?

I am pleased and honored to humbly but enthusiastically endorse and recommend the goals of Chemically Dependent Anonymous and the means that fellowship recommends to achieve those goals.
~*Chemically Dependent Anonymous* P XVII

February 24

Seeing ourselves in the aura of Grace, we will not be deceived by pride, but will ever humbly expect and get all things from the hands of an all loving God. ~Father John Doe

Of course, pride in and of itself is not bad. We ought to be proud of the good we do, our accomplishments, and the joy we bring into the lives of others. We even ought to be proud of our recovery. It is *false* pride, however, that is the deceiver. False pride tells us that we are better than others, that our solutions are the best, and that our opinions are "right." False pride tells us we know why others slip, and that we know what the group conscience should be. The old saying "Pride goeth before a fall" is true. When false pride deceives us, we will fall. But through prayer and meditation, we also know that we can find God's grace again. Prayer and meditation is the direct line that keeps pride from running our lives.

**There but for the grace of God,
goes my false pride.**

We must always remain a group of equals helping equals to attain sobriety through the grace of their Higher Power.
~Chemically Dependent Anonymous P 79

February 25

Sometimes we had to search fearlessly, but he was there. He was as much a fact as we were, we found the Great Reality deep down within us.
~Alcoholics Anonymous P 55

In recovery, we begin the search for our own Great Reality, even if we don't believe in organized religion or doctrine. Sometimes we do believe, but it is rather fuzzy and ill-defined. Sometimes our beliefs are not mainstream but more metaphysical or Zen in nature. Some of us are atheists and prefer to look in areas of science rather than the esoteric. No one can tell us what we believe or *should* believe. We instinctively know there is a Power greater than us, and our job is to define it for ourselves. Defining our Great Reality is a sacred task that is innately private and protected. Our search will sometimes go quickly, most times slowly, but eventually we must define our personal, private, and plentiful Great Reality.

**I don't need to *find* my Great Reality; He isn't lost.
My job is to *define* this Reality so
It works in my life.**

We have accepted the higher power concept and have begun to depend on this God to give us more love and the ability to continue to grow in open- mindedness.
~Chemically Dependent Anonymous P 92

February 26

Sometimes I go about pitying myself, and all along, my soul is being blown by great winds across the sky. ~Ojibway Saying

"Self-pity" is an all too familiar trap for many of us. It was exploited liberally in our using days. Yet now we see self-pity in an altogether different light. Is it really so horrible that we are chemically dependent and have found this great new way of life? Is it so horrible that we lost our job, but now have another, more terrific job as a result? Often, what we thought was the worst turn of events had a silver lining that brought us something wonderful. Self-pity is just another way of saying that we aren't getting our own way; it is throwing a temper tantrum with God. Since we can't see the larger picture, we need to have faith that God has our best interest in mind, even if we aren't immediately aware that our "soul is being blown by great winds across the sky."

**There's my plan and there's God's plan.
When I trust God's plan, the unfulfilled details
of my plan don't lead to self-pity.**

Am I consumed with self-pity when life is not as I wish?
~Chemically Dependent Anonymous P 38

February 27

God speaks in the language you know best — not through your ears but through your circumstances.
~Oswald Chambers

Do you think your recovery is an accident? That is like saying the fact that you are on earth is an accident. Sobriety is *never* an accident and once sober, we learn to live life on purpose, not by accident. We know that we are here for a reason, just as we know that each of you is reading this page, at this time, for a reason. Our disease, our recovery, and our present circumstances have a purpose, and they become our Higher Power's way of presenting His will to us. Our job is to meet these circumstances by practicing the principles we learn in the Twelve Steps and the Twelve Traditions. *That is God's will.* Our circumstances may be outside of our control, but the way we respond to them is not.

**The circumstances of my life are my
Higher Power's way of talking to me.
My responses show Him how well I listen.**

Even though I could not have recognized it for what it was at the time I know now that his adopting me was one of the circumstances that led to my being in Chemically Dependent Anonymous today.
~*Chemically Dependent Anonymous* P 314

February 28

Every day is a day when we must carry the vision of God's will into all our activities.
~Alcoholics Anonymous P 85

The "20/20 vision plan:" There is a simple vision plan we tell newcomers about when they are having a difficult time "seeing" what our program is all about. If they wonder why we have another 12-step program, why they need Steps, or why they need to share, we can suggest the 20/20 plan. We tell them, "Come to the meetings twenty minutes before they start and stay twenty minutes after they are over to SEE what happens." In fact, this plan is also useful for old-timers who are having difficulty "seeing" why they need to keep going to meetings. This 20/20 vision plan is so simple, and yet, it never fails to give us a brand-new perspective on our program, as well as our role within the Fellowship.

Situations don't change so much as my perception of them.

Not until I attended my first CDA meeting did I realize just how much I needed that program. I needed to be somewhere around people I could sit down with and talk about how it felt to do drugs.
~Chemically Dependent Anonymous P 146

February 29

Gratitude makes sense of our past, brings peace for today and creates a vision for tomorrow.
~Melody Beattie

Getting clean and sober is no picnic. Initially, there doesn't appear to be much to appreciate. Everything we do is laborious and very, very challenging. We soon realize, however, that challenges are opportunities in disguise. And for that we feel grateful. We are able to show our gratitude for such challenges:

- Each new twenty-four hours
- Each of our successes or failures
- Adversity through which we garner strength
- Dependence that brings us independence
- Our past that brought us this present

Let us remain grateful amid all our challenges, for it is because of life's challenges that we continue to grow.

When I am grate-full, I am grace-filled.

I want to convey this message to everyone reading this book: There is much in your life to be grateful for, just as there has been in mine.
~Chemically Dependent Anonymous P 205

March 1

You must go within or you go without.
~Friendship with God

Most people want a lot of "things" in the material world such as a beautiful home, a hot car, the perfect partner, and so on. Material well-being, we come to realize in CDA, always follows spiritual progress, never precedes it. The principles teach us that when our priorities lay with our spirituality and our integrity, all else falls into place. Many of us have thought that if we had abundance in material possessions, we would naturally be spiritual. But if we are not spiritual without them, what makes us think that gaining material possessions will add one wit to our spiritual progress? It is spiritual substance not material wealth that will cause the increase. Acquiring spiritual substance is cultivated by going within. The manner in which we cultivate our inner garden will ripen on the outside. We reap, as a by-product of the inner cultivation, all that we ever desired without.

When I seek inner spirituality over materiality, material gain usually follows.

We have found it absolutely necessary to separate the material from the spiritual, allowing nothing to divert us from our spiritual goal.
~Chemically Dependent Anonymous P 76

March 2

Problems call forth our courage and our wisdom; indeed they create our courage and our wisdom. It is only because of problems that we grow mentally and spiritually. ~M. Scott Peck

At one time, we didn't want to feel the pain or deal with the problems of our life, so we just simply didn't. We were irresponsible and selfish. We went about our business ignoring the serious issues, expecting others to fix things. Or, better yet, we blamed the problem entirely on another person which, of course, we believed absolved us from handling it. In 12-step recovery, we learn it's not only okay to face our problems, but *necessary* if we want to live a happy, joyous, and free life. Whether we are sober or not, life has problems. We face our issues and our problems by working through them using the tools of theProgram. What we find is the courage and wisdom to do what we must do. Our newfound wisdom will continually grow as we courageously confront new problems as they arise.

I will never have a problem that is worse than the old solution I found for it.

I'm dealing with my problems and I'm walking through them. I'm also dealing with the good times and walking through those.
~Chemically Dependent Anonymous P 227

March 3

Our hearts were made for God and they will not rest until they rest with God. ~St. Augustine

When we were using, we traveled through life like a ship without a rudder. If we went to one party, we spent the night thinking about what was happening at another party. We might have made plans to do something positive, but then our addiction called to us, and we made a change of plans. We usually had no clear path in work, love, or friendship. It was an exhausting existence to constantly be seeking something—something that we may not have even been able to name. In recovery we cannot say this. Our path is clearly laid out in Chemically Dependent Anonymous' First Edition. It is a twenty-four-hour plan based on a connection with our Higher Power. That something that we once sought after was God—the God of our understanding.

I rest, secure in the knowledge that my Higher Power has a plan for me, and that path is clearly covered in the First Edition.

The Twelve Steps are what Father Al G. once described as: "A master plan for living more accurately the Master's plan for living."
~Chemically Dependent Anonymous P XVI

March 4

And each heart is whispering, "Home, home at last!" ~Thomas Hood

Finding the similarities with the addict in the chair next to us was not usually our first choice upon entering the rooms of recovery. We wanted to be different, not like "them." Maybe we snorted coke, and they did painpills. Perhaps we drank every day, and they smoked pot. If we think we are unique then we think we don't belong, and sadly, the disease wins. The inner addict tries to divide and conquer by pointing out any differences it can find so that we will go back out and use. Yet, even if our minds don't listen, our hearts do. Our hearts listen to a fellow addict in a way that our minds cannot understand. When we are seated in a CDA meeting, listening with our hearts, we realize that we now are around people who "get us." We finally feel like we "fit in." We are home. We are home.

It is my heart that hears the message of recovery. Today, I choose to listen to my heart and not the addict in my head.

Our minds are warped into denial and sick thinking that support our continued use.
***~Chemically Dependent Anonymous* P 24**

March 5

Happiness can only be felt if you don't set conditions. ~Arthur Rubinstein

There will always be some group members who want to set their conditions on others—so that everyone works the Steps and traditions, runs the meetings, and practices sponsorship as per *their* interpretation of recovery. It gets messy when one member gets stuck on rules of what can and can't be said in meetings, read in meetings, and how the meetings are to be run. In this environment the group conscience is not the director, they are. We find that these people, although passionate, are not usually happy. How happy can a person be when all their energy is devoted to enforcing 12-step rules, *as interpreted by them*? CDA was founded on the principle of inclusiveness, not exclusiveness. CDA's spiritual richness derives from combining the spiritual concepts of each of its member's views.

**I carry the message,
not the mess, to my group.**

CDA is an extraordinary organization in that there are no rules governing individual membership and no requirements imposed on groups by our Area Assembly or Intergroups.
***~Chemically Dependent Anonymous* P 80**

March 6

If you stop doing the things that keep you in the program, you will go back to doing the things that brought you to the program.
~The Pocket Sponsor

"We do recover, but we are never cured," is often heard in our fellowship. Even those who have only attended a couple of meetings realize that it is not a secret that we must continuously work a program of recovery. That is why after Steps One through Three, collectively called the surrender Steps, and Steps Four through Nine, also known as the action Steps, that we find the wondrous maintenance Steps Ten through Twelve. It is in doing our Tenth Step with eternal vigilance that ensures us that we continue to do the work of the action Steps. Step Eleven keeps our direction in alignment with our Higher Power, and Step Twelve is where we share what we have learned in the other eleven Steps. Eternal vigilance carries a small price tag compared to the price we paid when using. We know, only all too well, that being clean and sober won't keep us clean and sober.

I keep doing what keeps me here.

Just because I've been clean and sober for awhile, I can't expect to live happily ever after by simply not doing what I did before I came into the Program.
~Chemically Dependent Anonymous P 272

March 7

Insanity: doing the same thing over and over again and expecting different results.
~Albert Einstein

Albert Einstein was a very wise man and his quote is one we use often in the 12-step Fellowships. But there are many things we must do *over and over* again in order to get it through our thick heads. It's not that we expect different results—we just expect any results! For instance, we have to read recovery literature and meditations over and over so recovery principles will sink into our very being. We must go to meetings over and over in order to bolster our support and continue to grow. We must call our sponsor over and over so that we "get" what it is they need to teach us. "Over and over" again isn't bad when we use repetition to support ourselves and grow in recovery. It is healthy when it supports the results we want, but repetition is insane when we keep getting results we *don't want*.

I do what I can, let go of what I can't, and leave the results to my Higher Power.

That is the insanity of this disease—that I did the same thing over and over and over and expected different results every single time. The results were always the same and always devastating.
~Chemically Dependent Anonymous P 219

March 8

There is only one key, and it is called willingness.
~Twelve Steps and Twelve Traditions

Releasing our reservations about recovery is the first step to finding the keys to our own personal kingdom. And releasing our reservations is called "willingness." None of us can claim true willingness, however, if we place conditions on what we are willing to accept in recovery. Our Higher Power may want us to delve deeper into our character than we want to or do types of service work that we don't like. It is acceptance of where we came from, where we are going, and what God's will is for us—acceptance *without reservation*—that becomes true willingness. Willingness opens many doors in a strong recovery. It is of no use to accept God's will in our lives if we reserve the right not to accept what we don't like! Strength lies within willingness. Self-will lies in the reservations.

I set my reservations aside, fully accepting God's will, so that my "willingness" is not actually "self-willingness."

If I had only been willing to change my lifestyle, I could have had a life worth living so much sooner.
*~**Chemically Dependent Anonymous** P 333*

March 9

This life's five windows of the soul,
distorts the Heavens from pole to pole,
and leads you to believe a lie,
When you see with, not thro', the eye.
~William Blake

It is said that love is blind, and along those same lines, we recognize that "hate is blind," "fear is blind," and "anger is blind," as well. Intense emotions obscure our sight and distort what is actually before us. Our perceptions become distorted, and we suffer from a type of "mind-blindness." When we see through the eyes of hate, we see enemies. When we see through the eyes of fear, we see danger. When we see through the eyes of anger, we see conflict. When we look *through* our *eyes* and not *with* our emotions, we stand a chance of seeing the bona fide reality. Our sponsors have the job of acting as our seeing-eye dog so that we may navigate these intense, distorted emotions. They help us see through life's "blind spots."

I do not allow my mind-blindness to keep me from seeing my spiritual possibilities.

I was completely blind to life {...}. I had no principles and no values. But those in the Fellowship loved me until I was able to establish some principles and values.
~Chemically Dependent Anonymous P 340

March 10

Men are disturbed not by things, but by the views which they take of them. ~Epictetus

Life is about ten percent of what happens to us and about ninety percent of how we react to it. Knowing that, it is easy to see that if all our reactions are cast in a positive light, then only about ten percent of our world can ever be "dark." How can we do this? The answer is a simple one: We need to see the glass half full as compared to half empty. Pollyanna received a gift of crutches instead of a doll. She could have been sad that she didn't get a doll, but instead she was happy because she didn't need to use the crutches. Let's not be bummed that we don't make more money, but rather be grateful that we have a job. Let's not be unhappy because our partner isn't perfect. How about being grateful that someone loves us, warts and all? We choose the way in which we see the world.

I don't have a problem unless I think I do.

I remember someone sharing that he had felt like such a loser and had no hope that the future would be any better. But after coming into CDA, all his problems had become challenges.
~Chemically Dependent Anonymous P 129

March 11

Living in Fellowship: Perhaps nothing else exists that can so completely multiply all our joys and divide all our grief. ~Day By Day

In Russian, the word for "share" means literally "to divide." Thus, it is no surprise that Russians in the Fellowship innately understand that to share with others means to divide our burden. Each time we share a trouble, we leave another little piece of the weight of our burden at the meeting or with another person in the Fellowship. This has several unexpected benefits for all. We allow others to practice the principles by reaching out to us, someone else might be experiencing the same burden and benefit from the discussion, and newcomers see firsthand how it works. So, from the Russian language we learn to share (divide) our burden and lighten our load. Thus, we understand the European Proverb that *shared joy is doubled joy; shared sorrow is half the sorrow.*

**My problems shared are
my problems halved.**

One man there spoke of his guilt about the way he's stolen from his mother {...}. When I shared, I related the remorse I felt about my mom in my early recovery. And I saw a little of the pain leave his eyes.
~Chemically Dependent Anonymous **P 108**

March 12

Sobriety often brings us effects we never expected, like becoming the person we used to resent. ~The Pocket Sponsor

Yes, many of us probably resented those people who lived decent lives. Sometimes we pretended we were living decent lives ourselves, but almost certainly we felt deep down inside that we were fakes. Other times we thought of ourselves as rebels or eccentrics, and we laughed at the straight world. But again, "me thinks he doth protest too much" because our higher self knew we were only acting the part, and we did a darn poor job of acting, as well. There always was an element in us that wanted to be reputable, creditable, and respectable. We may come into recovery to stop using mind-affecting chemicals, but we gain much more than that. We become the person we *said* we resented.

**If I don't change, I will use.
If I don't use, I will change.**

A change has taken place, one so fundamental that it will not yield to pain, doubt or denial. Whether one likes it or not, the change in self is here to stay.
~Chemically Dependent Anonymous P 63

March 13

> {T}he Realm of the Spirit is broad, roomy, all inclusive; {...}. When, therefore, we speak to you of God, we mean your own conception of God.
> ~Alcoholics Anonymous P 46-47

God, *as we understand him*, is such a beautiful concept. CDA does not have a preset description of our Higher Power, instead, we are free to choose our own spiritual source—be it God, Group, or Goodness. Chemically Dependent Anonymous holds fast to the precept of utilizing, as a foundation for recovery, a power greater than ourselves and *of our own understanding* as discussed in A.A.'s Big Book and CDA's First Edition. Our concept of God is not etched in concrete, but dynamic, flowing, and flexible as we grow and learn spiritual principles. For instance, God, used as an acronym, has been viewed by many of us at one time or another as: Get Out Devil; Group Of Druggies; Group Of Drunks; Giver Of Desires; Give Over Decisions; Great OutDoors; and Good Orderly Direction.

**What is my concept of a Higher Power?
It's a GOD thing.**

> The only thing remaining to do before we begin to delve into our former lives is open our hearts and minds to the concept of a higher power.
> **~Chemically Dependent Anonymous P 92**

March 14

If you haven't got anything nice to say about anybody, come sit next to me.
~Alice Roosevelt Longworth

When we were using, we often talked about people in negative ways behind their backs. Gossip was just a part of our daily life. Many of us were intolerant of the differences between ourselves and others. Even if we didn't talk behind other people's backs, we may have abrasively said unkind things directly to their faces! Once we begin working the Steps, the time arrives when we realize people are only doing the best they can, *just like us*. In CDA, we are a diverse group of people seeking recovery. At times, each of us falls short. Instead of taking others' inventories, both in and out of the Program, we would do better to focus on helping them up when they are down and rejoicing in their triumphs when they are on top of the world!

The only time I should be looking down on another is when I'm helping them up.

Obvious social and sometimes moral issues arise when such a diverse group of addicted people gathers in the CDA setting.
~Chemically Dependent Anonymous P 11

March 15

Anybody tell you today that they love you?
~Allen B.

Having destroyed much of our lives, we come to the Program as outcasts. We hit a hard bottom and wind up in CDA. How baffling to see so many people reach their hands out and offer us their help. This, for many of us, is the first time we witness unconditional love. It seems these people love us no matter what our past. As time goes on, we get in relationships with others in the Program that become very special. These can be relationships with sponsors, sponsees, or simply fellow members with whom we've formed special bonds. No matter how much time we have, we continue to talk openly about where we are and what we've done. We share emotions, get things off our mind, and don't hide skeletons in the closet. People we trust can offer advice or simply listen. This ability to be open is a very special gift. It's also howwe stay clean and sober for long periods of time. In fact, it is considered selfish and self-centered *not* to share on this level in order to help others.

Today, I will tell someone I love them.

I never thought I'd find people like myself but CDA is open to all addictive people{…}. Their love is what kept me alive for the first month.
~Chemically Dependent Anonymous P 197

March 16

The cure for boredom is curiosity. There is no cure for curiosity. ~Ellen Parr

Sometimes we find ourselves bored with recovery. We go to the same meetings and hear the same people say the same things. We may consider not going to meetings at all because we could be doing something else. This is a time when we need to make some changes. We can go to different meetings, get involved in service work, or find a sick newcomer and sponsor them. Finding out how the Fellowship is organized is also a good way to fight boredom in recovery. Starting a new meeting or taking meetings into rehabs and institutions are also ways to get excited again. The message is: *Get out of self*. We need to look around and see where we can give back. It doesn't even need to be in the rooms of recovery. We can get involved in our own communities, which could lead us in completely new directions. Before we know it, we will wonder how we ever could have said we were "bored."

Today, I look for ways to become curious about my recovery.

Having institution commitments is a Godsend especially when I've been feeling a little down.
~Chemically Dependent Anonymous P 108

March 17

And living and letting live contributes a great deal to sanity. ~Father John Doe

To live and let live, we have to get past surviving. "Surviving" is a desperate place where no energy is left for enrichment and self-nourishment. "Living" is when we finally learn to be good to ourselves, and truly enjoy what life on planet Earth has to offer. "Letting live" is the ability to allow others to nourish themselves without our direction. What a concept! Letting others make their own decisions *without our direction.* This is a form of true love; the unconditional type that so many of us strive to obtain. Until recovery, most of us never learned to really live life; we were only interested in surviving. Learning to live was the beginning stages of recovery. When we finally learn to *let live*, we truly begin to incorporate what our spiritual path is all about—love and service to others.

**When I live and let live,
I teach myself to love.**

We must now begin to take care of ourselves if we are to survive and grow in recovery. The Program provides us with the tools and the support necessary for us to become 'real people.'
~Chemically Dependent Anonymous P 77

March 18

The question is, how far down the rabbit hole do you want to go? ~What the Bleep do we Know?

Going down the rabbit hole is a metaphor for losing control. At one time, that loss of control meant being on psychedelics or drunk out of our minds. Today, our rabbit holes are character defects. When we lose our temper, are perpetually late, shamelessly criticize, or quick to condemn, we are falling down a rabbit hole. We know we are falling but knowing is not enough. Even thinking we won't fall again is not enough. If *having* the right thoughts were enough, we wouldn't need CDA. Few of us had a shortage of good thoughts when it came to controlling the use of drugs. And yet, when that craving hit, our minds cleverly found a handy excuse to use "just one more time." Then, down the rabbit hole we went. Ultimately, we see that our very best thoughts can't save us. Instead, we find it is only our very best *actions* that will keep us out of the rabbit hole. Recovery has little to do with thinking or theories; it is our actions that count.

**I don't think myself into right action.
I act myself into right thinking.**

I started to build a pathway of program action and that opened up the world for me.
~Chemically Dependent Anonymous P 235

March 19

When the student is ready, the master appears.
~Buddhist Proverb

Coming out of our drug fog makes it very hard to hear the message. Initially, we only half listen and use a few of the suggestions. This can be due to a variety of reasons ranging from confusion, prideful thinking, fear, or feeling overwhelmed. Some of us have thoughts that even doing half of a Step would be a mighty tall order. Some of us are concerned about opening old wounds and sharing them with another person. However, once we are finally ready to move forward, doors begin to open. Suddenly we find teachers everywhere. Every meeting we attend seems to speak directly to us, each page we read in our book addresses our situation, and our sponsor is magically "right on" in everything he or she tells us. We know we are ready when we are "in the zone" of recovery and everything flows—when nothing flows, we simply are not yet ready.

If I'm not ready to learn, CDA members can't say anything right. If I'm ready to learn, they can't say anything wrong.

Look the person in the mirror directly in the eye. Is the readiness there—all the willingness that can be mustered?
~*Chemically Dependent Anonymous* P 46

March 20

The people who gather are a tribe not of blood, but of spirit, for all are born into it. We are bound together by our desire to live in peace, to be in the cathedral of nature, and to heal ourselves through union with the earthly mother and heavenly father.
~Rainbow Gathering Flyer

In CDA we are truly a tribe, not of blood, but of spirit. Upon finding the Fellowship, it isn't "me" and "you" anymore, is it? It's "we" and "us." Twelve-step groups say that this is a "we" program, not a "me" program—and that means we are a family. Just look at our Steps. They all say, "We admitted" or "We came to believe." Doing it together makes us stronger and less likely to fool ourselves with dysfunctional ways of thinking. Many people say, "Our mind is a dangerous neighborhood to be in alone." But together we can become the "neighborhood block watch!" So, don't let your mind get the better of you. Turn that "m" in "me" upside down (just as we are asked to *turn it over*) and make a "we" out of that "me."

I may not have it all together, BUT together *WE* have it all!

But even as our diversity makes us unique, our addiction makes us all one and the same. In CDA, the emphasis is placed on this common ground.
~Chemically Dependent Anonymous P 11

March 21

We tried to carry the message—for it is in giving that we receive. ~Father John Doe

When we "carry the message," we are giving back what was so freely given to us. This is one of the maintenets and purposes for the Fellowship. This important principle is covered in Step Twelve and Tradition Five. But notice in Step Twelve that it is written "*tried* to carry," not "carried" the message! *Trying* to carry our message is all we ever need do, because it is not within our power to get anyone drunk *or* to keep them sober. Yet *trying* is not confined to 12-step calls and sponsoring new members. In CDA, "carrying the message" includes living clean and sober, keeping meetings open, voting in our home group, and living a meritorious life. So, it is not just a matter of carrying the message, but rather, it is amatter of living the message! Then, by living the message, we become the message.

Sometimes I carry the message.
Sometimes I am the message.

Newcomers and sponsees are put in our paths for many reasons, some of which we never know. This Step says that we only try to carry the message. The outcome of these encounters is always left to God.
~*Chemically Dependent Anonymous* P 67

March 22

Experience is the only teacher that gives the test first and the lesson later.
~Collection of Eastern Wisdom Philosophy

How many times have people tried to console us by saying something like, "Well, at least you learned a good lesson?" This *is* a good way to frame a not-so-happy event in our lives—if we actually learn from it. Yet, if we console ourselves by saying "good lesson learned" and then moronically turn around and do it again, the lesson isn't getting through to us. Maybe we lost a job because of chronic tardiness. If we learned the lesson, we'd get to work on time with the new job. If we didn't learn, then we'd find new excuses for being late. Have we gotten ourselves into debt with uncontrolled spending? If we accrue credit card debt again even after refinancing the house, then we probably didn't learn the lesson. In recovery we don't let experience be something we get only *after* we need it.

**I not only share my experience with others,
I share it with myself as well.**

One of the things I learned was that out of all bad can come good, if we're willing to recognize the ways to make that happen.
***~Chemically Dependent Anonymous* P 226**

March 23

The only place you can find success before work is in the dictionary. ~May V. Smith

"Bring the body and the mind will follow" is something we tell the newcomer often. What we mean by it is that if they keep coming back *and* stay chemical-free, soon enough their mind will clear up. Eventually, the newcomer will begin to understand that to truly recover they must *do the work*, not sit aroundand expect the Program to magically *work for them*. There is a distinction between the Program workingfor someone and someone working the Program. The next time a newcomer says, "The Program isn't working for me," we can agree with them. We can tell them, "The only people who stay sober are the ones who *work the Program*, not the ones who wait for the Program to work for them." We tell the newcomer to bring their body to more meetings until they get it!

I teach the newcomer that when they work the Program hard, life is easy. When they work the Program easy, life is hard.

...{I} had really tried to work the Program this time. Even though I had gone back out so many timesbefore, I was now clean and sober.
~Chemically Dependent Anonymous P 235

March 24

Sometimes it's best to use my teeth as a grill for my tongue. ~Joann M.

When using, everything was a reaction—usually an instant one and usually a bad one! If the other person said mean things, we would say meaner things back. If someone on the phone hung up on us, we might return the favor by calling back ten times just to hang up on them. It's a lot easier to react than it is to think. Part of our new way of life is practicing *rational* thinking. When the behavior of another catches us by surprise, we pause—think—take a deep breath—and act, *if necessary*, or perhaps not act at all. Sometimes it is better to do nothing than it is to react. Our action might include prayer, calling our sponsor, taking a walk, or attending a meeting. What it doesn't include is reacting willy-nilly to the world around us, hurting others because we are hurt, or lashing out before we pause and think it through.

When caught off guard, I take a moment to make contact with my Higher Power, so that I can *act*, rather than *react* to the world around me.

Of course, I reacted immaturely and, as a direct result, both my best friend and I were subsequently released from active duty and honorably discharged.
~*Chemically Dependent Anonymous* P 242

March 25

Whether one believes in a religion or not, and whether one believes in rebirth or not, there isn't anyone who doesn't appreciate kindness and compassion. ~Dalai Lama

Most of us arrived at 12-step recovery without expecting much compassion and kindness. Many of us thought we might be humiliated into abstinence or perhaps something worse. More than one of us has been shocked by the loving embrace of compassion and the words of kindness that we had long ago chased from our lives. These acts of love are most often what kept us around long enough to "get it." Therefore, it is imperative that when newcomers arrive, even straight from the crack house stinking to high heaven, we show them compassion. We match their belligerence with kind and patient words, their confusion with understanding, and their disdain with love. We help clean them up, find them a seat, and give them a hug. This is our way.

I give my gift away.

{G}od can still use this beaten-up, tired shell of a man to help someone else in recovery, to be of service to someone in need, to encourage the less fortunate, or to pray for a brother's salvation.
~Chemically Dependent Anonymous P 248

March 26

Most folks are about as happy as they make up their minds to be. ~Abraham Lincoln

In A.A.'s Big Book it says, "*We insist on being happy.*" So why do so many of us insist on being sourpusses? We really don't have forever to start enjoying this life. Whatever amount of time we wasted abusing ourselves in the past is over. We learn how to free ourselves from the firm grip of our past in the first three Steps. In the next six Steps, we learn how to stop abusing ourselves and others. We learn how to enjoy living in the present in the last three Steps. So, at this point in our recovery, if any of us are notexperiencing an abundance of true joy—*what are WE waiting for*? "Be happy—don't worry," as the songgoes. And let's not forget, if we have happiness in our hearts, we need to notify our faces. If we aren't feelingjoy, then we need to notify our sponsor. What are we waiting for?

**Happy memories never wear out.
I create one today.**

And that was how recovery started for me. I found people who were happy and content with smiles on their faces. And I said, "I want that, too."
~*Chemically Dependent Anonymous* P 267

March 27

Never forget that God is able to lift you from fatigue of despair to the buoyancy of hope, and transform dark and desolate valleys into sunlit paths of inner peace. ~Martin Luther King, Jr.

Unfortunately, people sometimes forget what God, the Higher Power of our own understanding, means in our lives. We forget how God works in our lives, how God feels in our lives, and how God manifests in our lives. We struggle so hard to get clean and sober, and then we sometimes forget how we got from there to here. We might even begin to take credit for things that manifested from a divine source and begin to think it was *us* who created this wonderful miracle. This is why having a conscious contact with our Higher Power is so important—so that we do not forget how God works, feels, and manifests. We remember: Our program will work for people who believe in God. Our program will work for people who don't believe in God. Our program will not work for people who believe they are God.

I know that it is me who creates the expression, but it is God who creates the face.

But I was miserable because I thought that I had all the answers.
~Chemically Dependent Anonymous P 322

March 28

Half measures availed us nothing.
~Alcoholics Anonymous P 59

Half measures do not avail us half, they avail us nothing. That's why they tell people in halfway houses that they must work a full program—not a halfway program. If we find ourselves restless, irritable, and discontent, *and* we think we are working a full program, *then* we are probably not working it to the best of our ability. Working a full program does not mean that we take one inventory and that suffices for the rest of our lives. As we read Step Ten, we realize it suggests that each of us needs to continuously take our own inventory, and when wrong, we need to make it right. "Half measures" means stopping halfway, while "full measures" means deeply integrating Step Ten into our lives. The Program teaches us that if we are to be happy, joyous, and free, we need to work the Program one hundred percent.

I understand there are no shortcuts.

As time goes on, we are reminded once more that: Half measures availed us nothing. Testing the waters is all well and good for a time but sooner or later we have to dive in.
~Chemically Dependent Anonymous P 33

March 29

Pain is the price we pay for being alive.
~Harold S. Kushner

No one promised us a rose garden when we stopped using mind-affecting and mood-altering chemicals. Yet, many of us feel betrayed when life's common tragedies strike: loss of a loved one, loss of a job, or a chronic illness. We wonder how this can be happening to us—after all, aren't we clean and sober now? Getting clean and sober does not mean we are somehow rewarded through the absence of pain or the continual challenges that life brings to every living person on the planet. Pain, as well as all of life's challenges, are life—*normal life*. We all feel pain when life's normal losses catch up with us. The thing we don't want to do is turn life's normal pain into horrible, intense suffering—a drama that addicts are good at. We remember that although pain is mandatory, suffering is optional.

**The world has not singled me out for pain.
The world has singled me out for progress.**

My life is not about pain anymore. It's about challenges, not problems.
~Chemically Dependent Anonymous **P 340**

March 30

If one is out of touch with oneself, then one cannot touch others. ~Anne Morrow

At times, we all get out of touch with ourselves. We may get hung up on what we ought to be, what we were supposed to be, or what we want to be. You canguess what the result is. When focusing on the "ought-to-be," "supposed-to-be," and the "want-to-be" thoughts, we have no time to be ourselves. If we can'tbe ourselves, then we can't see ourselves. If we can't see ourselves, then there is no way we can help others to see themselves. The cornerstone of our recovery is the ability to get honest and finally see ourselves as we really are, and not focus on the "ought-to-be," "supposed-to-be," and "want-to-be" thoughts. Staying in touch with whom and what we *really* are allows us to continue to effectively reach outto others. Today, and every day, we take the time to get in touch with ourselves.

I spend more time with myself than with anyone else. It makes sense to stay in touch.

Through the people who cared for me, and the God who, I know, loves me, I have been able to get to know myself.
~Chemically Dependent Anonymous P 130

March 31

When I am restless, irritable, and discontent, I'm wishing, wanting, or worrying. ~Billie M.

The most natural states for the chemically dependent person are being restless, irritable, and discontent. We come from a world where we always wished things could be different from what they were. We wanted what we could not have, worried incessantly about what we had done in the past or
obsessed about what might or might not happen in the future. What dissatisfied creatures we are when left to our own devices! So how do we neutralize the "wishing, wanting, and worrying" that is so characteristic of our unhealthy selves? It's called "BE HERE NOW." If you are *Being* who you really are, you're not wishing for something else. If you are *Here* in the moment, you won't want to be elsewhere. If you stay with what's going on *Now*, you can't worry about yesterday or tomorrow.

When I am being here now, I can't be wishing, wanting, and worrying.

The Steps allowed me to let go of my past and stop living in it.
~*Chemically Dependent Anonymous* P 235

April 1

If you have a problem, you have a choice: You can either take care of the problem now, or suffer longer and <u>still</u> take care of the problem later.
~Doug Kelly

Either way we choose to tackle the problem, we find that eventually *we will* have to take care of the problem. Time heals all wounds, but it does not solve all problems. The tricky thing about problems in our lives is that they usually do not disappear on their own. They usually require action on our part. When we procrastinate solving a problem, it makes the problem grow larger—like putting off paying taxes. When we ignore a problem, such as an unhappy spouse, it poisons us inside. When we blame others for our problems, we assume the role of the victim and empower our victimizer. After some time in recovery, most of us find that addressing our problems as soon as possible is the easier, softer way.

**By sharing my problem at meetings,
I make the solution bigger than the problem.**

By sharing our Experience, Strength, and Hope with each other, we solve our common problem and help others recover from chemical dependence which has made their lives unmanageable.
~Chemically Dependent Anonymous P 3

April 2

Nothing in the world is as important to me as my own sobriety. Everything I have, my whole life, depends on that one thing. ~Twenty-Four Hours a Day

By keeping our recovery first, we have a greater chance of maintaining the emotional balance we need to address the daily affairs of life. Without emotional balance, we become irritable, unreasonable, and discontent without even realizing what is happening to us. There are times when our focus wanders and we put employment before sobriety, dating before sobriety, or our egos before sobriety. When we place more importance on something instead of our recovery, we are unable to do the work that supports a clean and sober lifestyle. Let's face it, we put our efforts where our priorities are. All we need to do is look at what our life is revolving around, and we will easily see where our priorities lie. To keep recovery first, we must put a dedicated effort into our spiritual condition every day, one day at a time. Whenwe want to know what our priorities are, we can look at where we spend our energy.

I put my recovery first to make it last.

Morning and evening prayer have become vital to the ongoing sobriety and serenity of many CDA members.
~Chemically Dependent Anonymous P 61

April 3

Don't get mad and don't cuss a body out mentally or in voice. This brings more poisons than may be created by even taking foods that aren't good.
~Edgar Cayce

Because so many therapists assert that it is healthy to deal with our anger by "expressing it," many of us think that it is better to vent angry feelings than to suppress them. Yet, from A.A., we learn that anger is considered the "dubious luxury of normal men." Venting anger doesn't usually make addicts feel better; it makes us feel worse. If we curse someone, either verbally or mentally, our anger increases rather than decreases. Perhaps others find peace this way, but addicts have found that venting anger is like adding gasoline to the fire. Yet, we don't want to suppress it either. We can cope with our anger by expressing our feelings in writing or talking to our sponsor. With the help of our 12-step program, we can apply the appropriate principles without venting, cussing, raging, or even blaming.

By practicing Step Ten on a consistent basis, I do not develop a relationship with anger.

I was so full of anger, hurt and fear that I just started writing. Emotions poured onto the page; I had found a constructive outlet for my confused feelings.
~Chemically Dependent Anonymous P 37

April 4

I try hard to hold fast to the truth that a full and thankful heart cannot entertain great conceits.
~Daily Reflections

The disease of chemical dependency manifests itself as one based on thoughts of self-importance, smugness, and beliefs that we *know better* than others. Many of us have looked down on the person who helped us up out of the gutter. Snidely we say things like, "Yeah, and he thinks he is *sooo* perfect!" The superiority of conceit that tells us we are above the fray of other lowly drunks and addicts, *for whatever reason*, is an illusion that must be shattered if we are to maintain healthy recovery. That way of thinking can lead us back to that first fix, pill, drink, or snort. When we think we are "above it all," we are encouraging thoughts of superiority and conceit. When we simply fill our heart with gratitude that weare not a part of the fray *today*, we acknowledge the true nature of our disease. We cannot deceive ourselves with thoughts of superiority and conceit.

Today, I fill my heart with gratitude, and there is no room for attitude.

Our hearts become truly grateful and our spirits finally light.
***~Chemically Dependent Anonymous* P 56**

April 5

Shouldest not thou also have compassion on thy fellow servant, even as I had pity on thee?
~Matthew 18:33

As practicing addicts, we were selfish, creepy people. Even though we may have cared when someone we loved was sick or hurt, their suffering became just another excuse to use. In recovery, we have almost daily contact with those who are sick and suffering, but their suffering is no longer an excuse to use. It is an excuse to honor the newcomer as the most important person in the meeting. But it is not always easy to treat the newcomer like a VIP when he or she rambles on and on or is constantly picking up a desire chip. These people can be frustrating, but we remember that at one time we frustrated others in the same manner. So, we patiently bite our tongue. We behave kindly, rather than impatiently. We ignore our desire to criticize. We smile at the guy with the snot wiped over his cheek and never forget the compassion we received from others.

I live with compassion and gratitude instead of judgment. I am kinder than necessary.

Others gain a new level of self-acceptance when the response to their sharing is compassion rather than judgment.
~Chemically Dependent Anonymous P 43

April 6

Out of the Indian approach to life there came a great freedom, an intense and absorbing respect for life, enriching faith in a Supreme Power, and principles of truth, honesty, generosity, equity, and brotherhood as a guide to mundane relations.
~Wallace Black Elk

Many of us were taught that a "little white lie" was an act of kindness. But this lie can be an act of disrespect for another. We cannot attain the deep respect for life that Black Elk speaks of if we are showing inequity. When we tell "white lies," we are filtering information for people and placing ourselves above another. We are placing ourselves above them because we think we know what is best! We have been taught to think that this type of dishonesty with others is okay so long as we are sparing their feelings. We really don't know what will or will not hurt another. Being dishonest with other people deprives them of the information they need to run their own lives. Honesty is honesty, in any color.

I show respect for others by not filtering information for them.

The greatest element in the universe is truth and we can only find it by being honest.
~Chemically Dependent Anonymous P 90

April 7

I find that when we really love and accept and approve of ourselves exactly as we are, then everything in life works. ~Louise Hay

"You can change any cucumber into a pickle, but you can never change a pickle back into a cucumber." The old-timers tell this familiar adage to illustrate an especially important point that once we cross the line into chemical dependence, there is no going back. They tell us, "Once alcoholic, always alcoholic." As chemical dependents, we *have* crossed that invisible line between social use and addiction. There is absolutely nothing we can do to change the fact that we will always be addicted to mood-changing and mind-altering chemicals. The old-timers also tell us that we can be grateful or ungrateful. No matter which we choose, we are still chemically dependent. Doesn't it make sense to approve of ourselves exactly as we are and be *grateful* for that?

I fill my heart with gratitude for who I am, and then I cannot resent who I am not.

At last we understand what CDA members mean when they describe themselves as "grateful alcoholics and addicts." Were it not for chemical dependence, we may not have found this incredible, fulfilling way of life.
~Chemically Dependent Anonymous P 65

April 8

Do not forget the story of remembering.
~Seneca Traditional Story

People who can spiritually integrate the stories of the past become greatly gifted. Those of us who disregard the past are doomed to repeat it. We have heard it said many times, "Never forget your last drunk." Old-timers give this stern warning so that we do not forget where we came from. Many a newcomer would do anything to forget the insanity of what their last drugging experience was like. After all, the circumstances that brought us to the doors of Chemically Dependent Anonymous were usually ugly. We tell newcomers not to forget. We tell them to remember, and remember the story well, by sharing it with the rest of us. By recalling our stories, we can retain something to pass on to the future. It is by sharing our harsh experiences that we can begin to spiritually integrate the lessons of the past.

I live today as I want to remember my life, but I do not forget the past that created it.

Their thinking gets twisted and they forget where they have come from. Somehow they think that recreational drug use will be all right for them.
~Chemically Dependent Anonymous P 9

April 9

Silent love is like silent prayer, it is dead unless we speak it. ~Big Rob

If we care about someone, then we need to tell them that we care. This is especially true for those we have harmed due to the disease of addiction such as parents, partners, and children. Many of us think about saying "I love you," but then allow the thought to slip by without any action. We hug people at meetings all the time and say, "I love you." But do we give that same attention to those we love at home? It is very important to practice the same love and principles at home that we do in our service work. Love is not love, however, until we *say it out loud* to those whom which we are closest. Remember, they loved us even when there was little there to love. They said *and* demonstrated it many, many times. Now we get the opportunity to give the power of love back to them. We do not keep love locked up inside. We speak those words out loud.

I remember that love is a verb.

I am also glad I've been given the courage to say I love you to friends because they need it. When I'm able to do that, I find I lose my own fear of rejection.
***~Chemically Dependent Anonymous* P 114**

April 10

Being receptive means allowing your Senior Partner to handle your life for you. ~Wayne Dyer

It is not difficult to understand that recovery requires letting our Senior Partner run the show. The problem is that many of us don't understand exactly how that is supposed to work. Does it mean that we have nothing to do except surrender each day, and all else will be done for us? Although everyone's relationship with a Higher Power is different, we can usually agree that God does not do for us what we can do for ourselves. We can pray for potatoes but must pick up a hoe. So, being receptive means we allow our Creator to give us direction, but we must *walk* in the direction in which we are guided. We are not put through a Sci-Fi transporter. Guidance comes through sponsors, speakers, and meetings, as well as reading, meditation, and prayer. We see and hear our Higher Power speak through others. And, sometimes, our Senior Partner sends memos through *our own voice*, even when we thought we had nothing to say.

Today, I listen to God's memos that come right out of my own mouth!

There are many things I still want in life; there are also things I have to keep working on.
~Chemically Dependent Anonymous P 296

April 11

I get by with a little help from my friends.
~John Lennon

Actually, we get by with a lot of help from our friends. If it were not for our friends in recovery, we may not get by at all. During times of crisis, some of us become afraid that we are using our friends like we did in our old drugging days. We might find ourselves calling them at late hours knowing they have to get up early for work; maybe we ask them for a loan when we know things are tight for them too; or maybe we ask for rides to meetings a little too often. The difference today is that we are using a friend, and we expect them to use us as well. We are of service, one to the other. In our using days, we abused people—*we were not their friends nor were they ours*. It was our interests alone that concerned us, not mutual interests. Today we use the help of our friends with pride, because we trust that they will use us during their time of need, too.

I get by with a lot of help from my friends.

During active addiction, my dreams never included trying to recover, establishing friendships or caring about people. And they certainly never included being anything but hopeless and helpless.
***~Chemically Dependent Anonymous* P 338**

April 12

Being defeated is often a temporary condition. Giving up is what makes it permanent.
~Marilyn vos Savant

Whether it is physically, emotionally, or spiritually, we should never give up on ourselves, even when we seemingly hit a brick wall. Often, a brick wall only means it's time to look at our program differently. What worked for us at three months is probably not what works best at three years. Just as what works at three years isn't how we get the best results at fifteen years. Recovery is about progress. And we don't progress if we stay the same. When we hit that wall, rather than feel defeated, we try incorporating other approaches along with our Twelve Steps. The world is full of psychological theories, self-help books, and homemade wisdom. If one way to work a Step doesn't work for us, or it stops working (perhaps because we have changed so much), then we need to try another way. Ours is a program of *suggestion*, because a single technique with the Steps may not be effective for everybody at every stage of growth.

Rather than just give up, I try giving up my preconceived ideas, and then look at it again.

Sometimes we really feel stuck... We may be repeating an unwanted behavior or frequently going into emotional relapse... What then?
~*Chemically Dependent Anonymous* P 68

April 13

Now I realize that the present moment contains all time and within it is all that can be hoped for, done, and realized. ~Kahlil Gibran

There isn't a single member of a 12-step program who can claim to have not heard the slogan, "One day at a time." But what does this really mean? What we mean by this is that we live only in the moment. Right now is the only time we own. Living in the moment allows us to *apply lessons* from yesterday. If we are trying to *change the past*, there is no time or energy to apply yesterday's lessons. We certainly cannot grow today if we are locked in yesterday, regretting the past, or fixated on changing what has already happened. Likewise, living in the moment allows us to move fearlessly into our future. This way, we don't waste energy on planning for a future that we may never actually reach. Living in the moment means we take each thing in life one at a time, and one day at a time.

I can't carry a board 365 feet long, *but* I can carry a one-foot board 365 days in a row.

Slowly, one day at a time, we start to understand the concept of serenity that is expressed by so many in CDA.
~Chemically Dependent Anonymous P 34

April 14

Even if you're on the right track, you'll get run over if you just sit there. ~Will Rogers

Many members of the 12-step programs attempt to search for the *cause* of our disease of addiction. If we just get on the right track, they believe, the solution will be obvious. Yet, knowing where the train comes from does little for those stuck on the track! The origin of our disease and the origin of our shortcomings mystify us. We ponder whether it could be genetic, societal, environmental, or all three. If we just had enough knowledge about what went wrong, then things might be set right again. This is a common belief. Yet, knowing what went wrong does absolutely nothing for getting it right today. Knowing that chemical dependency is a disease of brain chemistry may put us on the right track, but it does little for our actual recovery. Rather than wasting our energy on figuring out "why," we figure out "what" to do now, so that we might avoid the oncoming trains of life.

Rather than "why" questions, I begin asking the "How do I change?" and "What needs to be done?" questions.

My friend thought it was hysterical when I gave her my theory about why I had gone crazy and had to attend group therapy.
~*Chemically Dependent Anonymous* P 329

April 15

"To thine own self be true" is an oft-uttered adage. But to which self? The higher or lower?
~Ralph Waldo Emerson

Learning how to be our true selves—the genuine, unique individual who is the rightful us—is an amazing gift of sobriety. Yet often we get carried away with this fabulous new gift. The joy and fullness of the freedom from mind-affecting chemicals can be quite intoxicating. Many of us have, at times, all too easily forgotten which self we serve. One of the ways we know how well we are practicing the principles of the Program is to notice how we treat people who can be of no service to us. Do we snap at the salesclerk who is fumbling, or do we ask if they are all right? Do we rush around the senior citizen taking their time on the stairs, or do we take their arm and help? In Chemically Dependent Anonymous it is very important to be true to ourselves—the sober self, not the self-centered self.

I will give my smile to the next person I meet.

For us, "straight" means that we don't drink and drug but stay true to our consciences.
~*Chemically Dependent Anonymous* P 90

April 16

A quotation at the right moment is like bread to the famished. ~Talmud

It has often been suggested that we adopt a favorite maxim, quotation, or slogan to repeat when we need to tide ourselves through a difficult time. Many of us use the Serenity Prayer in this way. We recite it in our car on the way to a difficult meeting or say the words slowly when something has angered us. Others, trapped in a baffling dilemma or tempted to do something stupid, often say, "Not my will, but Thine be done." In CDA, we have the ultra-simple but nonetheless profound statement, "I will to will Your will." Sometimes the simpler the saying, the easier it is to bring it to mind when we need it. One handy discipline is to tape post-it notes on our mirrors or refrigerators as quick reminders. Tucking notes in our books or pockets, to be brought out at opportune times, can also be helpful. Our slogans are wisdom in shorthand, and we make use of them as one of the many tools in our recovery toolbox.

**I decorate my life with the slogans,
not just my walls.**

In CDA, we employ the pure simplicity of such slogans to help us to stay on the straight line to success.
~Chemically Dependent Anonymous P 91

April 17

I used to settle for less, but now I choose to work for filet mignon versus macaroni and cheese.
~Steve M.

Most of us come to the rooms of recovery in an absolute despondent state, begging for little more than to just stop using. We may only want to stop hurting the ones we love, or maybe we are desperate to find a slight glimmer of hope in our dark lives. We came to CDA no longer able to live that ugly life. We seldom turn up at the doors of CDA expecting bright and promising futures. The "macaroni and cheese" recovery is what we asked for, and we might have been satisfied with just that. But, in due course, our sponsor and other members in the Fellowship tell us not to settle for mere abstinence. "There is more to look forward to than you can ever imagine," they say. Thus, our expectations are raised. Our expectations do not become real, however, unless we are willing to do what is suggested. It is important to understand the concept that being abstinent is the "macaroni and cheese" approach—and working the Twelve Steps is the "filet mignon entrée."

I do not settle for macaroni and cheese recovery.

We expected to be trapped in a narrow hallway but we found ourselves walking on a broad highway.
~*Chemically Dependent Anonymous* P 30

April 18

We learn to say, thank you, for these problems and feelings. Thank you for the way things are.
~Melody Beattie

Even though our greatest adversities in life become our greatest opportunities for growth, we can often be heard lamenting loudly over the hardships. There is a time in our spiritual growth when we realize that adversity has a purpose, and we learn to thank the Universe for *all* it offers us. Adversity is our opportunity to work the Program. It is our opportunity to grow and strengthen our resolve through action, not just words. After all, we don't think to work the Steps when things are going well, or when people are acting the way we think they should. But, let a crisis surface or someone thwart our efforts oversomething, and suddenly we are on the phone to our sponsors, on our knees to our Higher Power, anddelving into the Steps for relief. We *need* problems to learn how to live life on life's terms. Thus, we come to see how adversity, problems, and grief become our friend.

Today, I express gratitude for everything: the good, the bad, and the ugly.

Of course, there are problems. But the point is that now I am living life on life's own terms.
~*Chemically Dependent Anonymous* P 227

April 19

We will love you until you learn to love yourself.
~Walk Softly & Carry a Big Book

Most of us were starved for love and affection when we arrived at the doors of Chemically Dependent Anonymous. So, it was music to our ears to hear, "We will love you until you can love yourself." Yet, how many of us understood love? The newcomer, in all likelihood, will confuse love with sex. They may even "come on" to us in their desperate attempt to feel love. Although we cannot tell others how to handle these delicate matters, most experienced CDA members choose not to respond in a romantic fashion to any newcomer. Our principles tell us not to prey on the vulnerable. Yet, if the newcomer confuses sexual attention with love, they may feel highly rejected and seek the love they crave in risky environments. It is important to let single newcomers know that *not dating* them or sexually pursuing them is BECAUSE we love them. We must teach newcomers what love is; they honestly do not know.

Teaching the newcomer to live and love the CDA way is my responsibility.

Do I insist upon having my sexual desires gratified regardless of who might get hurt in the process?
~Chemically Dependent Anonymous P 38

April 20

Worry does not empty tomorrow of its sorrow, it empties today of its strength. ~Corrie Ten Boom

In CDA, we have found that worry is like a rocking horse—it keeps you moving but never gets you anywhere. So, when we worry, all it does is take our energy and zap us of our strength without producing any results! When it comes to troubles, there are really only two choices: worry or trust God. If we trust our Higher Power, then we pray. Prayer changes things and worry changes nothing. But why would prayer put us in a position not to worry? Understanding the nature of prayer might help. Prayer is not a platitude uttered to please God; prayer is an honest attempt to contact God. When we contact our Spiritual Source, we are acknowledged and divinely nurtured. With this nurturing, we understand that our Source has our best interests in mind, *always*. Therefore, why worry about God doing what's best for us? We can use our energy, instead, for enjoying the present moment.

I pray. It helps.

{After prayer}: There was always a better feeling, inside, that I was being taken care of. It might not, necessarily, always be in the manner that I would like, but I knew I was being watched over {…}.
~*Chemically Dependent Anonymous* P 178

April 21

God has no hands but yours. ~Mother Teresa

Helping another person who is still suffering from addiction to mind-altering and mood-changing chemicals is the very cornerstone of our continued recovery. Yet, how do we become the hands of God when there are obstacles? Today, with all the treatment centers, we aren't called out on 12-step calls as often as in the founding days of our program. What if we live far away from the CDA Fellowship, making it difficult to work with newcomers easily? What if we are unable to take people to meetings because we are disabled, or unable to talk effectively to the newcomer because we are too shy? The answer is that we remain willing by doing what is asked of us when we can. We can find alternative ways to show our willingness. We clean tables, write letters to inmates, become an internet sponsor, or donate time or money to group projects. When asked, *we do what we can.* Let us ask our Higher Power to guide us to those in need of help, and to empower us to meet their needs.

I say YES when asked to help.

One idea made a deep impression on me. It stressed how important it is to remember that God makes greater use of the channels that are the most willing and receptive.
~Chemically Dependent Anonymous **P 115**

April 22

We need courage to meet what comes and know that whatever it is, it will not last forever. ~Leo F. Buscaglia

There are times in all our lives when the pain is overwhelming, the tragedy is real, and all we can do is endure. Drinking and drugging are no longer options. Taking unnecessary medication is no longer an option. Running away is no longer an option. We endure. We find solace where and when we can: at meetings, from our sponsor, and in prayer and meditation. Yet, honestly, there are times when these actions don't ease the pain much. When real tragedy strikes, the only way out of the suffering is to gothrough it. We may have taken all the suggestions offered, received counsel from our sponsor, and advice from our friends, and, yet our suffering persists. It is in times like this that we can rest assured that "this too shall pass."

I do not use unnecessary pills to get me through what only time can heal.

I still go through a great deal of emotional pain, but I'm told that it's part of the growth. I do get glimpses of peace of mind and serenity.
~Chemically Dependent Anonymous P 151

April 23

They tell us that even if our ass falls off we should put it in a bag and take it to a meeting. There's a reason for that because there's a good chance your brain is in the bag too. ~Jumpin' Joe

Meeting Makers Make It is a popular 12-step slogan suggesting just how important meetings are. "Making it" doesn't mean staying clean and sober; it means living happily. You see, we have what is called an addictive-thinking mind. If we don't bounce our thoughts and actions off other people who are practicing the principles of the Program, a subtle shift occurs in our thinking. This shift happens so gradually that we often cannot recognize it without help. Maybe we get bored with the same old stories and the same old anecdotes. Maybe after 10 or 15 years of recovery, we feel as though we've become 12-step experts. Perhaps we're simply busy. By routinely making it to meetings, our family in the rooms will never let us rationalize away our shortcomings.

**Regardless of my clean time,
I make it to meetings to find out what
happens to those who don't.**

Go to meetings!
~Chemically Dependent Anonymous P XVII

April 24

My own disease would like to tell you that my 'isms' are now my 'wasims.' But {...} it's an ongoing process that leads to the sweetest spirituality.
~Steven Tyler (Aerosmith)

Just what are the "isms" of our disease? For many people, "ism" stands for "I, Self, & Me." Others claim that our "ism" is another way of saying, "Incredibly Short Memory." A particularly dangerous one is "I Sponsor Myself." The "ism" concept also proves useful in illustrating our various dispositions. Narciss*ism* is a version of "InSide Me," whereas pessim*ism* is the product of "I Sabotage Myself." On the other hand, optim*ism* results from "Incredibly Spiritual Moments." Which "ism," therefore, should we adopt for our program of recovery? The choice we make will either lead us to an integrated self with that "sweetest spirituality" or to an alienated self with a bitter separation from our soul. Because of our program of recovery, the choice is ours today.

**I remember myself
as the whole person that I am.**

Experiencing emotion is part of being human and emotions themselves are neither good nor bad. However, they manifest in healthy or unhealthy ways.
~Chemically Dependent Anonymous P 37

April 25

So we decided to let go of our own ideas at last and to let God take over. For again we read in the A.A. Big Book that "this spiritual life is not a theory." ~Father John Doe

"If God is your co-pilot," the speaker said, "we suggest that you switch seats." The speaker, of course, was referring to our Third Step decision. The decision we make in Step Three is to submit ourselves to the care of God; thereby allowing God to become our pilot. This requires the letting go of old ideas. Many of us are content to take our Higher Power along for the plane ride, but we are reluctant to give up the controls. By holding onto old ideas, we hold onto *our way* of doing things, and find it impossible to turn our will and lives over to the care of our Higher Power. Furthermore, when we don't completely integrate Step Three into our lives, we do not have the proper foundation for working the remainder of the Steps. Truly, the saying, "This spiritual life is not a theory," is the foundation of our spiritual life. For us, God cannot be the co-pilot. Our Higher Power is the pilot.

Today, I release my reservations.

I wasn't working the Program the way it was suggested. I still had reservations and the old mentality of the quitter.
~Chemically Dependent Anonymous P 281

April 26

Hug often. Hug well. ~Kathleen Keating

It is not the easiest thing in the world to let people touch us, especially if it wasn't a big part of our upbringing. We may feel like our space is being invaded when hugged. Sometimes we have been taught that touching is a feminine gesture and "unmanly." Some of us have been violated in the past and aren't sure how to feel when hugged. In CDA though, we are hug bugs. We greet each other with hugs at meetings, at sober events, and even in chance encounters in public. We often end meetingsin huge group hugs. Hugging is us telling each other, "You mean something to me, and I want to affirm that." A big old bear hug can also establish a sense of security in us. You may not want everyone hugging you in their attempts to comfort and communicate, butremember the Mom and Dad hugs of your childhood? Allow others to bring back those feelings of comfort. If you didn't get Mom and Dad hugs in your childhood, let us make up for it now!

**I will let the next person that hugs me
be the first to let go.**

It was so comforting to know I wasn't alone.
~*Chemically Dependent Anonymous* P 177

April 27

The Sleeping Beauty story is the best story to use in these Steps, but in other teaching stories like Beauty and the Beast, there is the same principle employed - that of facing fear and distaste and the change that is granted.
~Change With the Twelve Steps

Working the Steps does undeniably require that we face the fears of all our defects. We begin facing our fears the day we pick up the pen to write our inventory. We must own up to each of our shortcomings and then correct them. In doing so, we are healing ourselves. It is in this healing that great change is wrought within. Monsters turn into friends, frogs into princes, witches melt away, maidens become queens, and wooden dolls become living people. Eventually, the ultimate transformation takes place: a wretched, violent drunk, a using and abusing junkie, a pitiful useless cokehead is changed into a grateful, grace-filled human being. The story of our lives in CDA does indeed have a fairytale ending.

**I am not afraid to face my fears for
I believe in happy endings.**

Once again, fear is the ally of the disease. When we give it power, we act in ways that separate us from God.
~Chemically Dependent Anonymous P 47

April 28

Just for Today ~Narcotics Anonymous Slogan

In reality, of course, all we have is this day. However, the concept is sometimes misused. It's maddening to ask someone for lunch next week and they won't commit because, "I live in today," they answer. But isn't one of the promises of the Program to restore us to sanity? When we live in recovery, our ability to think clearly and make decisions is restored. If we never look past the end of our noses, we would be like the cricket who fiddled all summer instead of preparing for the inevitable. How would we fund retirement accounts, plan for taxes, get our kids through college, or make that lunch date for next week? So, the slogan was born *Plan plans, not results*. When we plan the plans, we are using our heads, and we are working Step Two. The results, however, belong in Step Three where we turn it over to our Higher Power. So, we can plan for lunch next week, but we cannot guarantee that the restaurant will have sushi that day, that our favorite waitress will be there, or that we can both get there right on time.

I do my best; my Higher Power does the rest.

A limited ability to affect when or how much one used created an illusion of control. But, in the end, it invariably failed.
*~**Chemically Dependent Anonymous** P 44*

April 29

Can we change our focus,
With no need to defend?
Acknowledging joy and sorrow,
Without judging foe or friend? ~Jamie Sams

To be a victim, one must have a villain. To have a villain, one must judge another as having failed us in some way. Thus, the victims judge the villains and, in essence, victimize the ones who victimized them! As our focus changes, we no longer want to be the victim asking, "Why me?" Neither do we want to shout, "It's your fault!" What we strive for is acknowledging our joy, sorrow, and growth without judging. This is done via the *action Steps,* Four through Ten. When working the action Steps, we cannot blame others. We must look at ourselves and take responsibility for our own actions, which is not consistent with victim mentality. We must compensate others for what we've done wrong, which is not consistent with villain mentality. By doing these, we cannot be a victim or a villain, only a victor.

I do not blame or judge my past so that
I am free to embrace my future.

Do I continue to think and act like a victim?
~*Chemically Dependent Anonymous* P 40

April 30

I don't understand this God stuff. I don't understand electricity either, but I won't sit in the dark until I figure it out. ~Mosses Yoder

For some, the definition of God is found in the doctrine of their faith; for some it is found in the glory of nature; for many God is plural; for others, God is simply the goodness that comes from humanity's best. According to Random House Dictionary, Life, Truth, Love, Mind, Soul, Spirit, and Principle are all synonyms for "God." Although the Steps suggest we define God *as we understand Him*, many of us get hung up on defining our concept of God. Many of us are looking for a concrete definition of who God is. Maybe we are shaking off an oppressive religion, or maybe we are afraid that God will be ticked off if we don't get it exactly right. However, experience has taught us that our concept of God changes along with our growth in the Program. How we understood God in early recovery is often very different from what we understand after a few years of working the Steps.

**Instead of defining God for myself,
I let God define Himself for me.**

And the major discovery I have made since coming into the Fellowship is learning how to get close to and become comfortable with the God of my understanding.
~Chemically Dependent Anonymous P 339

May 1

Resentments are like drinking poison and hoping the other person dies. ~Joyce Meyer

There will always be conflicts in life that cause us grief. There will always be someone or something that hurts us and leaves us feeling angry. We live in a complex world where there are many situations that will arise that don't always strike us right. However, if we are diligent in working the Twelve Steps of CDA, we will learn to look at many situations differently. We become willing to take responsibility for our own feelings. We learn not to blame the person, place, or thing we think is causing us grief. It's not about what is going on outside of us; *it is our reaction to it*. When someone has hurt us, first we must ask ourselves, "Is what they said about me true?" If it is true, then we think about changing it without forming a resentment about it. If it is not true, then we ask ourselves, "Is it my pride, ego, or self-esteem that is being affected?" Ninety-nine percent of the time, it's our pride and ego, and resentment is never the answer.

My emotional recovery is not about others taking it out on me. It's about me *not* taking it in.

But the people in "The Program," by now, CDA, kept assuring me that my reactions and anxieties were not atypical and that I could survive it all, clean and sober.
***~Chemically Dependent Anonymous* P 257**

May 2

Think of what you are doing as entering into partnership with Divine Intelligence, a partnership in which you begin to share your concerns with the understanding that there is an Intelligence receptive to what you're saying. ~Gary Zukav

Whatever we believe about the Divine Source is not going to change the nature of the Divine Source. But what we believe, and how we relate, *can* make an enormous difference in our personal program of recovery. For instance, if we believe God is looking down on us and passing judgment, then we will be looking up, trembling. If we think God only loves people of one faith, we will consider ourselves superior to people notof that faith. If we believe that God is harsh and unforgiving, we will be harsh and unforgiving with ourselves. If we see God as a Father, we will act like His children. Likewise, if we see the Creator as a Friend, a Partner, and a Helper—we will see this Partner everywhere in the Fellowship!

There is nothing I can do to make my Creator love me any less, but there is a lot I can do to love my Creator more.

{I}n Steps One, Two and Three we needed to examine our relationship with God.
~Chemically Dependent Anonymous P 57

May 3

God grant me the serenity to accept the things I cannot change, the courage to change the things I can, and the wisdom to know the difference.
~Serenity Prayer

In this, as in most prayers, our usual thing is to ask for something from God. Whether it is spiritual growth, money, the perfect partner, emotional strength, or insight, we are asking something of our Higher Power. In the Program, we are instructed not to ask for our own selfish gains, but only for things that will enable us to help others. Something like: "Thy will, not mine, be done." Although this is a good approach, the time comes when we must stop passively waiting for the will of our Higher Power to strike and, instead, make our relationship with God proactive. We begin to search for what we can do for our Higher Power, and not just ask what our Higher Power can do for us. The passive approach is asking God to do for us what we can do for ourselves; the active approach is asking God to help us to help others; and the proactive approach is asking God what we can do for Him.

God, what can I do for You today?

I know that the only way I can repay God is by passing on what I have received to someone else.
~Chemically Dependent Anonymous P 284

May 4

Know the power of Disciplina, the Roman goddess of discipline. ~Harvey Stout

After physical recovery, our sobriety depends largely upon how we discipline our emotions and live the CDA Program. Just acquiring knowledge of the Program is not enough. Our continuing growth requires discipline. Discipline begins with a few small things done daily: calling our sponsor, meditating, treating others with kindness and respect, going to meetings, and ending the day in grateful prayer. To discipline ourselves does not require tortured sacrifices that make our lives miserable. We simply require ourselves to adhere to some healthy standards, some consistency, and spiritual reliability. Discipline is the opposite of "self-will run riot." Simply to accept the reality of this force, whether internally or externally, is a primary step in resolving a condition which has been exacerbated by denial, dishonesty, and a lack of control.

Happiness is the by-product of my disciplined life.

As the literature says, I'm an alcoholic and I'm undisciplined. I let God show me discipline through the habit of prayer.
~Chemically Dependent Anonymous P 60

May 5

Human beings, by changing the inner attitudes of their minds, can change the outer aspect of their lives. ~William James

Many of us have spent our lives reacting to what was going on in our minds. Then we found recovery and we were told, "You have to have an attitude of gratitude," and "Either you control your attitude, or it controls you." But how does one "control" an attitude? Isn't it just an innate part of us—aren't we powerless over everything, including our attitude? Then our sponsors may tell us that the only thing in life we *can control* is our attitude! So, we ask, "How." One answer might be: "Fake it 'til you make it." That's right. We *fake* a good attitude until we *make* a good attitude. Then amazing things happen around us—even when we fake it, people treat us better, life looks better, and suddenly, life is better.

**Even when I cannot control my attitude,
I *can* control my actions and
my attitude changes.**

We see where our behavior is contributing to the difficulty or conflict, how our attitude is affecting our perspective, and what feelings are being triggered.
~*Chemically Dependent Anonymous* P 57

May 6

You will be happy to know that the universal law that created miracles has not been repealed.
~Wayne Dyer

God's business is making miracles. Each of us that has found recovery in CDA, or one of the other 12-step programs, is a living miracle. Not only have we been liberated from the chains of addiction, we also have been given the opportunity to make peace with our past. The consequences of the past may have been horrendous. There are those of us who have been involved in the death of another, have stolen large sums of money, or been involved in the exploitation of others. Every one of us has lied, used, and abused people to some degree. So, to find ourselves forgiven and able to forgive is a miracle, to be sure. God *wants* to create miracles for us. We just need to "Step" aside.

**I not only believe in miracles,
I rely on them.**

And this is the miracle. Lives once nearly lost in desperation and degradation are now lived openly, powerfully and joyously.
~Chemically Dependent Anonymous P 68

May 7

You can't get indigestion from swallowing your pride. ~A Grandmother's Wise Words

This is a succinct saying that any of our grandmothers might have recited to us. So, does this mean we can never take pride in anything? What this saying actually means is that we can't get indigestion from swallowing *false* pride. For pride in who we are, the ability to hold our head high, and look people in the eye are examples of the many benefits of recovery. When we work with newcomers and sponsees, we swallow that *false* pride that might make us think *we are the ones* creating the miracle of sobriety. Instead, we cultivate genuine pride by humbly realizing wehelp others because it helps to keep *us* clean and sober. False pride is a stumbling block, while genuine pride is a steppingstone. In our spiritual progress, we come to realize that genuine pride is one side of humility. Humility is the ability to acceptour virtues without embellishment and without embarrassment.

**I am proud of the unadulterated,
virtuous side of me.**

But, somehow I just didn't get the picture. I still had a lot of denial about letting other people help me—too much false pride. I thought I could deal with my problem on my own.
~*Chemically Dependent Anonymous* P 293

May 8

My program is based on the Father, Son, and the Holy Coincidence. ~Billy G.

Old-timers tell us, "There are no coincidences in Chemically Dependent Anonymous, only God incidences." A God incidence is a wonderfully serendipitous event that occurs just when we need it. Indeed, we have noticed that once a person releases all their reservations regarding recovery, the number of "coincidences" is astounding. For instance, we might be afraid of doing the Fourth Step. We go to a meeting and the topic is Step Four. We get a flat tire on a road trip and the AAA person that responds to our call just happens to be in recovery. We are hotter than a volcano about to blow its stack and the phone rings. It's our sponsor. The list goes on and on. The chain of events that "coincidentally" occur around us every day, protecting and safeguarding us, are like having our own personal CDA guardian angel.

**Even when I don't expect a miracle,
I do expect a God incidence.**

I could not have made such a coincidence happen. I believe it somehow symbolized how God's plan works in my life.
~*Chemically Dependent Anonymous* P 157

May 9

And he said, How can I, except some man should guide me? ~Acts 8:31

When we were using, we were so sure we knew it all. Our ego and distrust would not allow us to seek guidance from another man or woman. Ask for help from another—never! Instead, we used people as gullible targets to feed our egos, our pocketbooks, and our drug hungers. Coming into the Program, we found that our only hope was to learn to use people in a new way. Our old way of thinking was to use, con, and manipulate others. In recovery, we still use others, but in a good way. We use people by learning about recovery through their guidance and teachings. Part of the old thinking that needs to be set aside is our pride, our egos, and our thinking that we always need to be the expert. So, we learn to be humble. We listen to and take the suggestions and guidance of others. Thankfully, our Higher Power has given us a group of spiritual teachers; it is up to us to use them to graduate to a new life in recovery.

Today, I use people, places, and things to learn and grow in my recovery.

I couldn't have done that alone. I just did my part by doing a little bit of the footwork. The Program and the people of the Fellowship are responsible for the rest.
~Chemically Dependent Anonymous P 237

May 10

Live to make the child you were proud of the person you are.
~Collections of Eastern Wisdom Philosophy

During childhood, our parents, grandparents, aunts, and uncles (and maybe even ourselves) had such high hopes for our future. We may have wanted to be the president, a doctor, or a movie star. As time went on, we lost this hope in ourselves—our dreams squashed by what we called "reality." Maybe it happened because of our addiction, or maybe our addiction happened because "reality" was something we didn't know how to deal with. Either way, we know today that we do not have to be the president, a doctor, or a movie star to be special—we already are special. Today, in recovery, we shine by being the kind, hopeful people we knew we could be as children. We become our own heroes. We live by the principles of the Program. This makes that inner child very proud of us indeed.

I embrace myself like I did as a child.
I never give up on my dreams
because I am my dream.

I love the memories of my childhood. It was a healthy one.
~Chemically Dependent Anonymous P 325

May 11

Do not do unto others what they can undo for themselves. ~Anonymous

Doing too much for others resembles that of helping a hatchling out of its shell. If we pull a baby chick from its shell, not allowing it to use its leg muscles to push, the chick will be crippled and not walk. Similarly, if we pull a butterfly out of a cocoon and do not let it develop strength through the struggle, it cannot fly. Likewise, we cripple people by not letting them do for themselves what they can, and should, do. Being of service is a way of life for us, but that does not mean we take over another's life by getting them out of jams, telling the courts to go easy on them, paying their bills, or asking loved ones to forgive their unforgivable behaviors. Shielding him or her from the consequences of their own actions as they test this new way of life, is us playing God. Showing an addict how to live a good and decent life is our duty.

**I best serve the chemical dependent
who needs my help by caring
about them, not *for* them.**

Among the many pleasures of living a sober life is a growing awareness that we are capable of taking care of ourselves.
***~Chemically Dependent Anonymous** P 76*

May 12

But people who pray for courage, for strength to bear the unbearable, for the grace to remember what they have left instead of what they have lost, very often find their prayers answered.
~Harold S. Kushner

Having our prayers answered is no small matter. But unlike the wish granted by the genie in the bottle, we may not actually get what we expected. In fact, there may be times when we wished our prayer had not been answered. For instance, if we pray for patience, we are likely to be caught in traffic jams, wait in long lines at the grocery store, find our sponsor's phone continually busy when we need them, or sit in a meeting listening to someone jabbering on and on. All these situations may fray on our nerves, but remember, *we did pray for patience!* We develop patience by being in situations that try us. Being in frustrating situations allows us to develop the skill of patience. Patience isn't the world calming down; it'sus learning to calm down amid chaos. By placing us in the midst of chaos, God grants us that for which we prayed!

I am careful what I pray for.

Whenever we bring a request to God, we remember to add, "if it be your will," then let ourselves be open to that will.
~*Chemically Dependent Anonymous* P 62

May 13

Anger makes you smaller, while forgiveness forces you to grow beyond what you were.
~Cherie Carter Scott

We all find ourselves angry at times, and occasionally our anger is justified. While it is important to feel our feelings, we addicts cannot afford to get stuck in anger. We must push forward and neutralize it. This is done through practicing forgiveness. If anger makes us smaller, rather than running the risk of becoming even smaller, we need to learn to forgive. We begin by turning the person, place, or thing that we are angry with over to the care of our Higher Power. It is then that we must *act in a forgiving way* toward them—not in an angry way. For some of us this is difficult. Anger can be a high, in and of itself. But, if we are to grow and recover, we cannot afford to harbor those negative, destructive emotions.

As I control my anger by forgiving, I find that I do not have to be forgiven for my anger.

Today, I know that I can't hold on to anger and resentment because they will destroy me and any relationship that I might have with God.
***~Chemically Dependent Anonymous* P 283**

May 14

If the only prayer you say in your whole life is 'thank you,' that would suffice. ~Meister Eckhart

Gratitude creates joy. Being joyful does not create gratitude. And so, it is not for joyful times that we should save our gratitude—it is for the down times. However, during a crisis, it can be difficult to find gratitude. It is so easy to slip into a critical, whining way of relating to the world. "Why did this have to happen to me? Why isn't my life better now that I am clean and sober? People are getting on my nerves! The red lights on the highway are all out to stop me!" Gratefulness is a necessary ingredient to create a stable spiritual foundation in a joyful recovery. We can start to feel grateful by giving thanks, even if we only start small. We can give thanks for our breath, our food, our shoes, or our friends. If we cannot give thanks for what we have, thenwe give thanks for those things which we are grateful we don't have!

**When I can't make a list
of all I am grateful I have, I make a list
of all I am grateful I don't have!**

I am so grateful that most of the fear and shame is gone and I no longer feel the need to hide.
~*Chemically Dependent Anonymous* P 110

May 15

{J}oy and sorrow are inseparable ... together they come and when one sits alone with you ... remember that the other is asleep upon your bed.
~Kahlil Gibran

How could we know sheer joy if it were not for the comparison to sheer sorrow? Thus, life cannot be about eliminating sorrow, but learning to live well despite it. We all experience losses in life. For those in recovery it can be a major setback if we get "stuck" in the sorrow. Sorrow finds us through death, illness, and other tragedies. Yet, the only way out is to go through it. Sorrow and joy are cycles. We will never escape the cycles of life—not with drugs, isolation, or geographical solutions. It is *time* that guarantees our sorrow will eventually go to sleep, and joy will awaken us once more. Yet, the wise man knows that sorrow sleeps beside us. So, by simply hanging in there, in time, we *will* start to feel a little better. We realize that we can get through anything with the help of family, friends, sponsors, and our home groups.

When I suffer, I know: *This too shall pass*.
When I am joyful, I know: *This too shall pass*.

We have become so close this year and have shared a lot of our pain and joy together.
~Chemically Dependent Anonymous **P 111-112**

May 16

I remember talking to a psychiatrist who diagnosed everyone with the following diagnosis "chronic human imperfection."
~Bob & Pauline Bartosch

It is important to know deep in our hearts that this program is not going to make us perfect. Neither is it going to give us a perfect life, nor make us blame-free from this point forward. *We strive for progress, not perfection*, as they say in A.A. We will be sorely disappointed in ourselves if we think that working the Twelve Steps will make us perfect. Many an old-timer has been livid at facing their own shortcomings—as if their longevity should make them defect-proof at some point. It doesn't. As long as we breathe, we will find imperfections to address. Think about it. If we *were* perfect, what then would we strive for? Finding areas to work on in ourselves is actually a blessing. It keeps us vital, involved, and of benefit to others. For as we learn to overcome our deepest failings, we get to share what we learned with others.

**No matter how long I work the Steps,
I will never rise above the level of human being.**

Now I could start accepting the fact that I am human. Therefore, I will, at times, be less than perfect.
~Chemically Dependent Anonymous P 234

May 17

Part of our codependency is an obsessive focus on what's wrong and what we might be doing wrong—real or imagined. ~Melody Beattie

Let's look at what is right and good in our life. We have so much to be grateful for today. We are clean and sober. We are learning to use the tools of this program to live life on life's terms. Where once we were compulsive about our addiction, obsessing about how to keep feeding our chemical desires, we now may take that same compulsiveness to the opposite extreme and obsess on what we are doing wrong in our program. Some of us beat ourselves up when we don't work a Step exactly right, we don't run a meeting exactly right, or our share didn't have everyone transfixed on our words. Working our program *is* the right thing to do as long as we don't fixate on what's "wrong." When worked right, the Program allows us to start seeing the good in ourselves, too.

There is nothing I can do so wrong that God would ever love me less.

Indeed, a brief review of experience shows that the harder one "works" on what appears to be wrong—a character defect or a shortcoming—the worse it gets.
~Chemically Dependent Anonymous P 45-46

May 18

The things we call impossible may be only one more step away from where we are right now. Don't stop trying too soon. ~Joan Chittister

We often tell newcomers not to quit five minutes before the miracle happens. But what about the rest of us? The first miracle of realizing that *we can* live clean and sober is only one of many that our Higher Power wants to do for us. We tell newcomers not to give up when we should be telling ourselves the samething. Don't give up just before you find your perfect partner; don't stop trying until you land the job you were made for; don't give up on that chronic relapser on time number 20 when it may be the 21st time that he or she will "get it." If we give up the belief that we are deserving of the best that the Divine Source *wants* for us, as well as for those around us, then we have given up on God. We don't stop believing that the Divine Source wants to make miracles happen for all of us at all levels of recovery. If we just keep "trudging the road of happy destiny," eventually new miracles happen!

I keep going even after I think I can't.

Just about ready to give up and take my own life, I stopped in at a meeting place. One of the guys there came to my assistance {…}.
~Chemically Dependent Anonymous P 245

May 19

We are, indeed, far more conscious and capable on a soul level than we have been taught to believe, or have dared to express.
~Sonia Choquette, Ph.D.

We come to realize that our responsibility to the new member is to watch over their spiritual growth. Taking on this awesome responsibility does not mean we preach to them or push our concept of the Spirit on them. Instead, we nurture them by allowing their confidence to grow for them to find their own place beside their own concept of a Higher Power. We never push our religious beliefs on any member ofCDA; we never even insist they need a religion. We only provide spiritual nourishment. To satisfy their beginning spiritual needs, we show them kindness through listening. It is through personal sharing thatwe let them know they are not alone. We are genuine. We are connected to them and physically present for them. Their developing spirit needs us, as well as our continuing spiritual development needs them.

I watch over and nurture the spiritual hunger of new members in CDA.

What we are passing on is the possibility of transformed lives through the spiritual program of the Steps.
~*Chemically Dependent Anonymous* P 66

May 20

Acceptance is not submission; it is acknowledgment of the facts of a situation. Then deciding what you're going to do about it.
~Kathleen Casey Theisen (Each Day A New Beginning)

When we get clean and sober, we think that we will automatically be happy, and that serenity will be ours immediately! Our peace will indeed come … in time. We soon understand that we are powerless over everything. That means there is and always will be something that isn't exactly the way we want it to be or think it should be. We come to understand that we don't have to "like it" to accept it. It means that we accept it for what it is. This is usually quite challenging for us. But there is help. By listening and sharing at meetings, we learn how others handle similar situations. We learn acceptance and we learn how to live life on life's terms.

By working the Steps, going to meetings, talking to a sponsor, and learning to pray, we begin to understand the concept of acceptance.

When we see our limitations, we do our best to accept them as part of our humanity.
~Chemically Dependent Anonymous P 47

May 21

Be still and know that I am God. ~Psalm 46:10

Do we still feel that we need to do it all? We were messed up for a long time. It seems that recovery rekindles that need to stay busy and repair the damage we caused while using. Being still is difficult for many of us. Frantic activity has been the comfort zone for many of us for a very long time. It is difficult to switch gears if we have been the frantic type. Sit still? Stay in idle mode? If we sit still, things happen without us! We are not in control. Outcomes are not dependent on our actions! Just how do we let go of things we feel the need to correct when in the past we always jumped in and ran the show? After all, we think, "This is my life!" But what will happen if we do sit still? What will change? What *changes* is our comfort zone. We come to know that calm, deliberate, well thought-out actions bring about positive results. That quiet voice within speaks louder. We intuitively know what path to follow. We learn to be still, change our comfort zone, and grow!

I choose calm over chaos.

If we are to receive this guidance and strength, it helps to be still and open; thus, our meditation serves us here well here.
~*Chemically Dependent Anonymous* P 62

May 22

Every blade of grass has its angel that bends over it and whispers "Grow, grow." ~Talmud

Using provided no opportunity for us to "grow up." We thought like children, always wanting things to go our way, to get our own way, and to have what we wanted when we wanted it. Just like petulant children, when we realized our dreams weren't turning out as we envisioned, we felt cheated. In reality it was not life cheating us, but our own dependency on mind-affecting chemicals. When we first entered the rooms of Chemically Dependent Anonymous, we heard, "Grow or go." What did that mean? Were these recovering people kicking us out of the rooms of CDA if we didn't follow their suggestions? Absolutely not! Those friends in recovery were simply telling us that if we don't *grow* as recovering people, we will end up *going* out of the rooms. The Steps provide us with the perfect way to "grow up" into a continually recovering adult.

**I do not *go* to heaven.
I *grow* to heaven.**

We all have these little places within us that refuse to grow up, but we must do it. We have to constantly work at being "straight" with ourselves.
~*Chemically Dependent Anonymous* P 90

May 23

We can look the world in the eye. We can be alone at perfect peace and ease. Our fears fall from us. We begin to feel the nearness of our Creator.
~Alcoholics Anonymous P 75

Alone and lonely are states that most chemical dependents tend to think of as undesirable—who wants to be alone? Yet being alone, and even lonely, in recovery has an upside that we seldom examine. When newcomers are lonely, they find themselves attending more meetings than they would if they were not lonely. Living alone in the beginning stages of recovery also protects others from the insanity we live with until our program is more firmly established! When lonely, we are more likely to become involved in program activities and service work. What a blessing in disguise this can be for us. By being alone, we are more likely to participate in activities where we can meet others. Likewise, to deeply feel the presence of God, one must learn to be alone with oneself. We learn that being alone, and even lonely, can be a good thing.

**Lonely is only a problem when
I build walls instead of doorways.**

Then, when I was alone, I talked to God for the first time since my mother had died.
***~Chemically Dependent Anonymous* P 310**

May 24

Prayer takes practice, and we should remind ourselves that skilled people were not born with their skills. ~Narcotics Anonymous P 45

We do not want our *prayers* to be mindless repetitions. Repetitions are for meditations where the goal is to still the mind. Prayer is *talking to God* and these divine conversations must be kept vital. Wekeep our prayers vital by refusing to mindlessly recite words or phrases unless we are using them to still our mind. Our *conversations* with God remain alive when we say what we mean with *conscious intent.* We do not let our words become mechanical. This includes the Serenity Prayer, which can easily become mechanical if we don't keep our minds conscious when we say it. Our Higher Power knows what things we have need of, so our prayers do not change God's will for us. However, these holy conversations, prayed with *conscious intent*, keep our contact with God fresh, alive, and in keeping with Step Eleven.

**When my prayers mean little to me,
they mean even less to my Higher Power.**

And the Program became more a part of my life as I practiced praying, in the morning and at night.
~*Chemically Dependent Anonymous* P 178-179

May 25

Negative energy can have a powerful pull on us, especially if we're struggling to maintain positive energy and balance. ~Melody Beattie

As human beings, we believe other people think the way we think. If we are thinking negative thoughts, such as taking other people's inventory, judging, or criticizing them, then we will believe they are taking our inventory, judging, and criticizing us as well. If someone is outrageously jealous of their partner, it usually means their head is full of cheating thoughts. It is human nature to project on to others what is going on inside of us. But this works both ways. If we are thinking *positive* thoughts and thinking good of others, we automatically think others are thinking good thoughts about us. That is why an honest person can so easily be fooled because they can't imagine anyone lying to them. Understanding this human characteristic gives us one more tool to apply to self-introspection.

If people could hear my thoughts, would I be embarrassed or feel confident?

Am I obsessively caught up in negative thinking?
~Chemically Dependent Anonymous P 40

May 26

Instead of putting others in their place, put yourself in theirs.
~Collection of Eastern Wisdom Philosophy

We live in a world composed of many different personalities. Some personalities we love instantly, and others take a while to warm up to. Working with the ones we like is easy but working with the others creates challenges for us. Yet we are told that working with them *is our duty* if they reach out for help. Maybe we are uncomfortable with some because they whine, they do self-destructive things, or they don't listen to our good advice. We may fail to understand the choices they make. Our arrogance tells us that if this person would just do what we tell them, they would be a lot better off. Few of us want to waste our precious time listening to the whining and crying—especially when they won't listen to our advice! Yet, it is not us that have to live with the consequences of the choices they make—*it is them*. Why are we so arrogant in thinking that they would be happy living with the consequences of our choices?

**I don't give advice. I simply share my life.
Then it is never "hard" to work with anyone.**

The sponsor I've had ever since I first went into treatment was a real blessing through all of this. He listened to my crying {...}.
~Chemically Dependent Anonymous P 246

May 27

Life only demands from the strength you possess. Only one feat is possible—not to have to run away. ~Dag Hammarskjold

In the past we hid from our inner feelings, our friends, our families, and our everyday responsibilities. In other words, we *hid from today*. We ran from everything and everyone, including ourselves. Once we stop ripping and running, "today" may still seem like more than we can bear. After all, now we are in recovery attempting to meet the responsibilities and obligations that we ditched earlier. But the demand of each 24 hours is never going to be more than we can handle. How do we know this? Simple. First, we build on the knowledge that God has worked in our life in the past and will continue to work in our future. Second, no matter what happens, our Higher Power has *secured our future*—nothing that happens today can take that away! So we face today and all its challenges, knowing that tomorrow is secured for us.

Today is here. I get busy.

Rather, each of us eventually gets a flash of the truth. Regardless of what we're doing or what the issue of the day might be, we all have to make decisions in every area of our lives.
~*Chemically Dependent Anonymous* P 89-90

May 28

I am careful not to confuse excellence with perfection. Excellence I can reach for; perfection is God's business. ~Michael J. Fox

Generally, in recovery, each of us tries to become the very best individual that we can. Sometimes, in seeking perfection, we let those less-than-perfect moments get in the way of our progress. Perfectionism can be the downfall of an addict, driving us back to addiction when we cannot be that perfect person or create that perfect life. The basic idea here is to strive for excellence, knowing that our efforts will never be "perfect." We try to work toward being our best, in full knowledge that we are supremely human, and therefore flawed, incapable of perfection. There are, however, perfect moments. Let's be grateful for every one of them, knowing that "this too shall pass" back into imperfection. Excellence in our behavior is what we pursue—and we leave those "perfect" moments up to God.

God gives me tasks to do knowing I am incapable of perfection. Nevertheless, I give every task an excellent effort.

We may tell ourselves that we cannot do the Step unless we do it completely and perfectly.
~Chemically Dependent Anonymous P 36

May 29

There is a principle which is a bar against all information, which is proof against all arguments and which cannot fail to keep a man in everlasting ignorance—that principle is contempt prior to investigation. ~Herbert Spencer

We like to think we are above contempt, yet can we honestly say we don't, at times, hold contempt for:

- People who consider themselves above us?
- Our sponsors and their suggestions?
- Ideas that are not our own?
- Other 12-step programs?
- Relapsers, psychiatrists, cops, priests, bishops, gurus or circuit speakers?

When we are in contempt of court, we place our will above the judge; *we know better*. That is a closed mind. When we live with contempt, we place our will above God's; we know better. That is a closed mind. It is only when we open our mind to God's will that we can let go of the contempt found in a closed mind. All those "issues" we found that elicited contempt from us actually belong in God's court, not ours!

I open my mind before I open my mouth.

To make a beginning, all we needed was an open mind. We simply needed to look around us and see, without judgment.
~Chemically Dependent Anonymous P 30

May 30

Four laws of happiness: Count your blessings; proclaim your rarity; go another mile; use wisely your power of choice. And one more, do all things with love ... love for self, love for others, and love for me (God). ~Og Mandino

Choice! Do we choose failure and despair or success and happiness? Learning to love our self enough to choose success is often pretty tough. It is so much easier to stay in "failure" mode. We are used to it, it's familiar ground, and we get to whine about not getting "more breaks" in life. It's like the joke with the character Clyde who walks around with the perpetual cloud above his head believing that God is saying, "There's just something about you Clyde that pisses me off!" Clyde made a choice to believe that and to remain stuck in failure. We, however, can follow the laws of happiness, count our blessings, celebrate our uniqueness, go that extra mile, and choose to live a full and happy recovery.

**I count my blessings and
my blessings count.**

{I}'d let people, places and things control my happiness. I had no foundation of self. Once I finally made a decision for myself, however, I discovered that foundation of self, and it began to work for me.
~Chemically Dependent Anonymous P 198

May 31

Our feelings don't define us, our actions do. We are not bad because we have a quick temper—but we learn that expressing that anger hurts others. ~The Pocket Sponsor

At some time or another we all have ugly feelings toward the ones we love. Some of these feelings can be very negative and we might want to hold them in so we don't hurt others. But we can't let them fester. Letting these emotions fester makes life miserable, and, in the end, we usually take it out on our loved ones anyway. How awful to be trying to get well and in the process making our loved ones sick! However, the Program teaches us that we *can share* these feelings, thus preventing them from festering. We are free to share our "ugly" emotions with our sponsor and other trusted CDA members. We have witnessed others share similar "secrets" and recognize that this act helps set us free. No matter how negative or bad our secret emotions may be, we can share them and be released from their bondage.

I share my deepest secrets with other CDA members, and I am free!

Do I secretly wallow in shame?
~Chemically Dependent Anonymous P 38

June 1

Character is much easier kept than recovered.
~Thomas Paine

At the heart of character is integrity, and at the heart of integrity is wholeness. In recovery, we strive to obtain this wholeness. We learn that it is much easier to keep a vase whole than it is to glue it back together after it breaks. In order to keep our character strong and whole, it is necessary to stay whole in the first place. We do this by practicing the principles in all our affairs. Thus, if we value honesty, it is important *not* to take a "few envelopes" from work for our personal use. If we give our word today to a person that we like, but find we don't like them next week, we must still keep our word. Any break from what we know is right, keeps us from being whole, and damages our good character. With enough "breaks" in our character, we eventually shatter. To stay whole, we pay attention to the small stuff. We do what it takes *every day* to preserve our integrity.

**My true character is determined
by what I do when no one is watching.**

Does what I gain by lying really balance out the integrity I lose?
~*Chemically Dependent Anonymous* P 39

June 2

Many Christians wouldn't want to be the God they've fabricated; they'd be more likeable than that! ~Edmond Bonin

Do we struggle to understand our Higher Power? Is it because we think He's a mean old judge, recording how bad we've been in the Book of Life? Maybe we think He doesn't care about us. But how did we receive the gift of sobriety? We were at the bottom of the heap, alone and frightened, unworthy of anyone's love, and undeserving of any break. And that's when the miracle happened. That's when we first realized there is hope—we didn't have to die from our addiction! God was good, kind, and gentle with us. So, why do we attribute such stern attributes to this gentle and loving Power in our lives? Any being that would pluck us from the depths of despair has got to be loving and magnanimous! Perhaps we struggle to understand Him because we try to make Him what He is not. God is very likable … God is very lovable.

My Higher Power can't give me a new understanding of Himself until I let go of the old one.

And so I came to understand God, in a small, beginning kind of way, as a Force which would help me and guide me, comfort and strengthen me. God became a friend.
~*Chemically Dependent Anonymous* P 178

June 3

Necessary evils are never necessary and always evil. ~Collection of Eastern Wisdom Philosophy

When we were using, we did whatever we had to do to get what we wanted. We may have felt that it was necessary to steal, lie, cheat, break the law, or even hurt others. All of us compromised our morals at some point during our active addiction. When working the Program, we are expected to practice honesty, morality, and goodness—we are expected to be free from the "necessary evils." Yet, their allure may sometimes tug at our character. There may be times when we believe it is necessary to lie. Maybe we don't want our boss to blame us for losing a client. So, we lie. We may even have times when we feel it is necessary to hurt others. Did we put work first, making an appointment that now prevents us from taking the kids to the amusement park as we had promised? Our priorities must change in recovery. There is nothing worth having that we must compromise ourselves for.

Today's priorities do not include "necessary evils."

Indulging in old behaviors is a sure way to compromise our recovery. Some refer to this as 'emotional relapse.' It shows itself most clearly in our interactions with others.
~*Chemically Dependent Anonymous* P 57

June 4

I think a hero is an ordinary individual who finds strength to persevere and endure in spite of overwhelming obstacles. ~Christopher Reeves

Sometimes we find ourselves overwhelmed by circumstances in life that we cannot control. At times we feel depressed, afraid, and not in charge of where life takes us. We see the light at the end of the tunnel, but it looks like an oncoming train! These are the times when we need to borrow the faith of our friends, family, and fellow addicts. We rely on their view of the world and keep going despite how we feel. If we have made it to the rooms, we have been able to survive the biggest obstacle of all, *ourselves*. We encourage each other not to give up before our Higher Power deals with the obstacles in ways we can't imagine. We learn that although we are ordinary addicts, we can weather *anything* without the need to pick up. That is extraordinary in and of itself! Thus, we become our own heroes—leaning on the faith of our loved ones.

When I borrow the faith of my friends, family, and fellow addicts, I become my own hero.

I found more faith and that faith kept me going.
~Chemically Dependent Anonymous **P 236**

June 5

Nothing on earth consumes a man more quickly than the passion of resentment.
~Friedrich Wilhelm Nietzsche

We addicts have a lifelong, obscure, and dark relationship with resentment. We "loved" to harbor them, but "hated" it when others harbored them against us. This relationship may have started when we were young. We may have played hurtful tricks on the people who loved us just to get some attention, and when they ended up resenting us for it, we were crushed. Our natural reaction was to harbor resentments *back*—they were so mean to us! Those of us who were rebels went out of our way just to 'piss' off others. At times, our thinking was twisted. In our attempt to gain allies, we would spread gossip and talk behind people's backs. We may or may not have been to blame for what started the resentment, but we surely kept the cycle going. Now, it is our job to break that cycle. Working a thorough Fourth Step absolutely ruins our ability to hold onto resentments.

I break the cycle of resenting by realizing that it is better to be the resentment, than to have one!

Energy spent on the Serenity Prayer, instead of on resentment or judgment, reminds us of what's most important.
***~Chemically Dependent Anonymous* P 61**

June 6

I asked for a life raft, and they threw me a yacht.
~Ron R.

Expectations are like a two-sided sword. Some of us come into the Program with grand and glorious expectations, despite how we feel inside. We may have an attitude about how wonderful we are, but are soon humbled, and perhaps a bit humiliated. Honesty catches up to us. We were losers, users, and abusers of everything around us. Did we really deserve to be respected, admired, and loved, with all the abundance of a well-lived life? Usually, from the depths of despair, we finally reach a place of clarity about *our real condition*. Grandiosity turns to gratitude and what we expect *from* others turns to respect *for* others. Ironically, once that clarity comes when we honestly don't expect admiration from the Fellowship for being clean and sober, and once we are humble enough to do what CDA suggests we do, we find ourselves respected, admired, and loved, with all the abundance of a well-lived life.

**I don't go to a meeting looking for what I can get.
I look for what I can give.**

I could never begin to describe all the blessings which I have received from this new way of life, but they include friends, love, security, and, most of all, peace.
~Chemically Dependent Anonymous P 155

June 7

We should make a private chapel where we can retire from time to time to commune with Him, peacefully, humbly, lovingly. ~Brother Lawrence

We have lots of relationships in our lives—parents, children, siblings, friends, and our spouse. Each requires different amounts of attention at different times. How much time we set aside for each, and the intensity of our focus indicate how we feel about them. If we really love our children, we spend time with them. The same holds true with God. Some people believe they can multitask during their prayer time. Rather than set aside a period of time in their day for prayer and meditation, they "pray" while driving down the interstate with the radio blaring. They think they can catch up with the Creator. Prayer, however, is not a multitasking event. To be truly prayerful, we must give our undivided attention to the task. We set aside a special time and place for God to meet us. In this space, multitasking is not allowed.

**I need to be with You, my God.
Help me find a way.**

I must have a relationship with God. Without communication, there can be no relationship.
~Chemically Dependent Anonymous **P 60**

June 8

You must speak straight so that your words may go as sunlight into our hearts.
~Cochise, June 8th 1874

The dawn of our new lives began with the rigorous honesty found in Step One. After this *huge* admission, we had to chip away at all the other lies we lived. Even those of us who had considered ourselves "honest" had to admit to the deceit that was involved in using chemicals the way we did. Our lies took the sunshine from our hearts. To get the sunshine back into our hearts, we had to learn to "speak straight." Our addicted lives were built on dishonesty. Exaggerating our ailments to get pills was dishonest. Even our excuses for using in such excess were often based upon fraudulent claims. We spent years spinning lies and believing most of them. It is an arduous journey to work our way through the Program, unraveling the lies and deceit. Any measure of comfort and progress requires rigorous and continuous honesty from the bitter end of our using to the better end of our recovery.

I speak straight today—no embellishments, no exaggerations, no exceptions.

I then moved back in with my mother and told her that I was a changed man. That made two lies. Lie number one: I had not changed. Lie number two: I was still a kid, not a man.
~*Chemically Dependent Anonymous* P 154

June 9

Daniel was a man who practiced the Presence of God, not now and again, but constantly and regularly. ~Emmet Fox

Practicing the Presence of God is essentially asking for God's will for us through prayer and meditation. So important is prayer and meditation to the recovering person that an entire Step of our program is devoted to it. This is Step Eleven. It is as essential to us as the air we breathe. Of course, we often use the power of prayer to get us out of difficult times. More importantly, however, if practiced daily, prayer and meditation will *keep us out of difficult times*! Like Daniel, we strive to make prayer and meditation a part of our daily lives, constantly and regularly. As we perfect the regularity of this Step, we are improving our conscious contact with God, and we find that we are "practicing the Presence of God."

**I began praying to *get* out of trouble.
Now I pray to
stay out of trouble!**

Why are these {prayer and meditation} worthy of special attention? To answer that, we must first look at the importance of consciously developing and enlarging our relationship with God.
***~Chemically Dependent Anonymous* P 60**

June 10

And acceptance is the answer to all my problems today. When I am disturbed, it is because I find some person, place, thing, or situation—some fact of my life—unacceptable to me.
~Alcoholics Anonymous P 452, 3rd Edition

The hardest part of life for us to accept was that we didn't *want* to "accept" it. Nothing was good the way it was—it had to be accompanied with alcohol or drugs. We went out of our way to make sure that we could be loaded and that, in turn, meant we could "accept" whatever happened. Everything was "better" high. Ball games, movies, plays, amusement parks, picnics, the list was endless. We didn't like where we were, who we were, and definitely not who anyone else was! In recovery, we find that one of the old ideas that we must smash is the idea that things are not good just the way they are. When people, places, and things are unacceptable to us, we could drive ourselves crazy trying to manage, control, and change them. But that is not our job. Our job is us.

**Serenity comes when I stop
expecting and start accepting.**

How am I growing in ACCEPTANCE?
~*Chemically Dependent Anonymous* P 39

June 11

It is not about being better than anyone else; it's about being better than I used to be.
~There's a Spiritual Solution to Every Problem

Upon coming to the doors of CDA, many an addict will say to themselves, "If I can't be a better *good* guy than everyone in here, I'll be a better *bad* guy in my past." Such is the nature of our disease. We compare ourselves to everyone, wanting to stand out, be more unique, be a better sponsor, be the most rapturous speaker, or be the most devoted service worker. Anything just to stand out—get attention—not be just like everyone else! But we eventually learn that in order to be "better than" in any one thing, we give up skills in another. To be a better speaker, we probably aren't a very good listener, because we are thinking of what to say, not listening. If we are the best in service work, we are putting all our time into conventions and events with less time for sponsees. It does little good to compare ourselves to others because being the best in any one area invariably means we are not the best in another!

I compare my self to *myself*—not to others.
Am I better than I used to be?

My former roommate and best friend, Ronnie, was someone I'd always compared myself to, but only to the extent that if I ever got as bad as he was, I might think about doing something about it myself.
~*Chemically Dependent Anonymous* P 263

June 12

At a certain point in the drinking of every alcoholic, he passes into a state where the most powerful desire to stop drinking is of absolutely no avail.
~Alcoholics Anonymous P 24

We have all been in that place where the memory of that last drink, that last shame-filled degrading drug run, or that last ugly "high" is forgotten or minimized. We put it so far away that we are tempted to reach once again for that chemical that holds so many empty promises. We tell ourselves the most ridiculous things, "It won't burn me this time; I have at least one more "good time" left; It wasn't *that* bad; The doctor said it was okay." We must be ever mindful of who we are, where we came from, and how addiction manifests in our lives. If we are not mindful of these things, we can all too quickly *lose* what we have gained. We will *lose* our minds. We remain mindful by filling our minds with the words of others in recovery. That means routinely going to meetings, having frequent contact with clean and sober folks, and not reminiscing over the "good old days."

I do not romance the drink or the drug.

That's when I have to exercise faith in this program, remember how devastated my life was before and realize that it is God's will that I remain free of drugs and alcohol.
~Chemically Dependent Anonymous P 284

June 13

Clarity will come. The next step will present itself. Indecision, inactivity, and lack of direction will not last forever. ~Melody Beattie

A common characteristic of addicts is the fact that we have a hard time understanding that any given moment isn't "forever." The various twists and turns our lives take do pass. Things do not remain thesame for the rest of our days on earth. Yet, often our emotions act as if they do. Our path may appear dark,and we may not be sure where our next footstepshould fall. A dark path does not mean that our HigherPower is not giving us enough light. It means that we must *stand still* until the light is turned back on. And standing still isn't forever! It is for this hour, this day, or this week. When we do the work, we are given to doin our program, we can trust—without reservation— that soon the switch will be flipped and a clear, well-lit path revealed. God will not allow us to stand in the dark forever—just long enough to understand we are not in charge of the light.

**I remember that the darkest hour
is only sixty minutes long.**

Darkness Dispelled.
~Chemically Dependent Anonymous **P 173**

June 14

Great Spirit, give me your power whenever my weakness shows so I can live by spiritual decisions. ~Spirited Wolf

In order to understand spiritual matters, it is necessary to be faced with trials and tribulations, and then be asked to do the next right thing. We cannot fully comprehend what it means to do the next right thing, the God-thing, if we are never presented with circumstances that require us to choose between right and wrong. It is when we are weak, but do the right thing anyway, that we begin to understand the true meaning of a spiritual decision. Have we accidentally swiped a car in a parking lot? The damage is hardly noticeable. What to do? Do we leave the scene (after all, "It's just minor damage"), or do we leave our phone number on their windshield? We know what the spiritual decision is, but our weakness would like to "protect" us from higher insurance rates. Making the spiritual decision is trusting God. "Protecting" our self by making the non-spiritual decision is living in weakness, and not with the Power of God.

What would my Higher Power do?

Today, my power is God.
~*Chemically Dependent Anonymous* P 193

June 15

People have a tendency to find someone to blame when bad things happen. This behavior is certainly very prevalent and easy to observe in children. ~H. Tennen & G. Affleck

Like children, chemical dependents have a propensity for shifting responsibility and blaming people, places, and things for whatever happens to them: *Darn, it snowed last night, now I have to shovel the walks. This rain keeps me inside so I can't go out and have fun. If only they had acted differently, I wouldn't be in this mess.* We used "blame" (and sometimes still use it) as a focal point for not taking responsibility for our own actions: *This or that was wrong, so we used. That didn't go my way, so we used. You should have acted differently, so we used.* Even in recovery we can still act like children: *This or that is wrong, so we yell at someone. That didn't go my way, so we quit our service position. You should have acted differently, so we boycott that meeting.* We seldom blame ourselves before exhausting every other possibility!

**Today, I remember:
At the end of blame is *ME*.**

We are taking responsibility, not drowning in blame and shame.
~Chemically Dependent Anonymous P 36

June 16

When all else fails, read the AA Big Book (CDA First Edition or NA Basic Text). I think I'll take the short cut and read it first. ~The Pocket Sponsor

Although our First Edition is one of the greatest books in recovery, it is useless when it sits on the shelf, unread. The person who has the book, but does not read it, has no advantage over the person who doesn't even own the First Edition of *Chemical Dependent Anonymous*. It is like putting together a model of something. We would make little progress in putting together a model airplane without reading the instructions. By looking at the picture on the box or looking at other models, chances are high that our plane would not fly. Looking at the First Edition on our shelf is not enough. Just as relying on others to tell us what the book contains is not enough. Assuming we already know the Program because we've read other 12-step texts is to miss the richness contained in CDA. We are not "just like other 12-step programs." To find out why, we read the suggestions.

Today, I move my CDA Book off the shelf and into my heart and soul.

If you are looking for a new, drug-and-alcohol-free way of life, these stories are presented as examples of how that goal can be achieved.
~Chemically Dependent Anonymous P 125

June 17

For if ye forgive men their trespasses, your heavenly father will also forgive you.
~Matthew 6:14

Isn't it ironic that we so often expect others to forgive us while we hold onto our own resentments? Not all, but many meetings end in the Lord's Prayer. In this prayer we say, "And forgive us our trespasses, as we forgive those who trespass against us." Now, if our Higher Power really held us to this, we would be in a world of hurt. Most of us have resentments or a grudge or two that we haven't really forgiven the offender for. So, at times, we stubbornly withhold forgiveness that is due to others, forgetting where we would be if God had refused to forgive us. God does not constantly, unrelentingly accuse us—yet when weresent, we are constantly, unrelentingly accusing our offender. Holding in resentments takes a great deal ofenergy. This energy, we have found, is best spent on our growth. Today, we forgive our offenders, not for them, but for us.

**I pass along the forgiveness
extended to me, and I am free.**

I was never able to forgive {my father} completely. But as a result of working the Steps, I recently had a wonderful healing experience.
~*Chemically Dependent Anonymous* P 282

June 18

You may think of the simple life as an empty, boring existence. Think again. ~Bruce & Stan

Many people don't want to consider living a simple lifestyle because they think that means they will be poor—without the finer things in life. They see "simple" as taking away from—not adding to. Yet, we find that "keeping it simple" is actually quite the opposite. When we identify what is truly important and get rid of all the superfluous junk around it, we no longer waste energy on that which is not important to us. By identifying what is *really* important, our choices become simpler and more focused. Focused choices become better choices. That makes us richer, notpoorer! Bruce and Stan go on to say that for most of us, "Our problem isn't that we need *more*. What we need is better." And, thus, by learning to discern what is truly important, we choose that which will make our program, our relationships, our service work, and our lives *better*.

I am just as enriched with what I *don't* have, as I am with what I do have.

We will keep it simple.
~Chemically Dependent Anonymous **P 121**

June 19

Though our feelings come and go, God's love for us does not. ~C.S. Lewis

Whether we are a newcomer, an old-timer, or an in-betweener, we cannot escape experiencing the *full range* of emotions, including the ugly, nasty ones. Yet, with the right attitude, this can be a blessing. If we take responsibility for our feelings, we can actually use them to solve problems. That's right. When we used drugs to quell our feelings, emotions were useless to us. But today, when we *feel* the emotion, we can use our awareness to figure things out. When feeling anger, we ask ourselves, "What isn't going my way?" We use that answer to identify self-will. When feeling fear, we ask ourselves, "Why do I not trust my Higher Power?" Our answer is used to work Step Three. When frustrated, we ask ourselves, "What or who am I trying to control?" We can answer this by reciting the Serenity Prayer and practicing the slogan "Let Go and Let God." We soon learn that the feelings which we used to run from can now be utilized as a greenhouse for our emotional growth.

Today, I use my feelings for healing.

I drank to suppress feelings of loneliness, and inadequacy, and all the problems that come with drinking.
~Chemically Dependent Anonymous P 136

June 20

You are today where the thoughts of yesterday have brought you and you will be tomorrow where the thoughts of today take you.
~Blaise Pascal

This journey of recovery is about understanding our past thoughts and actions while using the tools of the Program to turn them around. Sharing in meetings helps us to understand how we think in relation to others. It gives us the feeling that we are not alone in our beliefs. To take responsibility for our actions we work the Steps. This helps us gain a clearer picture of ourselves and allows us to make different choices in the future. We begin to gain an understanding of what we can, and cannot, control. We realize that giving ourselves to this process will affect a real change in our thoughts. And a real change in our thoughts will directly affect our actions towards others. We, who have walked through it, can testify that, although doing the work is a challenge, the reward is worth it.

I align my actions, so they are in agreementwith the good thoughts I think about me.

Hi! My name is Max, and I'm an addict-oholic. I'm powerless over everything but my attitude and my actions.
~Chemically Dependent Anonymous P 167

June 21

It unfolds itself before whoever walks along it.
~Lao Tzu

Nothing in our recovery has to be forced, finagled, or fought for because our next step is always in front of us if we will only accept it. Our spiritual journey requires one small step, and it is always *right now, right here, right before us*. It isn't into the next hour or the next day. Our path is not a myriad of mind games where we have to guess what is—that is a game we only play with ourselves. And taking the next right step, right here, right now is always God's will for us. Is there a newcomer walking through the door? That's our next step. Is someone asking us to chair a meeting? That's our next step. Is it time to show up for work? That's our next step. Do the clothes need to be washed? That's the next step. In fact, there is only one step we *can* take right now. Any other step we think of is a theory until it is directly before us—then and only then is it a step we can take. God's will and walking the path of sobriety never has to be forced; it is always the next right step, right here, right now.

I take the next right step, right here, right now.

Help me to grow in trusting your path for me. Take away any obstacles that I have placed in the way; I release them now.
~*Chemically Dependent Anonymous* P 47

June 22

Happiness and contentment are not the result of getting what we want; they are the result of wanting what we get in life. ~Father John Doe

Naturally, as human beings, we find ourselves wanting things—attention, a house, the perfect partner, job, sponsor, child, etc. But there is a subtle difficulty with these desires. When we desire something, our energy goes into *wanting* it and *wishing* for it, not into what is present in our lives. When *wanting*, we are not free to be passionate about what we have. The wonderment is when we are *fully present* in the moment. When we are *passionate* about what we are doing *right now*, wants disappear. The ability to want what we have is directly proportional to our ability to be fully present. By being present, we are completely absorbed in what we are doing at the moment—sponsorship, gardening, feeding the dog, or talking to a loved one. When completely absorbed in a task, we feel passion for it. When we feel passionate about it, we will want what we have.

Instead of thinking about what I don't have, I become fully absorbed in what I do have.

As far back as I can remember, I always looked for a way to avoid the reality of living in the present moment. **~Chemically Dependent Anonymous P 273**

June 23

Keep coming back. It works if you work it.
~Closing slogan at many 12-step meetings.

These are the last words spoken at a lot of meetings, and because of the repetitiveness of hearing it, many of us tune it out. But, if we listen with the ears of a newcomer, what do we hear? *"Keep coming back"* tells us that we are never done. It is an invitation to stay the course. *"It works"* tells us that if we accept the invitation, we will get results. It is a promise of success that is based on the contingency *"if."* If what? If "*you work it,"* then a successful result will be the effect. We must *do something* to get the results we seek. Our slogan is the promise that the tools we are given will, in fact, work. We can imagine we are wearing a carpenter's tool belt or we're carrying a toolbox with the First Edition in it. We have a crew boss (HP) and a supervisor (sponsor), and we receive training with our fellow crewmembers in the Program. Just as carpenters are always building, we too, will always be creating our lives.

I'll keep coming back because it works.
Better yet, I'll stay because it works even better.

{T}hat fellowship's {CDA's} program of recovery from the disease of addiction, is viable. It works!
~*Chemically Dependent Anonymous* P XVI

June 24

Once we truly know that life is difficult—once we truly understand and accept it—then life is no longer difficult. ~M. Scott Peck

In large events like war and natural disasters, or even small events like disagreements and disappointments, we have all learned that life is difficult. In fact, adversity seems to be a condition for living life on Planet Earth. Now, we could fight it, wail against it, struggle with it, and wear ourselves out emotionally; *or* we can simply accept it. What a concept. Making the simple acknowledgment that, "Yes, life is difficult," and then putting one foot in front of the other enables us to stop fighting life. Life *is* difficult. *Your point*? Life, at times, can also be quite pleasant, often strange, laugh-out-loud amusing, frequently unfair, greatly successful, and full of adventure. Life is life, and it balances on a scale from horrific to terrific. God gave us the wherewithal to deal with anything on these scales. So, take two aspirin and adjust!

**The best way out is through.
Today, I accept it, and go through
what is before me.**

Walking into difficult situations with level-headed maturity is new stuff.
~*Chemically Dependent Anonymous* P 52

June 25

We are talking about a real friendship with God. Not a pseudo-friendship, not a make-believe friendship, not a part-time friendship, but an important, meaningful, close friendship.
~Friendship with God

Not everyone in Chemically Dependent Anonymous wants to be friends with their Higher Power. Some do not feel worthy. Some are atheists and agnostics who don't really see the Great Reality as a being. Some of us just never thought of God as a friend. Maybe He was thought of as a father, employer, teacher, chastiser—but friend? Whether or not we want to be friends with our Higher Power, it is a strong bet that our Higher Power wants to be friends with us. As the slogan goes, "If you want friends, be friendly." So, what are the attributes of a friend? A good listener? God is that. Always there to lend a hand? Yes. Shares in our joys and sorrows? Yes. Doesn't abandon us in hard times? No. Doesn't withdraw love when we act stupid? No. What better friend could we have? None that we can think of.

**God, when I accept You as You are,
and me as I am, then we can be friends.**

Now, I just want to get closer to Him. I know that my God is a great and loving God. I just can't say enough about my Higher Power.
***~Chemically Dependent Anonymous* P 194**

June 26

If I keep on turning my life and my will over to the care of Something or Somebody else, what will become of me?
~Twelve Steps & Twelve Traditions

Some people feel that turning things over to their Higher Power is tantamount to rolling over and exposing their belly to the forces of the world. The difference between Turning it Over and Rolling Over is this: To *Turn It Over* we say something like, "God, I know you are in charge, and this will work out for my highest good, even if I don't understand the means. After all, I once thought it was horrible that I was an alcoholic and addict, and now it has become my greatest blessing!" *Rolling Over* is saying, "Go ahead God, mess up my life some more. After all, you cursed me with alcoholism, addiction, and threw in a few relationship problems to boot." It is a question of attitude. Are we optimistic, gracefully *turning over* what we can't control? Or are we pessimistic, *rolling over* and eating worms?

Today, I turn it over. I don't overturn it.

As I began to work the Steps with her guidance, she {my sponsor} told me that "surrender" in the Third Step meant not only surrendering our drugs and alcohol but the rest of our lives as well.
***~Chemically Dependent Anonymous* P 282**

June 27

Everyone is kneaded out of the same dough but not baked in the same oven. ~Yiddish Proverb

Developing an active support system is essential to a good solid recovery, but that doesn't mean that we only seek that support in one group. We have found that developing a strong support system includes not only attending meetings but attending varied meetings. It means visiting different meetings near and far, and maybe even visiting meetings of other fellowships. Just as we would not want to lean on only one person for all our recovery needs, we do not want to use only a single meeting or group for our support system. Those of us in addiction recovery are more alike than we are different, and it is our way in CDA to be inclusive, not exclusive. We *are* all made from the same dough, and we become a part of each other's support system regardless of what oven we were baked in.

Reviewing my involvement daily helps me keep my support system active.

I realized that Chemically Dependent Anonymous was not merely an extension of Alcoholics Anonymous.
~Chemically Dependent Anonymous P 336

June 28

To the fearful, change is threatening because it means that things may get worse. To the hopeful, change is encouraging because things may get better. To the confident, change is inspiring because the challenge exists to make things better. ~King Whitney, Jr.

Change has a varied impact on the human mind, depending on our frame of reference. No matter how hard we may try, we cannot avoid change. In CDA, we are told that all we have to change is everything. Change everything? How is that done? It's done by first donning the right attitude. By embracing change with hope and confidence (rather than fear), a proper frame of mind naturally accompanies our change. This means that we trust in our Higher Power. When we walk in the Sunlight of the Spirit, it is impossible to meet change with fear. We meet it knowing that whatever happens will happen for our highest good. By trusting in God, we remain hopeful and confident.

I accept change because the possibilities are infinite.

We have only come to this point in our recovery because we have broadened our understanding of trust, change and love.
~*Chemically Dependent Anonymous* P 92

June 29

Walk in wisdom toward them that are without, redeeming the time. ~Collossians 4:5

One major influence that truly counts today is the example we set for the people we touch in our everyday lives. In our addiction, we manipulated, lied, and used people. We influenced them alright, but it wasn't with wisdom—it was with thoughtlessness and idiocy. Today, when practicing the CDA principles, we have the unique opportunity to be helpful to others. Not everyone has the gift of our principles. We couldn't be the people we are today if it weren't for thewisdom of our program being utilized in every detail ofour lives. Each day, let us walk with wisdom insteadof past foolishness. Let us seize each opportunity to demonstrate a value-oriented life. Let the beauty of the principles of the Program shine in our every action so that we may be a better example to those that still suffer. We have limitless potential to deeply influence the perception that others have of recovery. We are "walking in wisdom" today.

**I may be the only copy of the
CDA First Edition that someone ever sees.**

These approximately two hundred words of inspired wisdom, wisdom that transcends human wisdom, are the keys to sanity and sanctity, to wholeness and holiness.
~Chemically Dependent Anonymous **P XVI**

June 30

Pay It Forward. ~Movie Title

A few years ago, a movie premiered entitled "Pay it Forward." It was about a young boy who learned a very important principle of life: what we do *here and now* ripples forward and multiplies. In our old lives, we worried about how to pay people back for the rotten way they treated us. Maybe we wanted to "show them" for criticizing us, or we felt we needed to "put them in their place" for their arrogance. We paid them *backwards*. It was a sad and oppositional way to live. In "Pay It Forward," immediate gain was not the goal. The goal was to give something to someone, trusting that they would, in turn, give to others. The hope was that they would continue this act of giving until large chains of people were giving to one another. The film contains an important message. How we treat another person does not end there. So, we must examine how we treat everyone for we create a chain reactionthat eventually returns to us.

My job is not to worry about how to pay back those who have harmed me, but how to pay back those who have helped me.

They want to help us and we believe in them.
~Chemically Dependent Anonymous P 92

July

July 1

Don't stop thinking about tomorrow, yesterday's gone, yesterday's gone. ~Fleetwood Mac

Music is a profound force in our lives. Armies march to it, and lovers embrace to it while proclaiming their love. Music can call us to action like no other force on earth. Listen to a bagpipe, the beat of a drum, or the opening horns from Aaron Copland's "Fanfare for the Common Man," and just try to remain neutral. It can't be done. In the past, it may have been music with sinister and negative messages that was our partner in addiction. Maybe that music is still with us, a dark aura reminding us of days we want to forget. As we plot our way to a successful recovery, it is suggested we "clean house." We can let our minds and hearts be rejuvenated by songs that speak of a new us, a new life, and a new hope. It has been said that Martin Luther converted more souls with his music than all his preaching. He knew the power of music.

I find a song that fills my heart with hope and tell myself, "Yesterday is gone and tomorrow holds nothing but promise."

I go in and play and enjoy it because I'm always plugged in to my universe with my music.
~*Chemically Dependent Anonymous* P 295

July 2

Don't give up meeting together as some have, but continue to do it to encourage one another.
~Hebrews 10:25

The author of the book of Hebrews knew that trying to do something on our own is tough. The early Christians had many enemies who did not want them to succeed. The practice of meeting regularly to encourage one another in their faith was one key solution to avoid defeat. The founders of Alcoholics Anonymous, Chemically Dependent Anonymous, and Narcotics Anonymous knew that one of the key factors to success over our addictions was having the support of others. We can't do it alone. There is something magical that happens when we spend time with people who know our struggles and speak our language. It empowers us like few other things. Don't underestimate the power of meeting together. Don't underestimate the magic, either. The early church didn't, and their story lives on across the centuries.

Today I go to one of God's workshops. I go to a meeting of Chemically Dependent Anonymous.

Talked for a long time with someone I work with who is also in the Program. It was like having our own little meeting, using the language we both understand so well.
~*Chemically Dependent Anonymous* P 111

July 3

Upon being asked which is the most important of the Twelve Steps, one of the early members once replied with another question: "Which is the most important spoke of a wheel?"
~Back to Basics

We know that if one spoke of a wheel is broken, the wheel may go for a while, but eventually it will give way. This is especially true when one hits a bump in the road. That missing or broken spoke will cause the collapse of not only the wheel, but maybe the vehicle as well. What about us? Do we have a Step or two that is broken or missing in our program? The old-timers used to have an exercise to find out. Close your eyes and recite all Twelve Steps. The ones you stumble on are the ones you need to be looking at. On a subconscious level, if we are resistant to working on a particular Step, or not doing it honestly, or perhaps just procrastinating, we won't be able to recite it effortlessly. We don't need to wait for that bump in the road to find out if we have a weak or broken spoke in our wheel of recovery.

I take *all* the Steps to find out
where they will take me.

If you want what we have and are willing to make the effort necessary, then you are ready to take certain steps.
~Chemically Dependent Anonymous P 21

July 4

We will suddenly realize that God is doing for us what we could not do for ourselves.
~Alcoholics Anonymous P 84

All our unsuccessful attempts to get clean and sober were always powered by self-deception and sheer willpower. The Second Step of CDA tells us we must come to believe that a power greater than ourselves could restore us to sanity. The Second Step is indicative of a process, not an event. In this process, we learn that faith in a Power greater than ourselves is the cornerstone of a solid recovery program. By working the Twelve Steps, we develop a relationship with the God of our understanding. This relationship is varied and personal. Some call it friendship; some see God as a parent; others as an employer; and still others see Him as all the above. Whatever our perception or connection, through our recovery years, we gradually see how our God ultimately achieves His plan for us. The old-timers told us, as the plan unfolds it will far exceed anything we could have imagined.

**Everything that is happening is
God's plan for me today.**

I believe that God has a plan and that's why He spared my life.
~Chemically Dependent Anonymous **P 193**

July 5

He that is soon angry dealeth foolishly.
~Proverbs 14:17

We all know the short temper that comes with a hangover, and how cross and grumpy we were in-between fixes. Sadly, angry responses and short tempers don't automatically disappear in recovery. They say if you sober up a horse thief, you then have a sober horse thief! Sober up a rageaholic and you have a sober person who still rages. Hostility and rage hurt us, just as it hurts those around us. Acting angrily on impulse is the opposite of the serenity we seek. Although therapists tell us that a *burst of anger* is natural and should be felt, we know that our program tells us that angry *behavior* is always a choice. Ever felt road rage and started name calling? Ever punched a wall with your fist? Anger, when fed with the above reactions, tends to grow, not abate. That is why A.A. tells us anger is "the dubious luxury of normal men." When we are feeling angry, it is best to write it down to get it out and look at it tomorrow, so we do not hurt someone needlessly.

If I lose my temper, I lose.

If it had been the old days and I was still using, such an occurrence might have set me off like a stick of TNT. Instead, I talked out my frustration and anger with some friends.
~Chemically Dependent Anonymous P 338

July 6

We are all like one-winged angels. It is only when we help each other that we can fly.
~Luciano de Crescenzo

Our sponsors tell us to listen carefully to their words because the day will come when they may need to hear those words repeated back to them. In early recovery, we may not understand or believe that our sponsors may someday need *us* like that. They seem so wise and above it all. We think they are just trying to make us feel good. But, as promised, as the years go by, there will be times when we are able to comfort our sponsors and help them see a truth they missed. Amazingly, the advice or comfort we will give them is the very advice and comfort they give us now. We, in turn, tell our sponsees the same thing. The miracle is that they too will come back to us with our very own kind and loving words of advice.

**In our need, sponsors helped us up.
We listen, so that in their need
We will not let them down.**

To sponsor newcomers in CDA is to give back what we've been given many times over.
~Chemically Dependent Anonymous P 66

July 7

Your actions speak your truth.
~Collection of Eastern Wisdom Philosophy

Good intentions were probably not our highest priority when using. We had intentions, but no one could call them "good." We *intended* to have "just one." We *intended* to get home on time. We *intended* to pay the bills. Maybe we protested, "But my intentions were good." Only they really weren't good. The truth is, if an intention is good, it is accompanied by good action. In recovery, we may still find it difficult to followthrough with the personal goals we set. The "follow- through" is what intention is all about. Didn't we just share about not gossiping at that meeting? Yet, the very next day we found it impossible to resist a juicybit of news. Did we say we were going to exercise,but instead end up snacking in front of the TV? When we do something other than what we say we aregoing to do, then our intention is not good. To be considered a "good" intention, it must be accompanied by good action.

It is not my intentions that define me.
It is my actions.

Action! That's what our sponsors keep telling us. Either take positive action and move forward or sit around and be drawn backwards.
***~Chemically Dependent Anonymous** P 35*

July 8

Burn the idea into the consciousness of every man that he can get well regardless of anyone.
~Alcoholics Anonymous P 98

The analogy "burn" is a good one because learning to stay clean and sober is not unlike learning to keep our body parts out of the fire! We learn not to touch the stove because of the way it physically feels. It hurts! Just as our physical body teaches us through feelings, our emotions do too. We learn to be even-tempered, honest, and social because of how our emotions *feel*. Example: When we put our hand in the fire, the physical pain warns us not to do that again. When we do something ignorant, like throw a fit in front of the group, we *feel bad*. The emotional pain warns us not to do that again. Hurting *can* be a good thing. It is an early warning system which sends a signal that something is burning us, like a character defect. The hurt and pain we feel in recovery doesn't mean the Program is not working—it means it is! It is teaching us to feel and, thus, learning to do things right.

When I feel bad, I am grateful that my early warning system is working.

CDA does work. But you've got to want it. I wanted it because I was tired of hurting.
~Chemically Dependent Anonymous P 194

July 9

Unless the medicine stuns you, it won't cure the disease. ~Zen Proverb

Coddling newcomers is not how our founding fathers carried the message. We often hear feel-good things like: Let the newcomer lead meetings; the person with the most sobriety was the one who got up first this morning; relapse is a part of recovery. Those are "coddle the newcomer" platitudes, not recovery. The founding fathers told newcomers to Suit up, Show up, Sit up, and Shut up. They didn't take time to build their self-esteem. They told the truth and expected the newcomer to listen. None of us arrived at a 12-step program because we were so brilliant. Nor did we get here because we had high or low self-esteem! We got here because we were sick in body, mind, and spirit. If lack of self-esteem or self-knowledge was the causeof our addiction, then our family could have loved and educated us right into recovery without the aid of the 12-step programs! They certainly tried hard enough!

I can love a newcomer without coddling him or her. It's called "tell it like it is."

I decided to give the Program my best shot and I'm going to keep coming back. I hope that the newcomer does the same.
~Chemically Dependent Anonymous P 194

July 10

I don't work the Program to get my life back; I work the Program to get my life forward.
~The Pocket Sponsor

When we first start coming to meetings, we think we just have a problem with drugs and alcohol. Once we set down the drugs, some of us start getting our lives back almost immediately. Then we hear that "drugs and alcohol are but a symptom of the disease," andwe may not understand what that means. Gradually, though, we find out that what we really have is a *living* problem. We learn that recovery is not just about abstinence. We learn about "getting a sponsor," "working the Steps," "taking suggestions," "going to meetings," "finding a Higher Power," and "praying." Our lives move *forward*. We begin to say, "I want todo this … go there … make that …," and our dreams become incorporated into our lives. We find out who we really are, how we tick, what we like, and what we don't like. This is recovery. We get our life *back* by stopping the use of drugs and alcohol, but we move our lives *forward* through the Program of CDA.

I am grateful to have my life forward.

And they too were looking for a better way of life. They were willing to give living a chance.
~Chemically Dependent Anonymous P 197

July 11

What are the three hardest words to say? The correct answer is "I was wrong." ~Bruce & Stan

Few of us relish admitting that we have made a mistake. It is so much easier to shift the blame to someone or something else. Yet, we know that without admitting the mistakes, we are likely to keep on makin' 'em! It is usually pride that plants itself between us and our honesty about the things that we botch up. If we admit to ourselves that we blew it, then we think that makes us less than perfect! How can our egos handle that? Maybe we think that "blowing it" means our program isn't up to snuff. But the truth is, our program is not up to snuff when we are failing to acknowledge our mistakes! Maybe we need to review the guidance from the wise book of Alcoholics Anonymous, "We claim spiritual progress, not spiritual perfection."

I talk to my Higher Power about my mistakes. After all, He already noticed them when I made them.

The only way to understand the mistakes I've made is to see them as part of my growth.
~Chemically Dependent Anonymous P 198

July 12

In doing the best that we can for today, we are doing all that God asks of us. ~Daily Reflections

There is a lot of good living in life, and we believe that God wants us to enjoy the heck out of it. We are not asked to build monuments and cathedral clubhouses to the glory of our program and leaders. Our Divine Source does not ask for gold or glory from us. Nor are we asked for continual penance and self-flagellation. Most people in recovery are secure in the knowledge that all our Higher Power expects is for us to do the next right thing. How do we know what that is? The blueprint for doing the next right thing is in the Twelve Steps of Chemically Dependent Anonymous that was so lovingly handed down to us from Alcoholics Anonymous. We must remember that we are working toward spiritual progress in the Twelve Steps, not penance. The wonderful thing is, nowhere is it written down that we have to claim spiritual perfection—*thank God*! We only claim to do our best, and God does the rest.

**I do the next right thing,
so that the wrong thing doesn't last.**

{I}f we do our best today, we'll have a good tomorrow. I know that because it's been happening for me day after day after day.
~Chemically Dependent Anonymous P 227

July 13

It is not only wrong to worry, it is unbelief; worrying means we do not believe that God can look after the practical details of our lives.
~Oswald Chambers

Step Three is an all-the-way Step, or it's no Step at all. Once we turn it over to our Higher Power, there is nothing left to worry about. If we are worrying about anything, then we haven't turned it over, have we? To worry about something is to focus on events that have not yet happened. This means that we don't trust our Higher Power to take care of life's details. If we don't believe that our life is in good hands, then we *should worry*—we haven't worked Step Three! It has been said that when you work Step Three, you take your life out of the hands of an idiot. That makes us smirk a little, but the underlying principle assures us that there *is* a divine plan for the details of our lives. When we honestly and deeply take this Step, we *know* that the details are being handled. We just have to show up and do the next right thing.

**I only have two choices: Worry or trust God.
Today, God gets the job.**

But I wasn't really willing to surrender to a God. I just didn't trust enough, yet.
~*Chemically Dependent Anonymous* P 133

July 14

Today I will wait in peace and rest in the knowledge that God is working for me while I am resting. ~Ruth Fishel

There are days when we might have to sit back and wait. We might have to wait for the right time ... the right energy ... the right answer. Waiting patiently may put us a little bit further down the line, but we will probably get what is meant just for us. When we move too fast or force solutions, we might get what is right in front of us, but absolutely wrong for us. Sometimes other people are involved with our answers, and *they* are not ready to be in our solution yet. There are days when we might have to wait for the right person to take the other side of our burden so we can lift it together and get it through the door. We don't always have the energy we desire, the necessary answers, enough time, or the right person in our life. So, we learn patience. We learn to hang in there until the "right" solution presents itself. Waiting is when we pause and rest, knowing the right solution will appear, when ready.

If I have to force a solution, it's not the solution.

{P}rayer enables us to become grownups...{W}e can sense what our true course of action must be, even if it is just waiting at that moment to let other circumstances change.
~*Chemically Dependent Anonymous* P 90

July 15

If you love something very, very much set it free. If it does not return, it was never meant to be yours. If it does, love it forever. ~Bancro

Nothing is more troubling to the chemically dependent person than romantic relationships. Fear of abandonment often keeps us determined to control our love interests. We try to force them to love us or behave in a manner we deem acceptable. And, as crazy as it sounds, rather than let go of a person that does not hold a genuine reflection of love towards us, we have been known to "hold them hostage" and coerce an unhealthy relationship. Something we learned from the Al-Anons and Nar-Anons is that we cannot force our will on others. We cannot force them to love us, stay with us, respect us, agree with us, or share our vision of the future. Although it is easier said than done, we must learn to let go. We consider this analogy: A seed germinates, breaks ground, sprouts, grows petals, and blossoms all without *forcing* anything.

**I cannot make someone love me, but
I can become someone who is lovable.**

And they asked me, "What makes you think you know anything about love? 17 years, all you've been doing is grasping and taking everything you can get out of your relationships."
~Chemically Dependent Anonymous P 351

July 16

Beware of the "geographic cure" and the simple "spouse-ectomy." ~Newcomers Handbook, Co-Dependents Anonymous P 47

Unless we address all the issues in recovery by working the Twelve Steps, our problems will dog us from place to place and relationship to relationship. One of the reasons our sponsors tell us, "Don't make any major decisions in the first year," is so that we can change what is on the inside before we starttrying to change what is on the outside. They are not out to make life miserable for us by denying us the ability to change and grow. But they know something we probably don't in the beginning, that changing spouses, changing houses, or changing jobs won't make a lick of difference in our lifestyles unless we have made the necessary changes on the inside. Wherever we live, whatever we do for a living, with whomever we find ourselves, if *we* haven't changed ourselves, our problems will remain the same.

Wherever I go, there I am.

I went for a "geographical" cure by moving from one side of town to another {...}.
~Chemically Dependent Anonymous P 293

July 17

Everything has its beauty but not everyone sees it. ~Confucius

One of the things we have to admit in recovery is that we all tend to judge not only ourselves, but the people and situations around us. We hear in the rooms not to be so hard on ourselves because we are our own worst critics, but we are pretty harsh critics of everything else, too! Having a positive outlook and appreciating the good in everything and everyone around us is one of our recovery goals. It is important to take the focus off the negative and judgmental voices we hear from that committee in our head. We need to listen to that loving, kind voice that seeks to appreciate—not depreciate—the life that surrounds us. What we focus on is what we feed. "If you can't say anything nice, don't say anything at all," could be changed to, "If you can't judge anything nice, don't judge anything at all." By taking the focus off the negative in others, we take it off ourselves, too.

As I focus on appreciating people and situations around me today, I learn how to appreciate me.

Do I appreciate the good people and things in my life?
~Chemically Dependent Anonymous P 38

July 18

A ship in port is safe, but that's not what ships are built for. ~Grace Murray Hopper

Our meetings, clubhouses, retreats, and conventions are our ports and safe harbors. But we are not meant to stay docked for the rest of our sobriety. Staying clean and sober is simply the beginning of our vast journey. Starting from our safe harbors, we venture out to our families, jobs, relationships, religions, and communities. We have been taught how to communicate, share, and walk among those we used to devastate. Our program has given us the gift of living in our world as whole human beings able to participate, contribute, and even enrich those lives around us. When we falter as the inevitable storms in life prevail upon us, our safe harbors remain for us to dock in.

CDA is not my whole life, but I accept today that it keeps my life whole!

{D}iscover the new life of health, sanity and sobriety that CDA has to offer.
***~Chemically Dependent Anonymous** P VIII*

July 19

A journey of a thousand miles begins with a single Step. ~Lao Tzu

It is through movement that we find out who we really are. We cannot stand still physically or spiritually and expect to recover from this disease. Thus, when we enter recovery, we begin with the First Step. It is our job then, to move forward in a positive direction by taking each new step as it is revealed to us. This is an incredible journey of self-discovery that gradually takes us to new places in life and love that we never dreamed possible. However, this is not an instant journey—there is no "Beam me up Scotty," and we get zapped from newcomer to old-timer NOW. There are no shortcuts either. Although we may stumble as we move forward, the path is *clearly* marked. Reading the literature, listening at meetings, and believing in our sponsors have become our road signs for the journey. Our Higher Power is what powers us for the trip. That power is waiting to unfold within us and fuel us for this incredible journey of self-discovery.

I embrace my journey.

I have observed that the members of Chemically Dependent Anonymous are bonded together, merrily traveling the road to freedom.
~*Chemically Dependent Anonymous* P XVII

July 20

He who rejects change is the architect of decay. The only human institution which rejects progress is the cemetery. ~Harold Wilson

Changing the way we felt was a 24-hour pastime in our old life. As the pain mounted, we used drugs to change the way we felt. As the joy mounted, we used drugs to feel *more* joy. As the boredom mounted, again, we used drugs to change from boredom to *anything*. Fortunately, the drugs stopped working, and we couldn't change fast enough and often enough. Yet, the only constant in life is change! We can count on that. Even though some think we addicts are afraid of change, this is not true. We're not afraid of *change*; we sought change all the time. What we are afraid of is that now we are *responsible* for the type of changes we make! We can't leave it to drugs to take us to "La La Land." It is our *responsibility* to make the desired change happen without the aid of drugs!

**If I don't change, I remain the same
and become the architect of my own decay.**

But such willingness begets change and change begets learning. Learning begets growth and growth, in turn, begets recovery.
~Chemically Dependent Anonymous P 334

July 21

A lot of these things you can't really teach. All you can do is create a situation where if people want to learn, they can. ~The Horse Whisperer

Once we become sponsors, we soon find out that we can't force our sponsees to *get* clean and sober, nor can we *keep* them clean and sober. All we can do is be a model of recovery, make suggestions, and gently guide them toward healthy choices. We've heard of the horse whisperer and the dog whisperer. As sponsors, we could call ourselves "sponsee whisperers," or we could even say "pigeon whisperers." We help to tame the addiction-gone-wild in our sponsees, calm them down, and quiet their noisy lives. If they aren't hearing the voice of God, we help whisper it to them. If they are in the midst of chaos, we whisper suggestions about where to find solutions. If our sponsees make ready to bolt, wewhisper words of encouragement and hope. We create situations for them so that if they do want to hear the voice of God, they can become quiet and listen for God's whispers.

I show my sponsees how to turn off the noise so they can hear God's gentle whispers.

Communion with God gives me peace, hope and confidence.
~Chemically Dependent Anonymous P 60

July 22

Never discourage anyone who continually makes progress, no matter how slow. ~Plato

We certainly could write a book about how persistent we addicts and alcoholics were despite all the hell we put ourselves through! We tried again and again to make our using work with different drugs, different combinations, different geographical cures—but nothing worked until we used abstinence and the 12-step programs. What a concept that was! Then, we learned to persevere in the *opposite direction*. We persevered to stay clean and sober, *no matter what*. Perseverance, as part of our recovery means that we are diligent in our efforts and patient in expecting results. We should not be discouraged that we don't change for the better overnight! Our Higher Power is not discouraged by it. There isn't going to be any judging about how long it takes us to learn new things as we apply these principles. And there isn't any graduation. How long must we persevere? Only one day: *today*.

I am diligent and patient. It is more important to get it right than get it now.

It also helped me not to have expectations of having this after one year or that after three years and something else after five years.
~Chemically Dependent Anonymous P 236

July 23

Courage is very important. Like a muscle, it is strengthened by use. ~Ruth Gordon

Courage plays a large role in our recovery. It is the tenacity to work our way through the Steps despite the great fear and pain we sometimes experience. Courage is not the absence of fear and pain; it is the ability to act in the presence of fear and pain. But we do not act alone. We have allies. Because of ourallies in the Fellowship, we do not allow ourselves to become paralyzed by the trials and tribulations that accompany the many changes we make—changes such as a divorce, the loss of a loved one, being victimized by crime, having our past catch up with us, losing a great job, or facing our inner demons. Our courage means we remain clean and sober day after day, always acknowledging the stumbling blocks and continuing to do the next right thing, even when fear screams at us to run. Our continued sobriety is the reward for this courage, and the Fellowship is our incentive.

**Courage is not a one-shot deal.
I work at it day after day.**

If it weren't for those first few commitments in CDA, I don't know that I'd have had the courage to do some of the other things that I've been able to do since I have been in the Program.
~*Chemically Dependent Anonymous* P 146

July 24

We are not human beings seeking a spiritual experience but spiritual beings seeking a human experience. ~Wayne Dyer

We may have thought we had wonderful spiritual experiences under the influence of psychedelics or in drug-induced trances, but the results of that "spirituality" was the addict inside us agreeing that more drugs would create more "spirituality." Many of us seek spirituality in CDA and soon find that we can't force it. Spirituality is not a matter of trying harder— we can't *make* it happen. This is because it's already happening. It is only through a lack of attention that we fail to see our true selves. The mask on our human body, and in our human activities, that makes us appear to be less than we are consists of our egos, desires, and self-will. But by paying attention to the details of our spiritual program, the mask becomes a casualty of our true self. We cannot make ourselves spiritual, we already are.

The biggest obstacle to realizing my true spiritual being is a lack of attention to my spiritual program.

When I don't get to a meeting for one or two days, I feel very insecure, not necessarily that I'm going to goout and use, but just spiritually "out of practice."
~*Chemically Dependent Anonymous* P 167

July 25

We are accepted and loved for who we are, not in spite of who we are. No one can revoke our membership or make us do anything that we do not choose to do. ~Narcotics Anonymous P 59

Unity, love, fellowship, and recognition are what we are given when we walk through the doors of CDA. When we are so freely given this gift, we sometimes wonder, "What's the catch?" There is no catch. We don't care what substance the newcomers used, nor do we ask them to leave because they're still using. If their behavior is so bad that they disrupt the meeting, we are instructed to take them aside, and present the Program to them one on one. It is then that we tell them to *Keep Coming Back*. And we sincerely mean it. We are a family of the body, mind, and spirit in recovery. Just as no one can revoke family membership, no one can revoke CDA membership either. This is our gift to each other.

I do not determine which newcomers have the right to membership in CDA, *they do*.

There are so many potential candidates for either A.A. or CDA out there, now. And, after all, both programs are really proclaiming the good news of the same hope {...}
***~Chemically Dependent Anonymous* P 181**

July 26

Lots of people want to ride with you in the limo, but what you want is someone who will take the bus with you when the limo breaks down.
~Oprah Winfrey

One of the benefits of fellowship is that whether we ride in the limo or take the bus, we do it together. However, there are times when we might feel a bit stifled from too much fellowship, and so we branch out. There is nothing wrong with getting into the mainstream, but it can be daunting. Maybe we mention the Twelve Promises, and our "normal" companions look perplexed. Or we tell a troubled friend to "turn it over," and they ask, "Turn what over?" Maybe we mention our Higher Power in normal conversation and someone remarks that they don't believe in astrology! It takes very little "branching out" to realize that we *want* to be around our CDA family who speak the same language and live by the same values we do. Whether we own the limo or ride the bus, we are there for each other through it all!

I give as much or more to my CDA family, as I do to those in my mainstream life.

All my close friends are in CDA and my whole social life revolves around that fellowship. I not only get what I need but what I want from their program.
~*Chemically Dependent Anonymous* P 226-227

July 27

My body is a temple.
Caring for my body gives me a place to worship.
Listening to my body brings me wisdom.
Challenging my body fulfills my potential.
~Hummingbird Words

Our disease is one of body, mind, and spirit, and it is in each area that we must find recovery. Sadly, once we stop using mind-affecting chemicals, we may think the "body" part of our disease is taken care of. That is akin to saying, "Well, I have my high school diploma, and so I don't have to learn anymore." Our bodies continue to need attention and care, just as our mind and spirits do. The idea that our body is a temple was once totally foreign to us. The only time we ever listened to our body was when it told us to use some more drugs. But, for our mind, emotions and spirit to stay healthy, we must also listen to what our physical body needs. The secret of a healthy body is paying attention to the details. We watch our diet, our weight, and keep in shape. We do it now!

**What I get out of my body relates
directly to what I put into it.**

My great foe is laziness, spiritual and physical, the deadly sin of sloth. I am more afraid of it, in myself, than the compulsion to go out and use.
~Chemically Dependent Anonymous P 171

July 28

{W}e confirm our values by resolving to change our behavior and by making reparations. These reparations might include paying back any ill-gotten money, or offering an apology, or taking another action that would restore the dignity of all involved (including ourselves). ~Harvey Stout

Step Nine, the amends-making Step, is as much about forgiveness as it is about making things right. But this forgiveness is not *them* forgiving *us*. It is about us forgiving us. We cannot possibly learn to forgive ourselves for all the damage we have caused until we take responsibility for our past. In taking this responsibility, we do not anticipate getting pats on the back for our "goodness" by saying we are sorry or paying back money we stole. Making amends gets a lot easier when we stop trying to extract forgiveness from everyone to whom we make amends. What they choose to do with our attempts to make things right is up to them. Amends is about how we see ourselves, not how others see us.

I restore my dignity when I take responsibility for what I have done and make my amends.

We let go of others' actions and take ownership of our part in things.
~*Chemically Dependent Anonymous* P 51

July 29

The best way to do ourselves good is to be doing good for others. The best way to gather, is to scatter. ~Thomas Brooks

When we are in pain, it is quite natural to lean on the Fellowship, and ask others to help us out. In CDA, our Fellowship is based primarily on the principle that we can ask for and receive help when we need it. The concept of one addict helping another is a proven and powerful tool that enables us to get our feet on solid ground. But, if we only receive and never give, we are acting like children that refuse to share. Others need us as much as we need them. Our fellowship is based on receiving the help of others. But personal recovery is based on us helping others. When we are feeling the need to run to others for help and comfort, there is a helpful spiritual exercise. It is to *do the opposite*. We search out someone *who needs our help*, and we serve them. We do what is needed to help them make it through another day. Gradually, what upset us is replaced with something more important.

Today, I give myself the spiritual gift of "service to another."

The Fellowship is what really put me on the road to recovery.
~Chemically Dependent Anonymous P 266

July 30

Talking about a path is not walking that path. Talking about life is not living. ~Lao Tzu

From a spiritual manuscript known as the Tao-Te Ching, Lao Tzu gave this teaching to mankind over 2,500 years ago. Today, this same bit of wisdom, "walk like you talk" is still heard. When referring to a hypocrite, many of us have rephrased the words to say, "They say one thing but do another." However, "walk like you talk" also applies to the person who never manages to really live their program. They only *talk* about living the Program. Could this be us? We talk about how important service work is. What position do we hold in the service structure? We talk about carrying the message. When was the last time we bought a First Edition and gave it to a newcomer? We talk about being patient. How do we react in traffic? We talk about having fun in recovery. When was the last time we made someone laugh?

Am I living the Program right now, or am I only *thinking* about living the Program?

We have so many other "things" to do in our lives sometimes that living the Program seems more difficult than it used to.
~Chemically Dependent Anonymous P 297

July 31

Don't despair over the darkness that is beyond your control. Instead, shine your own light so brightly that the darkness is overwhelmed.
~Jamie

In today's "self-help, find-your-inner-demons" culture, we are not obligated to be miserable in order to grow. We can *choose* where we want to focus our energy and attention, thus growing towards the light. When we focus on areas where we have a positive impact, such as what we can do today to be a part of the solution, we don't seem to *despair* about things. It serves no useful purpose to get stuck on things which we cannot control such as the past, other people, or the weather. We only have control over *our* perspective and *our* behavior. We are living in darkness if we keep going over the past actions of ourselves or others. It makes more sense to *act* on our own behalf, living in and growing towards the light, than it does to let the darkness overtake us. It is in this way we keep moving forward, becoming the people we were meant to be.

I overwhelm the dark thoughts with positive actions.

Do I take positive action in my life as I am guided to do so?
~*Chemically Dependent Anonymous* P 40

August

August 1

Autonomy gives our groups the freedom to act on their own to establish an atmosphere of recovery, serve their members, and fulfill their primary purpose. ~Narcotics Anonymous P 64

Before recovery, there were few of us who wouldhave used the word "autonomy," much less understood it. Today, we know that autonomy, on a personal level, pretty much means being true to ourselves. For a group, that means making decisions for their members' benefit. For CDA members, it means making decisions that benefit the groups without ruling them. We are a diverse group of people who find ways to adhere to our primary purpose and stay true to ourselves. We do not judge another group's conscience as "wrong." In fact, according to Tradition Four, as long as another group doesn't affect CDA as a whole, their group conscience *cannot* be deemed "wrong." Even if the decisions are completely different, we support our home group's decisions, as well as support the decisions of other groups.

**I support my home group's decisions,
or I find a new home group.**

In actuality, our Fellowship is a democracy with aloving God as our director as He may express Himselfin our group conscience.
~Chemically Dependent Anonymous P 72

August 2

A strong person takes responsibility, a weak person blames. ~David R. Hawkins, M.D., Ph.D.

Blame is an intoxicating and powerful defense mechanism. When we are in "blaming mode," we create the illusion that we are always right, and we become irreproachable when things go wrong. In actuality, blaming others is the same as giving our power away. It doesn't make us better people to find excuses why this or that happened: "My grades were low because_____. I didn't pick up the newcomer because_____. I was late because_____." It's a very primitive mechanism to blame a co-worker, a neighbor, or a family member when *we* don't measure up. There have even been times that we placed the blame on God for *our* shortcomings. We make ourselves the hapless victims of other people when we give our power away. And let's remember that blaming others is the same as giving our power away. Instead, we need to find strength in owning up to the choices that "caused" our circumstances.

When I look in the mirror, I look hard.
This is the person who got me here.

For many years, I still attached some blame to my father for what I believed was his part in my addiction.
~Chemically Dependent Anonymous P 282

August 3

Recovery through the program is simple. It will work if we live it. ~The Little Red Book

Life on life's terms can be confusing, intimidating, and overwhelming, to say the least. This not only goes for the newcomer, but also for the more seasoned in sobriety. We lug around our duffle bag of insecurities when dealing with our Step work, meeting someone new, the pressures of life, complexities of relationships, work, the PTA, children, bills, school, etc. We crawl further and further up into our head, all the while analyzing, justifying, and rationalizing. Whether we make mountains out of molehills or, conversely, molehills out of mountains, our sponsors encourage us to *Keep it Simple*. At the most basic level, keeping it simple boils down to two measures:

- Don't put the chemical in our bodies.
- Go to meetings.

It's that simple.

Today, recovery is simple. I go to a meeting, chemical-free, and the rest falls into place.

There are plenty of tools and people here to help me: my beautiful wife, my wonderful friends, all the co-founders of CDA, all the new people and Phil C., my sponsor in A.A., who keeps it simple for me.
~Chemically Dependent Anonymous P 297

August 4

If a bad word comes in your ear and then comes out of your mouth, it will go someplace and hurt somebody. If I did that, that hurt would come back twice as hard on me. ~Wallace Black Elk

Spirituality is the basis of our program and, once we have a few 24 hours, foul language and rumor-mongering should not be considered a part of our spiritual language. Words from the heart are said tobe the language of the soul. We may believe that our heart is full of spirituality and love for our fellow man. Yet, to know what's truly in our heart, we need to listen to our mouth. What are we and others hearing from our mouths? Do we sound haughty when we're talking about so and so relapsing on prescription pills just like we had warned? Do we take on a superior tone just because our sponsees seem to be doing better than *their* sponsees? Are we speaking words of condemnation when somebody doesn't do it our way? Our true measure of spirituality is heard by everyone.

**I monitor what's in my heart by
listening to my mouth.**

The CDA picnic is always so much fun. Sterling shares from his heart and speaks in a low-pitched, soft voice as hungry people eat hamburgers.
~Chemically Dependent Anonymous **P 119**

August 5

The way you deal with life each day depends on what you bring to life each day. ~Bruce & Stan

When someone asks us, "How are you?" or "How's it going?" chances are we just say, "Fine. How's it going with you?" Chances are, they reply the same. It is such a mindless social habit. Greetings often become boring repetitions that reflect a lack of enthusiasm about our daily routines. But recovery is not about being apathetic and boring. Recovery is infused with blessings, self-exploration, and turning impossibilities to possibilities. Recovery is fun and adventuresome. We find that a good exercise to remind us that life is not boring is to *really answer* the question, "How are you?" by telling the person who asks it at least three blessings we woke up with that morning. An example, "I'm clean and sober, I have a great job waiting for me, and my family is healthy. How 'bout you?"

When asked how I am today, I answer with a list of three blessings.

I have a love for life. I look forward to getting up in the morning. I love my job; I don't believe there is a better one in the world. I help people for a living. I enjoy watching, listening, and interacting with people.
***~Chemically Dependent Anonymous* P 130**

August 6

This is what I think heaven'll be: reexperiencing, in a blaze of light, the wonderful moments of our earthly existence. At each step along the way, we'll stop short, astounded by God's generosity and ashamed of our past heedlessness.
~That Man is You

It seems we go through life in a haze, always searching and striving for more. Indeed, it has been said that we suffer from the disease of "More." Even in recovery we find ourselves still wanting "more" of something. Perhaps it is recognition that we are seeking. Do we sit in a meeting waiting to hear if anyone might refer to what we just said? Maybe we want a raise, a higher-priced car, or lengthier sobriety. Do we want to have more sponsees that adore us, quoting us at other meetings? Is this the life we want to live? If we could only see and feel that all we really need is to know that we belong right here, right now. We are part of a Master Plan. We don't *need* more of anything. We *are* MORE—more than enough—God made us that way.

I don't need more. I am already more than I could have ever hoped for.

All of us who have grown up together in these Programs are living more now; experiencing more and have much less free time.
~Chemically Dependent Anonymous P 297

August 7

You see, in the final analysis, it is all between you and God; it was never between you and them, anyway. ~Mother Teresa

Doing the right thing isn't always easy and it doesn't always feel good. Excuses to *not do* the right thing can creep in insidiously, and seemingly feel good at the time. Maybe we choose that which we want, rather than that which we know is right. We can make selfish choices and then "excuse" them away. We "choose to excuse," so to speak. We say, "The cashier won't know she gave me $20 dollars extra in change," or "I don't have to say I'm sorry, he already knows it." Our program teaches us that these self-serving choices are contrary to Step Three. Step Three is based on the principle that our Higher Power is in charge of our life, not our self-will. Our Higher Power wants us to do the right thing. Thus, doing the right thing *is* doing God's will. As Mother Teresa says, "It is all between you and God, anyway." How does that make you feel?

**I choose to do right because
that is who I am today.**

Herein lies the beauty of Step Three. After our desire for control has taken us in so many destructive directions, we are offered the opportunity to do something healthy and life giving with it.
~Chemically Dependent Anonymous P 33

August 8

Life is difficult. ~M. Scott Peck

When we look back on our lives of drinking and using, we reflect on just how "difficult" times were. As much as we hated those times, we relished in them just the same. No matter what the situation was we could always find a way to justify our actions. There were even times when we sought out difficult situations to justify why we needed chemicals. "This wasn't *just* right," "That should have been different," "You should have acted in this manner," ... and thelist goes on. Life being "difficult" *was the perfect excuse for using!* The irony is that *life is difficult*, just as life is wonderful, miraculous, amazing, boring, raw, unpredictable, fun, not-so-fun, and so on. Life is everything we know. A good chemical dependent will use any of these reasons to justify drinking and drugging. A good *recovering* chemical dependent will use all these same reasons NOT to drink or drug. Life is difficult; so, what's your point?

There are a million excuses to drink, but no *good* reason I can think of.

Oh, surely they experienced difficulties. Yet, they believed that they would make it through such times, even grow from them, and so they did-without using.
~Chemically Dependent Anonymous P 30

August 9

If you want to have what you have not, you must do what you do not. ~Author Unknown

How many times do we find ourselves wishing for something we don't have, or at least for something different? In order to acquire something we want, we can't just sit and wish for it—we have to *do something* to acquire it. We need to do things that we have not done before—not the "same old same old." If we do the same old things, then we won't get the new thing we were hoping for, will we? We couldn't get sober without first putting the drink or the drug down; just as we can't run a marathon without putting on our running shoes. Change comes from *action*. "If you want what we have, you must do what we do." If we don't have friends, it is no doubt because we are not being friendly. So, to get the friends we want, we must do what we have not done—*be friendly.* Whenever we find ourselves wanting something, we need to ask ourselves what we need *to do differently* to acquire it.

I define one goal today and do one thing differently in order to reach that goal.

I was incapable of setting realistic goals and then working a plan to achieve them. All I had were grandiose fantasies {…}.
~Chemically Dependent Anonymous P 132

August 10

In spite of our best efforts to work our programs and lean on God's guidance, we sometimes don't understand what's going on in our life.
~Melody Beattie

Sometimes it may feel like we are not on the right path, that we are not working our program the "right way." Despite all our best efforts, we aren't producing the results *we want*. The key to understanding this is to understand that what *we want* is not necessarily what our *Higher Power wants*. How many times has it happened? We hastily obtain something we wanted desperately, only to have something even better pass us by the very next week. Unlike God, we only see what's laid out in front of us. When we look across the street, all we see is that shiny, red sports car, whereas a satellite can see all the vehicles in that region. God sees that region, the Western Hemisphere, the Galaxy, the Cosmos, and the future. We *are* on the right path if we are working our program to the best of our ability.

**My Higher Power wants for me what
I would want for myself IF I had all the facts.**

That meant so much to me, when they said that they understood, because I didn't understand, myself. I didn't think anybody could.
~Chemically Dependent Anonymous P 176

August 11

Nothing has changed but my attitude. Everything has changed. ~Anthony DeMello

Attitude is everything. When we were using, our attitude was like a horribly infectious disease. Who could stand us? Could we even stand ourselves? But darn it, if everyone else would just behave the way we knew they should, then we wouldn't be bitter or angry! How shocked we were when we learned that it is *our attitude* that needs to be checked. What does this mean ... it's *our attitude* ... it's *not them*? It's not *their behavior* that is making us bitter and miserable? It's *our attitude*? It is tough to swallow that all along it was *our perceptions* that colored our world. "Change your attitude and change your life," the old-timers tell us. When we accept that we are the very persons making ourselves miserable, we open the door for change. We can't change reality, but we can change how we look at it.

Whatever happens today, it is my attitude that determines whether I feel bitter or better about it.

I continued to harbor many of the old feelings, ideas, and attitudes. I knew that the Big Book of A.A. said that we had to let go of our old ideas but they were all I had ever known. I didn't trust people.
~*Chemically Dependent Anonymous* P 281-282

August 12

The feeling of affection calls forth the awareness of an inclination to share the desirable state. The spirit is nourished. The feeling of rejection calls forth the awareness of having been refused. The spirit is diminished. ~Patricia Evans

The primary concern of every meeting is to be open and available for the newcomer. We want CDA to be there for the newcomer, just as they were for us. And yet, newcomers can be hard to take at times. If they are actively using or coming in just off a long drug run, they can be disruptive, often smell bad, look terrible, or act belligerently. So often, without meaning to, we judge them. The purpose of judging someone is to reject them. Maybe they are so unreasonable that we get frustrated or so disruptive that we don't get what we need. So, we silently judge them as unworthy of this meeting. We think, "Maybe they should be asked to leave." There is no addict born that is worthy of rejection from CDA. When we judge someone as unworthy in a meeting, the best remedy for the situation is to become their sponsor.

I reject rejection.

If I had felt rejected when I first came into A.A., I might not have come back.
***~Chemically Dependent Anonymous* P 180**

August 13

It's not that some people have willpower and some don't. It's that some people are ready to change and others are not. ~James Gordon

The word "change" seems to be a formula for panic in early recovery. It is akin to torture. It can leave us feeling out of control in a different and unfamiliar world. Humans by their very nature resist change, and so it is no surprise that those of us in recovery find it uncomfortable too. The process of change is scary because it leaves us feeling powerless and out of control. We may even attempt to justify continuing old "druggie" patterns of behavior so that we don't have to enter the unfamiliar world of change. Eventually, we hear in a meeting, "If you keep doing the same thing over and over, you'll keep getting the same thing over and over." We eventually come to understand that life will only get better as our behavior changes. We can finally say that "change" is our friend.

I embrace change because the possibilities are infinite.

I was afraid, from the stories people told, that if you didn't work the Steps, if you didn't change, you would end up back out there.
~*Chemically Dependent Anonymous* P 178

August 14

"Life" is what happens to you while you're busy making other plans. ~John Lennon

Sometimes we are so busy making plans and saving for the future that we forget that life is happening today. How many of us women have that expensive outfit we're saving for a special occasion, only to realize that it's out of style before we ever get to wear it? How many of us men have put in so much extra time at work in anticipation of that big promotion, only to find that the kids grew up without ever really knowing who their dad is? Did we get clean and sober to make life wonderful just for some future date that we may or may not even make it to? No. We found recovery to get our life back. And today, we stay in recovery so we can learn to savor life to the fullest. Living in these 24 hours is simply a matter of paying attention to the details. What are we grateful for? What can we do to make a difference? Who can we spend time with? Wake up and smell the recovery.

I find one thing today that will make me deep-down happy, and I do it.

People in the Fellowship told me that happiness comes from within and it is from within that I am happy now. I have a successful life, but my happiness is where my true success lies.
~Chemically Dependent Anonymous P 236

August 15

He goes to meetings for three primary reasons: to learn, to avail himself of the much needed group therapy and to give, by his presence, encouragement to all. ~Father John Doe

If you come into a CDA meeting looking for recovery, you will find exactly that. If you come looking for a reason to continue using mind-altering and mood-changing drugs, you'll eventually find that too. Those of us who choose recovery go to meetings willingly. We do this simply because we know that it is in the meetings that we continue to learn how to give *and* how to receive. We must stay in a receptive, learning mode if we want to stay clean and sober. When we are receptive to new ideas, we will continue to progress in our recovery. We learn what it is that we need to know in order to turn around and give it away. We tell the newcomer, "Don't act out, don't use, and go to meetings. The answers to all our problems are contained in our sharing. Meeting makers make it."

**Today in CDA, I choose
to be a meeting maker.**

They didn't seem to be hurting the way I was. They were even smiling. They told me, "Meeting makers make it," and said that I should get to a meeting every day.
~*Chemically Dependent Anonymous* P 151

August 16

When one devotes oneself to meditation, mental burdens, unnecessary worries, and wandering thoughts drop off one by one; life seems to run smoothly and pleasantly. ~Nyogen Senzaki

Our Higher Power is fully capable of getting our attention if need be. But why wait for a spiritual slap in the face? Making a regular appointment to meditate is the easiest way to work Step Eleven. It doesn't matter whether it is dawn or dusk. What matters is that we schedule it. If we don't schedule the time and place, it is all too easy to put it off. When we have a standing appointment, we are showing respect for our Higher Power. We are saying, "You are important enough for me to set aside time to listen for guidance." For those who have other spiritual beliefs, we can make an appointment to relax, focus, or just time to be still. When we take this scheduled time each day, we set a great foundation to center ourselves in our program. We show ourselves respect when we reserve a time and place for meditation.

I record my daily appointment for meditation in my day planner or on my calendar.

Some of us find the word 'meditation' rather intimidating.
~Chemically Dependent Anonymous **P 62**

August 17

The greatest good you can do for another is not just share your riches, but reveal to them their own. ~Disraeli

Our riches in CDA are the Twelve Steps and the Twelve Traditions. Sharing these riches at a group level is covered in Tradition Five: *We carry our message to the chemically dependent person who still suffers.* It is the primary purpose of our organization. We once were the addicts who needed the message carried to us. We couldn't stop using, but our family and friends kept telling us that we *could stop,* "if only we really wanted to." We tried to stop on our own but, sadly, we would always start using again. Then CDA, as well as other 12-step groups, found us and we were no longer alone. Members revealed their riches and made it possible for us to see that we *can* stop using and, thus, stop suffering. Even those of us that are clean and sober for years can sometimes find ourselves suffering and in need of the riches of CDA. The message is for all of us, all the time.

I make sure my home group holds fast to our primary purpose.

We in CDA believe that our recovery is a gift from God and that the primary purpose of that gift is for us to give it away to those who need it.
~Chemically Dependent Anonymous **P 75**

August 18

Taking a mini break of ten minutes here and five minutes there can change the mood of our day and turn what might have been a pressure keg experience into a more bearable one.
~Ruth Fishel

There are times when days get so full that anything more than taking 10 minutes alone feels impossible. Some days it might seem too hard to squeeze in even 10 minutes. At times like these, mini breaks can be refreshing. Mindfulness, simply being fully present with whatever is going on in the moment, can make 10 minutes feel much longer. We can experiment with something we do every day. Bringing our awareness to whatever we are doing in the present moment, at least a few times a day (especially in busy times), can be very peaceful. We can practice this during our walk to the car, or when we stop for a cup of coffee, or during our morning routine. Eventually, we get into the habit of being mindful of everything we do! That's when we always have peace within us.

I focus my awareness on the colors, sounds, and shapes around me, and feel peace.

Whether one's experience is sudden or gradual, whether struggled against or hurried along, eventually it just is. One is awake and alive, aware of the world and of one's own participation in it.
~Chemically Dependent Anonymous P 63

August 19

"What would spirituality give me?" said an alcoholic to the Master. "Non-alcoholic intoxication," was the answer.
~Antonio De Mello

Celebration. Joy. Wonder. Happiness. Conviviality. Ecstasy. Bliss. Laughter. Companionship. Yes, spirituality brings us non-alcoholic intoxication. Not every moment. Not every day. And, in fact, in the beginning stages of recovery, it seems we will never know pleasure again. But it does come. It creeps up slowly. We find ourselves smiling for no good reason. We feel the satisfaction of a well-made amends. We feel an inner spark when we realize that our family respects us again. This happens because we are now practicing spiritual principles. We don't have to "hang on" and "white knuckle" our recovery once we agree to a spiritual program as our way of life. There are folks who stay abstinent without our joy, and that is their choice. But, for us in CDA, we embrace the intoxication of a well-lived, well-practiced spiritually- based recovery.

**Any past unhappiness now becomes
a casualty of my spiritual growth.**

Our parent fellowship, Alcoholics Anonymous, tells us of Twelve Promises, among them freedom, happiness, peace and spiritual fulfillment. At last, we are alive.
~*Chemically Dependent Anonymous* P 56

August 20

Nothing we ever get, see, taste, smell, touch, hear or think about, is going to bring us the peace we really seek. ~Buddha

Chemically dependent people seem to always be chasing some form of gratification. When using, we were always chasing the next high. In recovery, we *continuously* seek different forms of satisfaction: a new job, the perfect partner, or a "bling-bling" SUV. As a newcomer, we might want to be respected like the old-timers. Whatever it is we have, we seem to always find ourselves wanting more. We seldom see beyond the veil of desire when we are consumed in chasing that gratification. But, ah! Once we stop seeking and start accepting, peace finally catches up to us. It has been hidden *within* the journey all along. Our journey of recovery is one of discovery with peace, not at the end of the road, but paving the road beneath us.

My recovery is not about the acquisition of some desire. It is about the peace I finally find as the very foundation of my journey.

I have peace of mind and that's what I never had before. I never dreamed I would ever achieve it. That's what I'm truly grateful for today.
~Chemically Dependent Anonymous **P 228**

August 21

You will learn more from adversity than from prosperity. ~ Bruce & Stan

ADVERSITY—is it a negative or a positive? In our old life, adversity was something we could capitalize on, giving us the OK to keep on using. So, in a sense, adversity was a positive force that helped fuel our addiction. While practicing our addiction, it was a common reaction to take any adversity and run with it. Negative thinking was the preferred way of looking at any situation, and we could always find a way to do it. But, once we're clean and sober, we no longer want to use adversity as an excuse to get loaded. This can be a hard habit to break. Something goes wrong— use. Someone is disrespectful—use. Adversity becomes a *negative* in which we have to fight our old reaction. On the upside, adversity can be a sure-fire way to grow spiritually, learn to practice our principles, and snatch opportunities to help others. A problem blesses us when we learn from the lesson it teaches. Adversity then becomes a positive.

**I watch for big problems;
they disguise big opportunities.**

My Higher Power has now given me CDA so I can work on the drug-addict personality problems that I have been ignoring.
~Chemically Dependent Anonymous P 158

August 22

God is the friend of silence. See how nature--trees, flowers, grass--grow in silence; see the stars, the moon, and sun, how they move in silence? The more we receive in silent prayer,the more we can give in our active life. We need silence to be able to touch souls. ~Mother Teresa

Meetings often begin with a moment of silence for the addict who still suffers. Some meetings begin with a moment of silence that is not dedicated to anything in particular. Silence *is* golden—a golden opportunity to become centered. It can be time used to do the Tenth Step and reflect on self, or, perhaps time used to pray and listen to our Higher Power, as in Step Eleven. It is when we shut off the noise in our head that we can actually hear from the Divine Source. That moment of silence that begins many meetings should not be used to think about Aunt Bessie's Chihuahua, that cute person next to us, or dinner plans. It should be used to pray for the addict and to quiet our busy mind so we will be able to touch souls.

**I pledge to use my next meeting's
"Silent Moment" in the way intended.**

I know the soul remains constant but it is what I never listened to before.
~*Chemically Dependent Anonymous* P 198

August 23

The best choices are those left up to God.
~Brother Alexis

It wasn't too long ago that many of us thought we knew what God should give us and *when* we should receive it. Most of the time, we acted as if we should receive the blessing we asked for right NOW. After working the Steps, especially Three and Eleven, we come to realize that God answers all prayers in *His time*. Four ways He answers our prayers are:

- No, not yet.
- No, I love you too much.
- Yes, I thought you'd never ask.
- Yes, and here is more.

What we ask for in prayer may not be for our ultimate good. Thus, we need to accept that "No" can be an answer to a prayer as well as "Yes."

What I pray for may not be in my best interests. I agree to accept "Yes," "No," or "Wait" as answers to my prayers.

We are instructed to ask for knowledge and power, to whatever degree God sees fit.
~Chemically Dependent Anonymous **P 62**

August 24

From weakness (adversity) comes strength; we forgive to be forgiven; we give it away to keep it; we suffer to get well; we surrender to win; we die to live; we serve to lead; from dependence we find independence. ~The Recovery Paradoxes

Many a chemical dependent has delayed asking for help because they didn't want to be "weak." Then they learned that *not asking* for help is actually the sign of weakness. We have suffered to find our health, and we had to die a thousand deaths to find our life. We also find that once we throw in the towel, it is at that moment we can begin to win. We eventually learn that the truth is full of paradoxes. For instance, we must give away what we find in order to keep it! Other than those based on the Twelve Traditions, what other organizations say that to lead you must be a servant to the group? Sages tell us that all true wisdom is found in paradoxes.

**The paradox of my recovery is that
I am a clean and sober chemical dependent!**

We want nothing from you other than the chance to share with you our experience, strength and hope.
***~Chemically Dependent Anonymous* P 97**

August 25

We must all obey the great law of change. It is the most powerful law of nature. ~Edmund Burke

"I'm flexible as long as you don't change anything," the saying goes. Why are we so afraid of change? People are afraid of change because they think God won't give them what it is they think they want. We would rather keep the mess we have than let go of the reigns. Maybe God *won't* give us what we want! Maybe God has other plans! Being afraid of change is actually saying, "I'm afraid of God's will for me." Overcoming fear of change is simple. It requires trusting our Higher Power. We always have the option of continuing to hold on, but change *will still happen.* It is when the pain of holding on becomes greater than the fear of letting go that we finally let go. So, rather than feel the pain of resisting change and holding on, we learn that it is easier to simply let go. We try not to leave claw marks in everything that passes through our lives.

When I allow change, I get better.

But doing what I sometimes don't want to do has been a big change in my attitude since I have entered the Program.
~Chemically Dependent Anonymous **P 350**

August 26

Fear of people {...} will leave us.
~Alcoholics Anonymous P 84

Chemically dependent people are often described as egomaniacs with an inferiority complex. We have a fear of being surrounded by sober people because we might be asked to take off our "mask" and reveal who we really are. In our addiction, we were chameleons changing into whatever we needed to be, blending into our surroundings. In the process of properly working the Twelve Steps, we become "real" people with real lives. Attending meetings also helps to bring us out of our "shell." Recovery is a process that happens at different rates for everyone. Slowly but surely, this transformation takes place with everyone who incorporates the Twelve Steps of CDA into their life. Losing our fear of people in the Fellowship is promise number nine of the Twelve Promises of recovery, as given to us from Alcoholics Anonymous.

With the help of the Twelve Steps, my sponsor, and God, I rid myself of the "mask."

We feel a lessening of the fear that has consumed our lives and know the beginnings of real freedom.
~*Chemically Dependent Anonymous* P 34

August 27

Many men go fishing all of their lives without knowing that it is not fish that they are after.
~Henry David Thoreau

For many of us, adolescence represented the threshold to adulthood that we felt would save us from a boring, dull, or fitful childhood. We sought some type of change, anything, to make us feel whole. A lot of us saw chemicals as the vehicle to this change. By using these chemicals, we tried to save our soul and ended up slowly killing our spirit. Some of us eventually realized we were embracing a remedy that caused us to lose the very thing we were seeking— ourselves and a relationship with God. Maybe we didn't understand that we were seeking a relationship with God with our usage of chemicals. Although, once in recovery, we realize that the "wholeness" we wanted could only exist within a spiritual context. Because of the guidance of the many recovering addicts before us, perhaps we now can learn what we are really after.

When I can't find God, I know today that it is not God who has moved.

{B}ut I'm sure that God will be with me and with anyone in CDA who is looking for Him, always, even until the end.
~Chemically Dependent Anonymous **P 248**

August 28

No one can escape from prison without the help of those who have escaped before.
~G.I. Gurdjieff

Whether or not we were the addicts that got caught and put away in prison, every person in recovery was, in a sense, a prisoner. We built walls to keep others out to "protect" our fragile selves. Isolation became an intimate partner, whether we separated ourselves physically or simply isolated in our minds. Even if we didn't do it to ourselves, the community often built those walls, putting us behind them to keep us away from those we would hurt, intentionally or not. It matters not whether isolation is self-imposed or community-imposed, a prisoner is a prisoner. Recovery offers hope for escape from the prison of isolation: "a new freedom and a new happiness," as expressed in the Twelve Promises from A.A. How do we find that freedom? That freedom is found by allowing those who escaped before us to unlock our prison doors.

In CDA, I am a regular person in a whole world, not a prisoner locked in my own restricted world.

Another celebrates giving instead of taking, being thoughtful instead of selfish and breaking down the walls to escape the isolation.
~Chemically Dependent Anonymous P 56

August 29

Never worry about numbers. Help one person at a time, and always start with the person nearest you. ~Mother Teresa

Sometimes, we spend more time worrying about how we can help those who have not even made it to the rooms of CDA than about the ones standing right before us. At other times, we try to communicate our experience, strength, and hope to *everybody* in the room, thinking that we must reach as many people as possible because no one else can communicate the message as well as us. Sometimes, we concentrate only on the newcomer, forgetting that someone with five, ten, or more years may also need our help at any given time. Are we helping too many and neglecting our family? Are we not helping enough and neglecting our service work? Just how many people can we work with at one time? Too often, we overlook the fact that by slowing down and helping just one person—the one next to us—we can do so much more in our service to CDA, our fellow man, and God.

I value the person God puts in front of me.

We can only hope and pray that our Higher Power will continue to allow us to be used as instruments to help people still suffering from the disease of alcohol and drug addiction.
~Chemically Dependent Anonymous **P 121**

August 30

My flexibility keeps me from getting bent out of shape.
My laugh lines are life lines.
I listen to my heart.
I have an attitude of gratitude.
~Hummingbird Words

Are we open to being flexible, able to laugh, and listening with a grateful heart? Being uptight and rigid or ungrateful and stressed is the opposite of a grateful heart. Having a grateful heart sounds a lot like the serenity we seek. Some of us confuse serenity with somberness. To be serene, we think we must be removed from the chaos, climbing to a mountain top like a monk. But serenity is not a dead word; it is a living word. Serenity can be ours when we laugh, when we listen, when we love, and when we live. Serenity is remaining grateful even when things don't go our way. Serenity is being able to go with the flow, being flexible where our old self would have been demanding. We are spontaneous, intuitive, and we smile. This becomes our living serenity.

My serenity is expressed in how
I live life, not in how I hide from it.

However, some of us find quietness as alien as sobriety once was.
~*Chemically Dependent Anonymous* P 62

August 31

I am an old man and have known a great many troubles, but most of them have never happened.
~Mark Twain

Aren't we something? We get inside our heads and commence worrying about the small stuff that will probably never happen anyway. And what if it does happen? Well, if we've worked Step Three, we can assume that it was meant to be. So, why worry? We wear ourselves out worrying about outcomes, the path of our recovery, where we fit in, how we will fit in, and so on. We need to remind ourselves that our recovery is a process. It is a process that we can enjoy as we learn to trust our path and our Higher Power. The oft quoted Melody Beattie, like Twain, warns us not to "think too hard about things. The flow is meant to be experienced." We don't need to think so hard anymore. Worry is a choice and only occurs when we leave God out of the picture.

**I do not worry about what I can't do.
I think about what God can do.**

We could waste a lot of time and energy worrying or intellectualizing about methods.
~Chemically Dependent Anonymous P 37

September 1

> *How poor are they who have not patience! What wound did ever heal but by degrees?*
> ~William Shakespeare

Patience NOW! Serenity NOW! A symptom of our disease is that we seek instant relief, instant progress, and demand what we want when we want it. Newcomers want to be old-timers, we want our family to trust us immediately, we want our employers to reward our worth though we have been unworthy, and we demand respect before we become respectable. In this fast-paced world of ours, a lack of patience is not just the addict's problem—people, in general, honk at red lights, fidget when our computers load, and flock to "fast-food" restaurants to avoid a 20-minute wait for dinner. But some things, *important things*, cannot be rushed. When we heal from addiction it has to come in degrees. Each step and each new lesson will come in God's own time, and God doesn't wear a watch.

**I slow down my expectations.
Everything is right on time.**

To those of us accustomed to instant gratification and quick chemical cures, Step Two is dismaying to say the least.
~Chemically Dependent Anonymous **P 27**

September 2

If you hear a voice within you saying, "You are not a painter," then by all means paint ... and that voice will be silenced. ~Vincent Van Gogh

We *can* do what we think cannot be done, despite the malicious voice that claims we "can't" do this or that. When finding the Program, how many times did we argue with the voice that claimed we could never get clean and sober? But we *did*, and that voice was silenced. What about the voice that says, "You are not a good speaker?" We *speak,* and that voice is silenced. Maybe it says, "You are too old to be a student." Then by all means go to college. The way to silence the voice is to do the very thing it tells us cannot be done. There is a part of us that wants us to fail—that is our inner addict. The inner addict, the voice that says, "You can't," attempts to discourage us to such a degree that we will go back and feed it. But, instead of feeding the inner addict, we learn to feed our future—we do the very thing we tell ourselves we cannot do.

I identify what my inner addict tells me I *cannot do* and I make plans to do it, today.

Even though the thought of speaking before such a crowd is frightening, I know that I have to trust in God and confront my fears.
~*Chemically Dependent Anonymous* P 111

September 3

Yesterday is but a dream and tomorrow is only a vision. Look well therefore to this day.
~Sanskrit Proverb

Living in the turmoil of regret and remorse of yesterday, dread of today, and fear and trembling of what tomorrow might bring is an indicator of our disease. A good definition of the chemical dependent person is a person that makes plans for the past and regrets for the future. Part of growing up spiritually for us is to deal with the past by completing the action Steps Four through Nine, and then *not looking back*, unless we intend to go that way! It isn't long before werealize how successful our past is becoming. After all, the longer we've been in recovery, the more successful we've been in the past. The past thenbecomes our pride, not our shame, as we demonstrate to others that recovery is about building one chemical-free day on another.

My yesterdays become good memories and, in CDA, I need have no fear of tomorrow.

Letting go of my past has been worth it.
~Chemically Dependent Anonymous P 198

September 4

Humility is a perpetual quietness of heart.
~From Dr. Bob's desk plaque

We can be sure that our Higher Power wants us to be humble because we are told that it is one of ourspiritual principles. Yet, the moment we think we've got it, we don't! None of us strives to be arrogant, but it's difficult not to shout from the rooftops that we are clean and sober, and that we've done such a great thing by cleaning up our past! And indeed, it's not wrong to be proud of who we are, if we don't forget *Who* we are. In Step Three, we submit ourselves to the care and direction of a Higher Power.In that submission lays our humbleness in recovery,in our everyday lives, and in our service to others. When we allow our Higher Power to direct us, and weremain honest about Who runs our life, we gain that "perpetual quietness of heart," and serve God in a humble manner that we can be proud of.

**I need not think less of myself to be humble.
I simply give the credit to Whom it belongs.**

As Virgil guided Dante through the inferno, I humbly beseech my Guide to lead me out of the hell of marijuana.
~*Chemically Dependent Anonymous* P 172

September 5

Lord, grant that I may seek rather to comfort than to be comforted—to understand, than to be understood— to love, than to be loved.
~Prayer of St. Francis

This prayer of comfort prepares us to be proactive in our recovery. Rather than sit and wait for others to care for us, we are asked to begin caring for others. The irony of this is that once we become proactive and do for others, we then receive it back tenfold. It has been said that if we want friends then we must befriendly. Likewise, if we want comfort then we must give comfort. When we pray to understand rather thanto be understood, we are asking God to help us get outside ourselves and not be so wrapped around our own axles. In unwrapping ourselves from our axles,we then become untangled enough to go where we want to go in recovery. In each circumstance of our recovery, when we give comfort we get it back, when we understand others they understand us, and when we give love, we are loved.

I do not struggle with my need to be comforted, understood, or loved. I give it away to get it.

I also have to pass what I've received on to others, in order to keep it. {…} And it seems I feel my best when I try to give it away.
~Chemically Dependent Anonymous P 151-152

September 6

Kindness is the inability to remain at ease in the presence of another person who is ill at ease, the inability to remain comfortable in the presence of another who is uncomfortable, the inability to have peace of mind when one's neighbor is troubled.
~Rabbi Samuel H. Holdenson

The Golden Rule, to treat others just as we would like to be treated, is often taken for granted. When was the last time we vented our frustration on a salesclerk, even though we wouldn't want them to do that to us? When was the last time we gestured unkindly to an absentminded driver when we know we have done the same thing? Everyone—even rude people—should be treated with kindness, not because of whom they are, but, instead, because of whom we are. There once was a reporter who asked President Lincoln why he treated his enemies with such kindness rather than trying to destroy them. "My dear fellow," said Lincoln, "I do destroy my enemy when I make him into a friend."

I may have to say I'm sorry for a multitude of sins, but I'll never have to say I'm sorry for being kind.

He was as kind and patient a person as I have ever met. Our short association has proven fruitful for me especially in these past few years of attempting sobriety.
~Chemically Dependent Anonymous P 205

September 7

Freedom is not a proclamation, but a way of life that demands self-restraint and some sacrifice on the part of all those who wish to enjoy it.
~Harold Roy Brennan

Freedom from addiction is God's will for us—this we know. Yet, freedom is not just something we say ("Hey, I'm free to live a new life now"). We have to learn how to sacrifice our old habits and put some discipline in our lives in order to enjoy freedom from mind-affecting chemicals. The sacrifices include giving up old playgrounds and playmates and, in some cases, we must give up high-risk jobs with big salaries. In order to continue to enjoy our new freedom, we need to use self-restraint and not subject ourselves to risky situations such as doing business inlounges, being in a car while our "friend" smokes pot or failing to let our physician know we are chemically dependent. Today we have the freedom of choice, butone of the things we better choose is not to put ourselves at risk. Our freedom is not free.

My freedom in recovery is not free. I earn it by making right choices on a daily basis.

However, I have found that freedom does come with the responsibility that I accept.
~Chemically Dependent Anonymous P 236

September 8

Your faith has strengthened mine. ~Ann Spangler

"Lean on me when you're not strong and I'll be your friend. I'll help you carry on ..." is a very popular line in a song that describes how we relate to each other in Chemically Dependent Anonymous. One of the reasons we work so well in this fellowship is precisely because it is a "we" program. We watch our friends deal with pink slips, divorce, birth and death, or tragic events. They get through all of life's trials and remain sober. How? Through the faith borrowed from the Fellowship. We hold their hand, sit with them in court, attend funerals, watch their kids, or loan them money. We give them strength and hope. It is our way. We help them get through it without using mood-changing and mind-altering chemicals; and they make it through each trial or joy day by day *because of us*. Then, when the loss of a job, the birth or death of a loved one, or divorce happens to us, we make it through *because of them*.

**I strengthen the faith of others by
being an active member of the Fellowship.**

We know through our own experiences that spreading hope and faith is the single most important factor in our program.
~*Chemically Dependent Anonymous* P 77

September 9

For our group purpose there is but one ultimate authority—a loving God as He may express himself in our group conscience. Our leaders are but trusted servants; they do not govern. ~CDA's Tradition Two

There are few more satisfying feelings in CDA than taking a position in a group, or even helping to start a new group. In fact, it is so satisfying that we might even say it's intoxicating. Members appreciate us, we help shape group conscience, and we may even have a measure of respect that was never enjoyed before. It can be hard to let go. Who hasn't seen a group or club run by someone's ego? He or she may be sincere in adhering to traditions, but it becomes tradition *according to them*. Ego and self-will can destroy a group if left unchecked. It is our group conscience that keeps egos in check. No group member is the boss. Through group conscience we align ourselves with the Authority that is our boss. Eventually, even those loudmouths who tried to take over come around and see the value of Tradition Two.

I do not allow my ego to separate me from the group, God, or the good of the Fellowship.

No CDA member can issue an order to any other member or try to force adherence to his or her own beliefs.
~*Chemically Dependent Anonymous* P 71-72

September 10

God made us all special. ~Mindy P.

It is not our job to point out other people's faults, yet we spend a lot of time and energy doing just that. How often have we lingered after a meeting making small talk with other members, mentioning how "so- and-so forgot the cake," "how long the old guy rambled on," or "how we hate that the leader didn't come prepared with a topic and the group had to pick it at the last minute"? Sometimes we pick apart others who don't do things as we want them done. Instead, we should appreciate that we are all different and special. Do we think putting others down will somehow bring us up? Our Higher Power gave each of us unique gifts so that we may help each other out—not pick each other apart. By seeing the positive gifts that God bestowed on others, we can embrace that positive gift in ourselves. We are all special cases.

**At the next meeting I attend,
I will only say positive things about
God's special people.**

They were talking about positive things so I kept showing up.
~Chemically Dependent Anonymous P 346

September 11

A man may criticize or laugh at himself and it will affect others favorably, but criticism or ridicule coming from another often produces the contrary effect. ~Alcoholics Anonymous P 125

The truth is we seldom criticize others for their benefit; we criticize them to make ourselves appear more important. What was it Jesus said about the speck of dust in another's eye and the log in our own? It seems that we often amplify the faults of another while minimizing or ignoring our own. We all know that criticizing is not considered a spiritual gift, yet we succumb to it so often. The Big Book of A.A. tells us that we do, and should, talk about each other in order to help one another. So, when we talk about another, we must check our motive. Are we concerned about what they are doing so we can *reach out* to them, or are we concerned about what they are doing so we can *reach over* them in stature? This is a question we must explore in our Tenth Step work and with our sponsor.

**Today I motivate, not denigrate,
my fellow members in CDA.**

Do I offer empathy rather than criticism to those in need?
~*Chemically Dependent Anonymous* P 38

September 12

If you know how to worry, you already know how to meditate! ~Reverend Guy Williams

Meditation is the ability to focus on something—or nothing—and still our minds in order to hear from our Higher Power. The first part of meditation is very similar to worry if we think about it. What do we do when we worry? We focus on a problem with intense concentration, possibly for hours or perhaps days. What if we use that same energy and focus on something spiritual instead of worry? The difference between worrying and meditating is that when we worry, we focus on the problem, and when we meditate we focus on the solution. Seasoned members of our 12-step program tell us that whatever we concentrate on becomes larger. We feed it energy and it grows. What are we feeding in our thoughts today?

I don't tell God how big my problem is by concentrating on the problem. I tell my problem how big God is by concentrating on God.

By such simple measures, we begin a habit of meditation. With some experience, we may find ourselves able to slip into a calm, meditative state whenever we need a short break.
~Chemically Dependent Anonymous **P 62**

September 13

When one door closes, another door always opens—but those long hallways are a real drag.
~Patty Wooten

Man! Those hallways are like airport runways—endless at times! We trudged the hallway to happy destiny impatiently looking for the right door, and at times felt like we entered Hell! Sometimes we forced locked doors open, only to find that when we had to force the solution, it wasn't the right solution. When our relationship doors, job doors, or legal doors snap shut, we may foolishly try kicking down some other doors. There are so many obstacles that seem to pop up deterring us from opening our own doors—but the real obstacle is simply impatience with God. It's like the popular game show that asks which door you choose. You don't know if it's the car, the million dollars, or a can of Campbell's soup behind it. If we have to force the door open, then it's not the one for us. It's best to wait in that hall of spiritual patience for our Higher Power to open the door meant just for us.

**I accept God's direction by waiting until
the right doors open in my life.**

{God} has opened up other doors in my life which far replace any void {...}.
~*Chemically Dependent Anonymous* P 165

September 14

So watch the thought and its ways with care, and let it spring from love, born out of concern for all beings. ~Buddha

Metta is a wonderful Buddhist practice that helps us to love ourselves and others and become our own best friend. Basically, metta is an unconditional attitude of love and friendliness distinguished from mere agreeableness based on self-interest. Through metta, one refuses to be offensive and renounces bitterness and resentment. Instead, one develops a benevolence which seeks the well-being and happiness of others. The practice of metta has three branches. The first is practicing loving kindness in one's day-to-day conduct. The second is to meditate, which leads the mind to a higher consciousness. The third is to commit to this way of life in our physical, mental, and verbal activities. When we think about it, metta embodies Steps Ten through Twelve. It is uplifting to know that we in CDA are incorporating solid truths found by spiritual leaders throughout the ages.

Today, I have the willingness and the desire to be a loving person.

They are happy people living useful and productive lives, loving and serving God as each understands Him.
~*Chemically Dependent Anonymous* P XVI-XVII

September 15

You can change your life by changing the choices you make! ~Dave Carpenter

Every waking moment we make choices. We choose when to get up, when to eat, and what to wear for the day. We choose whether to walk the dog or let it out the back door. We choose what thoughts to put in our head and what people we are going to associate with. We choose whether we are going to be kind, short-tempered, tolerant, or impatient with others. We make several choices from moment to moment. All these choices have a large bearing on the "quality of our life." Dave Carpenter says that "Everything we choose to do either supports our life purpose, or works against our purpose." What is our purpose? If we choose to hang out in a lounge, does that support our purpose or not? If we choose to donate to a charity, does that support our purpose or not? Defining our purpose in life gives us a yardstick for measuring our choices—does it support our stated purpose or not?

I define my purpose *on paper* so I can evaluate if my daily choices support it.

We have one primary purpose: to meet together, share in recovery and spread the message to the still-suffering individual.
~*Chemically Dependent Anonymous* P 77

September 16

Guilt is the Godfather masquerading as God.
~Bob Mandel

To escape the "Godfather Guilt" that has plagued so many of us, we must understand the difference between feeling bad about something we did and what it means to set it right. In Step Nine, we learn all about this from a practical standpoint, and it is a major turning point in our lives. We may indeed regret something we have done, but until we make it right, guilt will plague us. And when we honestly look at it, guilt *should* plague us. But once we right these wrongs, guilt no longer serves any good purpose. If we continue to work the Steps and practice the principles in all our affairs, we begin to enjoy more of what the Ninth Step suggests. Step Nine suggests that we will enjoy restored relationships; we will clean away the wreckage of our past; and we will become responsible adults instead of selfish brats. Working Step Nine eventually delivers us from the burden of "Godfather Guilt."

I am not guilty. I am accountable.

One member speaks of "restored relationships, wrongs set right and freedom from guilt."
~Chemically Dependent Anonymous P 56

September 17

The floo floo bird, that peculiar and special bird that looks backwards so as to see where it has been rather than where it is going, is very much like us. ~Frank Lloyd Wright

Legendary architect Frank Lloyd Wright spent all his creative life looking forward. It should not have been a surprise to his audience of Federalist architects in 1938 that he failed to address their love for the past. Instead, he compared them to a bird that was more concerned with where it had been than where it was going. Those who embrace recovery should heed his words. Where we allow our minds to roam is likely the land we will inhabit. If we spend our time dwelling on the past and reliving what went wrong, it is likely we may visit there again. If we focus on the challenges of today and, more importantly, the visions of tomorrow, we will most likely never again visit the dark hours of the soul we once knew so well during our active addiction.

Frank Lloyd Wright dreamed of an exciting future, and so do I!

All in all, I have a great deal of hope for the future because of the Program. Thank you CDA for giving me back my life and my sanity.
***~Chemically Dependent Anonymous* P 152**

September 18

Children begin by loving their parents; as they grow older they judge them and sometimes they forgive them. ~Oscar Wilde

For those of us with children, our addiction caused us to be irresponsible parents through neglect, abuse, and desertion. Our kids had to endure a lot because of us. Even if they understand the disease of addiction *now*, all they knew *then* was their pain. Part of our restitution is to seek counseling for us and them—*and paying for it*. We learn to forgive ourselves only after we have made restitution. We can make direct amends where possible—like paying child support, acknowledging their pain, and asking for their forgiveness. One of our direct amends is to stop the behaviors that caused so much grief. We stop using! We cannot change the past, but we show our children we are here for them now. Of course, occasionally they won't forgive us. Nevertheless, we remain ready and willing to be the parent we know we should be and leave the results up to God and our children.

The love in my heart for my child inspires me to stay clean and sober one day at a time.

When my 6 year old son saw the condition I was in, he was heartbroken. He packed up his suitcase and put his coat on.
~Chemically Dependent Anonymous P 309

September 19

He shall call upon me, and I will answer him. I will be with him in trouble; I will deliver him and honor him. ~Psalm 91:15

Calling on our Higher Power to take care of us only when the chips are down is not the way to build a good relationship with Him. "God, if you just let her come back to me, I'll be different this time." "Just let the judge give me probation and I'll never use again." We expect God to keep us from the consequences of our actions. Through our suffering, we call out to the God of our "mis"understanding. Are we understanding Him if we only call on Him during a crisis? Of course, when things go well, we feel good about God—but feeling good about God does not bring us closer to Him. We feel good about the fireman who got us out of the burning building too, but that doesn't mean we have a close relationship with him. We must continue to call upon our Higher Power every day, so that when a crisis does happen, we know who we are talking to.

**My Higher Power is with me during trouble.
I am with Him between troubles.**

The people in the Program talked about a God as you understand Him. I had to admit I didn't understand God, at all.
~*Chemically Dependent Anonymous* P 178

September 20

As has been indicated, a little more patient, a little more tolerant, a little more humble. But ... not a tolerance that becomes timid--this would make rebellion in self. ~Edgar Cayce

Just about all of us could stand to be a little more patient, a little more tolerant, and a little more humble. Only, we don't want to take these merits to the extreme where they become a liability. Then, patience turns into martyrdom, tolerance turns us into a doormat, and humility makes people pity our wretchedness. Any virtue carried to an extreme becomes a defect—too much open-mindedness makes us wishy-washy, just as too much caring turns into controlling behavior. Turning our lives around means we are striving for balance. Just because we used to be "bad" doesn't mean we have to be better than good—that *would* create rebellion inside. We learn to do the right thing— not the self-righteous thing.

Recovery leads me to balance.

We are told that recovery is "progress, not perfection." We see our progress when we affirm healthier behaviors.
~Chemically Dependent Anonymous P 58

September 21

What we give multiplies and circulates back to us through the dynamic law of giving and receiving. So, not only the time, talent, dollars, and love that we give, but also the resentment, the smallness, the bitterness, will do the same.
~Mary Manin Morrissey

"As you sow, so shall you reap," is one of those universal laws that has not been repealed. We find that if more than one person is being unusually bitchy with us, or petty and unreasonable, we must think about what *we* are putting out to the world. Whatever effort we put out comes back tenfold or more. For example, if we expect drivers to move according to our timetable and then go into a road rage whenever they don't, we will be experiencing the rage back froma lot of nasty drivers. On the other hand, if we go out of our way to let people in lanes and go around us, they send waves and smiles our way. When we do acts of good, it isn't necessarily returned from the same people, but rather, it creates an energy of goodness from which we draw.

**I plant seeds of kindness
and reap peace.**

As we become spiritually awake and alive, our actions cannot help but reflect our awakening.
~Chemically Dependent Anonymous P 64

September 22

Many times, no matter what the position of our bodies, our soul is on its knees. ~Day By Day

Getting on our knees to surrender and submit to the guidance of our Higher Power is a tremendous spiritual discipline. Sometimes we have to get on our knees in order to rise. Yet, getting on our knees is only one of a multitude of ways in which to pray. We can use words, or we can pray silently through careful, mindful, spiritual acts. We can pray for the betterment of ourselves or the benefit of others. An act as simple as nourishing a child can be considered a living prayer. Some people sing for the glory of the Universe and some dance as a magnificent offering of gratitude to their Higher Power. In fact, we can make a prayer out of most anything we do. When we keep the highest good of all concerned as our primary motive, our acts are sacred. These then are our living prayers.

**I keep my soul on its knees
through mindful, spiritual acts and
I become a living prayer.**

However imperfect we are, when we are spiritually fit, we bring the best of ourselves to the relationship, the job or whatever our area of concern may be.
~Chemically Dependent Anonymous P 65

September 23

Learn to say no. ~Author Unknown

Although our fellowship is based on service, that does not mean we do not have the right to say "No." Of course, saying "No" for purely selfish reasons is not operating from our principle of service. Yet, if we never say "No," it is just as harmful to others as if we always say "No." It is a matter of respecting ourselves to know when to say "No." It is proper to say "No" when someone asks us to do for them what they should do for themselves. Another time to say "No" is when we are already over-committed. When we say "Yes" just so that people will like us, then we probably should have said "No." In order to have healthy boundaries, we must learn to say "No" at the right time. We can't do everything, nor are we expected to by anyone—except maybe ourselves. We shouldn't let others use us or drain us dry, nor should we drain ourselves. We learn to check our motives and move away from the idea that we need to do everything asked of us.

**Before I say "Yes" today, I check my
motives so that I learn to know my "No's."**

We have to continue evaluating our motives and position on a daily basis and the Twelve Steps are the tools that enable us to rise above our own egos so we can see the truth.
***~Chemically Dependent Anonymous* P 90**

September 24

Knock on the sky and listen to the sound!
~Zen Saying

Though we may never see a burning bush, the Ultimate Force in the Universe, that force that many of us choose to call God, *does* speak to us. He (*or She*) may speak to us in prayer or when we least expect it. The messages of our Higher Power come in varied sources such as the right timing of a song on the radio, intuitive thoughts when we're quiet, the words from a book, an intense dream, or from someone's sharing in a meeting. The voice of the person we meet in the grocery store may be the voice our HigherPower uses to talk to us. The Ultimate Force may put someone in our path that needs help just to pull us out of ourselves. We may be stuck in a traffic jam onlyto find that it's just what we needed to refocus and regain serenity. The question is not if God speaks to us. The question is, "Are we are listening?"

I do not look for burning bushes to know God is talking to me. I look at what is in front of me.

I was also told to pray to a God of my understanding. I chose a loving, caring God who speaks through the people in the Program, and my recovery was well on its way.
~Chemically Dependent Anonymous P 151

September 25

In the treatment of alcoholism, Karl Marx's aphorism, 'religion is the opiate of the masses' masks an enormously important therapeutic principle. Religion may actually provide a relief that drug abuse only promises. ~George Vaillant

Few people in 12-step recovery programs use the word "religion" to describe what the basis of our program is. We much prefer saying that our program is spiritual in nature, *not religious*. However, few of us would argue that we rely on a Divine Universal Source as the basis for our meritorious way of life. Compulsive use of mind-affecting, mood-altering chemicals *did promise* a sort of relief when our addiction overwhelmed us. Yet, any relief we found was always short-lived and usually created more problems than it temporarily relieved. People who accuse us of being religious or a cult don't understand that the joy of accepting a spiritual way of life *is the relief that we sought*. Some even accuse us of being "brainwashed" by the Twelve Steps. We have to agree—after all, our brains needed the washing.

As the Twelve Steps "brainwash" me, I get clean.

The alternative to denying this power is insanity and death.
~Chemically Dependent Anonymous P 27

September 26

The proof is not in the bottle but in the blessing.
~Walk Softly & Carry a Big Book

It is uncommonly easy to filter our thoughts so that we magnify the burdens and minimize the blessings. If we look closely at our lives, however, we see we are given similar amounts of blessings and burdens—even perhaps a little heavier on the blessing side. So, why is it that we often manage to forget the blessings and lament the burdens? Why do we demand "proof" that recovery is better than the bottle? We often hear in the rooms that we would be so much better off if we could only magnify our blessings the way we do our burdens. Part of turning into a 12-step optimist, rather than a program pessimist, is learning to magnify and concentrate on what is *right* in our lives—not on what is wrong. It would be wise to write down three "proofs" a day—proof that recovery is working in our life. Then, when we're down, we'll have multiple points of reference to realize how much good there is all around us.

I write down three blessings *right now* to magnify my grace rather than magnify my troubles.

I have so many things to be grateful for, so many blessings. My new life is a real gift from God.
~Chemically Dependent Anonymous P 227

September 27

One day at a time doesn't mean we shouldn't plan. ~Anne Wayman

The *One Day at a Time* philosophy has benefits far beyond the early days in recovery. It helps keep us grounded in the present—that Holy Instant that is so easy to miss in a busy, productive life. Unfortunately, some people in 12-step groups have taken this philosophy to mean we shouldn't plan. This is patently false. A major promise of the Program is to *restore us to sanity* which includes the very human blessing and curse—planning. We need to set goals, to make appointments, and to design our lives. But we don't leave *One Day at a Time* behind. It's one thing to plan, and quite another to demand that the plan work out the way we require it to—in that we have nocontrol at all. When our plans bring unintended results—and they often do—all we need do is reevaluate, accept where we are in this moment, and start anew.

As I plan my plans today, I accept that God is simultaneously planning the results.

If we ask for help and let God's plan, timing and will be ours, we can let go of our old ideas. Fear of the future will leave us.
~Chemically Dependent Anonymous P 96

September 28

Get over the idea that only children should spend their time in study. Be a student so long as you still have something to learn, and this will mean all your life. ~Henry L. Doherty

If any of us want to be the same person as we are right now five years from now, the best thing to do is not read and not make any new friends. But, if we want to grow, learn, and progress, then we need fresh interests and an influx of new information. The alternative is to do as little as possible: always go to the same meetings, don't read the CDA First Edition, don't read A.A. and NA literature, definitely don't listen to anyone else's views about how our program works (because you already know), and whomever your circle of clean and sober friends is, don't enlarge it. The best way to stop learning is to already know it. If we already know something, then why read new ideas or talk to new people? But, if we know that we *don't know* and are open, then we are able to continue to expand our mental, physical, and spiritual selves.

I didn't get sober to stay the same. I am willing to hear, read, and absorb new ideas.

What should I read to help me learn how to grow in this program?
~Chemically Dependent Anonymous P 102

September 29

When we stop to think more, we stop to thank more. ~Author Unknown

We don't acquire all the blessings in the Program because we are *entitled*. We have them by grace. Sometimes when we don't stop to *think*, a primal response goes off inside that cries, "It's mine—I want it—give it to me." We must stop and *think* about what we really have coming to us. If we were paid back tit-for-tat for all the havoc our disease caused, what would we have coming? Even though we are warned in meetings not to "think too much," there is a difference between stinking thinking and positive thinking. When we take a *real* look at ourselves, others, and our lives, we can list how much we have to be thankful for. At the top of that list is how the Universe doesn't "pay us back" for all the damage we caused. When we stop and think about the ways our lives have changed—all the ways we have changed—we will stop *wanting* and start thanking God. It isimpossible not to.

I take a moment, stop wanting, and then thank my Higher Power for Grace.

I really thank God for the Program. Before CDA, my life was a mess and I felt that there was no place in this world where I belonged.
~Chemically Dependent Anonymous P 187

September 30

The truth is that our finest moments are most likely to occur when we are feeling deeply uncomfortable, unhappy, or unfulfilled. For it is only in such moments, propelled by our discomfort, that we are likely to step out of our ruts …. ~M. Scott Peck

Look around the rooms and pick out the people who don't want to grow. You recognize them because they are comfortable staying as they are. Who wants to delve deep inside and rock the comfort boat? Maybe we find that the *person is us*. With a dose of deep-down honesty, we may realize we avoid situations that enable growth just because we are afraid of the discomfort growing entails. But our sponsors tell us that we cannot coast in this program for long. A plant is growing or dying—it doesn't "coast." So, even if we try to maintain a "comfort zone," we cannot remain in that neutral space for long. We are propelled by our discomfort to find new solutions and grow. Our finest moments are not inspired by coasting—but by the solutions we seek from the "discomfort zone."

My Higher Power makes life uncomfortable when it's time for me to change.

It was not easy to give up these old ways; we had become comfortable with them.
~Chemically Dependent Anonymous P 29

October 1

This business of resentment is infinitely grave. We found that it is fatal. For when harboring such feelings we shut ourselves off from the sunlight of the Spirit. ~Alcoholics Anonymous P 66

It becomes apparent that our resentments harm *us* even more than the people, places, and things we resent. They're so powerful that they stick with us even after the person has died! We can upset our entire equilibrium just by thinking about someone we resent. Our blood pressure skyrockets, and we don't think clearly. So, how can we best handle those pesky resentments? Well, there are many things that are best *not* to do. It won't do us any good to rehearse the resentment. Going over it in our minds hundreds of times simply gives that person more power in our lives. Plotting revenge isn't particularly effective either. The more we think of the situation the worse we feel. If our thinking is not resulting in positive action, then it's fruitless. The most effective action is prayer. Pray for the subject of the resentment to receive blessings *and* for the willingness to let it go.

Resentment is my enemy—not the one I resent.

I was up frequently because of troubling dreams. This always seems to happen when I harbor a resentment.
~Chemically Dependent Anonymous P 109-110

October 2

Serenity! That upsets me! ~David R. Hawkins, M.D., Ph.D.

Some people look at the word serenity and they see "seriousness" superimposed over it. They don't understand that being serene includes being light-hearted and humor-oriented *as well as* calm and tranquil. Taking ourselves way too seriously is a problem for many of us. Some of us have misguided thinking that serenity means being serious. We learn we can be tranquil and laugh too! Humor acts as a shock absorber—taking away the harshness in the bumps of life. The comedians are the healers of our hearts. Recent research has demonstrated that laughter can lower our blood pressure. It is also said that people who use comedy therapy (watching funny movies after surgery or chemo) have a faster and higher rate of recovery. This "laughter therapy" can work for recovering addicts as well. So, by learning to add some light-heartedness to our serenity we won't act so serious, and we can truly feel serene—and who knows, we may even lower our blood pressure!

I learn to enlighten up.

Bobbi and Sterling smile and laugh as the speakers share their experience, strength and hope with all of us.
~Chemically Dependent Anonymous P 118

October 3

It's up to each of us to get very still and say, "This is who I am." No one else defines your life. Only you do. ~Oprah Winfrey

Morals and values are not physical things that can be touched, put in our pockets, or bought and sold. They are the very foundation upon which our character is built and that which defines our life. When Oprah says that only we can define our life, she is saying that our character is determined by the morals we incorporate into our thoughts and actions. It is our morals that help answer the questions that we are here to answer. Do we stand up for what we believe? Do we look for the lessons in life's difficulties? Or do we cower—afraid that anything but following the crowd would be dangerous? Do our morals tell us to take theeasiest path or the path that brings the greatest good to all? Do our values tell us to watch out for number one or to reach out to others? No one can tell us who we are or what morals and values to live by. Only we can define ourselves.

Defining myself is an awesome responsibility. God gave me this gift with free will.

That is why we now place spiritual values first in our lives; when they are attended to, everything else falls into place.
~*Chemically Dependent Anonymous* P 64

October 4

Many people I have observed on the path focus so intently on spiritual growth that they ignore the needs of their bodies. ~Bill Austin

Spiritual growth is what our recovery is based on, but we must not forget that chemical dependency is a threefold disease affecting body, mind, *and* spirit. Like the legs of a stool, we need all three to be of equal length and strength. Without proper attention paid to each leg, the stool becomes wobbly and collapses. What good does it do to be a spiritual super-giant if our bodies are depleted and our minds feeble? Balance is what we strive for, wholeness in our wellness. Each of us has our own preferences for taking care of the body and mind along with the spirit. We may exercise, walk, eat nutritious foods, or play sports. Some of us dance, do martial arts, jog, or swim. Mentally, we might continue our education, read books, or learn a new language. It doesn't matter how we keep the legs of our stool strong—just that we do—so we don't topple.

**I nourish myself as the whole person
that I am, in body, mind, and soul.**

My life not only had become unmanageable; it, like my body, was seriously, gravely damaged through years of constant abuse.
~*Chemically Dependent Anonymous* P 168

October 5

There will come a time when you believe everything is finished. That will be the beginning.
~Louis L'Amour

Ancient lore states that from the ashes of the Phoenix a new bird arises in all its glory. The old dies so the new will be born. In dream interpretation, when a character in a dream dies it doesn't usually mean death. Instead, it signifies a new birth—for the old must die for the new to be born. Along these same lines, in A.A. they say that all our "old ideas have to be smashed." Why is this? We cannot get well using the same mind and the same behaviors that we used when we were sick. We must rely on new thought patterns and new behaviors. We operate based on our experiences and knowledge. It is that experience and knowledge that got us sick. So how can we expect them to get us well? We must let the old go so the new can be born within. Therefore, it is only when we smash our old ideas, kill them off, and end our old ways that we can truly find the beginning.

I avoid getting a new set of old ideas by allowing what doesn't work for me to end.

When we were ready to give up the use of chemicals, we also had to be ready to give up the beliefs and behaviors that went with our use.
~Chemically Dependent Anonymous **P 30**

October 6

If you want to be respected, the great thing is to respect yourself. ~Fyodor Dostoyevsky

There is no way we can respect ourselves if we have not yet learned to stop abusing others in our life. When we abused drugs, we abused people; and when we abused people, we abused drugs. It became a vicious cycle: we used mood-changing and mind-altering chemicals that numbed our conscience allowing us to easily abuse people; then we turned around and hated ourselves for hurting the ones we loved. For an addict, the natural thing was to pick up more drugs to forget our despicable behavior. The irony was that instead of forgetting our bad behavior, we once again abused them! Today, instead of picking up the drugs, we pick up the principles of the Program. By practicing these principles, we earn the respect that was once so elusive to us during the active state of our disease.

**Self-respect is the most
important respect I can earn.**

...{T}he ability to respect ourselves. We knew that we had lost or were losing these things due to our actions under the influence.
~Chemically Dependent Anonymous P 28

October 7

It is easy to love those you love. There is no virtue, no saintliness in that. But to love those you do not love, that is the attribute of an evolved soul. ~Silver Birch

It's natural and easy for us to love those who love and admire us. Just try to love the jerk down the street that keeps letting his dog out to poop on our lawn and then laughs about it—now that's the challenge! The guy or gal who hates us, taunts us, ignores us—they are the ones we can practice on to find out what true love is. Our lower, self-centered, addict self would relish in getting even, settling the score, or exposing the bad guys. Yet, we know that the spiritual response is not one of revenge or "getting to" others. Not only are we told to pray for those that bring out the worst in us, but we are also told to treat them with love and kindness. These saintly acts may confound and confuse our enemies, but that's not why we do them. We do them to help our souls evolve and develop a loving and kind spirit.

My kind and loving response may not change the heart of the one who taunts me, but it certainly changes mine.

In the Program, they tell me that if I pray for the willingness to pardon others, God will provide it.
***~Chemically Dependent Anonymous* P 110**

October 8

My friend suggested what then seemed a novel idea. He said, "Why don't you choose your own conception of God?"
~Alcoholics Anonymous P 12

Those words were Ebby's. He was the man who brought the Oxford message to Bill Wilson of Alcoholics Anonymous. Although the Oxford Movement was basically Christian, God, in His wisdom, guided Ebby to present the idea of each person finding their own path to their Higher Power. His words, "choose your own conception" are one of the 12-step program's greatest gifts. It is the gift of spiritual freedom. It is the gift to believe in our own personal guidance—not a particular doctrine. We can believe whatever we want to believe as long as it makes sense to us. Today in Chemically Dependent Anonymous, we are free to love the God we believe in. We must honor this spiritual freedom for ourselves *and for others*. God answers to any name we choose to use.

My Higher Power answers to whatever name I choose to use, and I honor this freedom by passing it on to others.

We may invoke our God by whatever name we see fit {...}.
~Chemically Dependent Anonymous P 34

October 9

Show me a completely smooth operation and I'll show you someone who's covering mistakes.
~Reverend Mother Superior Dsowi Odade

Even in recovery, we can become disconnected and distressed when overwhelmed by the consequences of past conflict arising in current problems. *Shouldn't I have a better handle on this? Why can't these problems just solve themselves? I must not be as well as I think I am. Am I doing something wrong with my program?* Not only can these thoughts plague us, but they can also keep us from sharing honestly about our less-than-perfect lives in recovery. We are promised "progress not perfection." When we share our experience, strength, and hope, we share the good things in our lives, as well as the struggles with situations that baffle us. Most of us would like only good things happening in our lives, but that is not the way life works. We gain practical and valuable lessons as we allow ourselves to learn by the life experience of others.

I am willing to share my mistakes because others are willing to learn from them.

{W}e can learn to avoid mistakes in areas we never would have thought of as problematic.
~Chemically Dependent Anonymous P 12

October 10

If you don't find yourself in your own backyard, you never will. ~Dorothy, *The Wizard of Oz*

Somewhere along the way we got the message that we were "less than." We felt (and sometimes still feel) unliked, unloved, or unappreciated. Maybe it's the negative messages we gave ourselves in active addiction; maybe it's from the negative messages in our childhood; or maybe it's genetic. But it is not by going back to our childhood, our addiction, or cursing God for our genetics that we find our true nature. It is by going into the backyard of our own character and burying that negative self, and then planting our positive self, that we can begin to change the negative messages. By working Step Four we dig up the negative. In Step Five we show God that we have found it. In Steps Six and Seven we ask God to turn it into fertilizer, and in Eight and Nine we plant our new positive self. Steps Ten and Eleven are where we nurture our new growth, and Step Twelve is the fruition. It's in our own backyard that we find our true selves and real growth is found.

I like myself today.

Today, at times, I feel so strange and confused. It's as if I'm meeting a new person in myself. I'm scared, happy, sad and lost.
~Chemically Dependent Anonymous P 198

October 11

Fear of {...} economic insecurity will leave us.
~Alcoholics Anonymous P 84

In recovery some of us have grave economic insecurities. At one time, most of us could not hold a steady job, and had little or no savings coupled with overwhelming debt. Yet, employment skills were not necessarily the problem for most of us. Our problems involved not being able to follow orders and our inability to get along with our fellow co-workers and managers. In sobriety, our recovery principles teach us to be team players as well as responsible members of society. We stop trying to get the better of our employer, creditors, and friends. We strive to be fair in business dealings. By improving our marketable skills, spending less than we make, and placing God in charge of our decisions, economic insecurity will become but a distant memory. Losing the fear of economic insecurity is promise number ten of the Twelve Promises of recovery, as given to us from Alcoholics Anonymous.

**I ask God to remove all my
economic insecurities.**

Similarly, we mirror the same attitude of responsibility in our groups when we support the Program with our money, time and energy.
***~Chemically Dependent Anonymous** P 76-77*

October 12

You know that there is a way out of any difficulty whatever, no matter what it may be, through the changing of your own consciousness by prayer.
~Emmet Fox

When we wake up and get out of bed, we hit our knees in prayer. We ask our Higher Power for the strength to surrender to the process of recovery. We know that by raising our consciousness with prayer, every conceivable form of good that we desire can be ours. Nobody can take this away from us because the good we create is from within. Yes, we do ask our Higher Power for the strength and power to not pick up a drink or drug, but we ask for so much more than mere abstinence. We ask for good things so that we might benefit others. We also ask for His care, guidance, and protection. We pray because we are told to; we pray because it works; we pray because prayer changes *us*.

**Prayer does not change things.
Prayer changes me.**

Time in the morning talking to God puts the day into perspective and gives us a chance to reaffirm that our will and our lives are in God's care for another 24 hours.
~Chemically Dependent Anonymous P 61

October 13

I am made up entirely of character defects stitched together with good intentions.
~Augusten Burroughs

Before finding recovery, many of us could have been poster children for "Character Defects." Although we probably had good intentions to pay the bills, show up at our child's school functions, or be faithful partners, our actions proved otherwise. Getting drunk or high always came first and we were labeled as unreliable, heartless, and selfish. Our "using" brain wanted others to judge us on our "good" intentions, not our actions. Confused because people didn't seem to see the "real" us, we became resentful and, with a vengeance, withdrew even further into active addiction. Our lives were run by character defects. In CDA, through working the Steps, our character defects are transformed into character assets, and our actions become aligned with our intentions. Miraculously, those same people we used to react to now begin to see the persons we always wanted them to see—the *real* us.

**Recovery affords me the opportunity
to just be me—warts and all.**

I have many character defects but I'm working on them.
~Chemically Dependent Anonymous P 194

October 14

The more honest one is, the easier it is to continue being honest, just as the more lies one has told, the more necessary it is to lie again.
~M. Scott Peck

Honesty is just one of the keys to living a successful life in recovery. We start going to meetings and we hear the words honesty, open-mindedness, and willingness. Old-timers say we must get honest with ourselves and others, but it's not an easy task. Not only were we lying to others, but to ourselves as well! Oh, how we could rationalize (anyone would do the same), manipulate (I need $10 for formula), and justify our behavior (I had a tough childhood) to rid ourselves of shame or guilt just to get something we wanted. We then lied to support our defensive position. But it takes so much energy to keep lying; lies compound on one another. Not only do you have to think of a lie, but you also have to *remember* the lie— forever! It's much easier to remember the truth because *it's the truth.* Slowly, once we learn *how* we are dishonest in our life, we can open the doorway to truthfulness and lead a life of honesty.

I am only as healthy as my honesty.

I put the pen down and thought to myself, "This is really ridiculous. Here I am, trying to do this Step and I'm lying, instead of trying to help myself."
~Chemically Dependent Anonymous P 270

October 15

There must be more to life than increasing its speed. ~Mahatma Ghandi

Time seems to have been lost when we first get clean. There is an overwhelming desire to play catch-up for the amount of time that we wasted while using. Spending time and energy obsessing about what we didn't do makes it hard to move forward. Likewise, rushing around trying to stuff in all the experiences we missed in our active addiction will leave us little serenity to enjoy life in depth—rushing around is only surface living. When we cram and hurry, rather than slowly playing catch-up, we actually lose the quality of life that we seek. By following suggestions and living in the now, we can say good-bye to the wasteland of lost opportunities and be grateful for the privilege of getting a second chance. It turns out that *now* is the moment we've been waiting for.

**Today I focus on the present
and breathe in the wonder
of the universe.**

I learned to become comfortable with myself. I started living for today instead of in the past.
~Chemically Dependent Anonymous **P 234**

October 16

A moment is to one's day as a day is to one's life.
~Author Unknown

Many of us dealt with "time" very strangely. We may have dwelled on our past and feared our future. We had the illusion that getting high might freeze time, allowing us to stop time in a moment of our choosing. Possibly we thought that we could make the *good old days* the *good now days* last forever. When we got high, we ignorantly thought we could erase our regrets, forget our guilt, and escape the consequences of the future. We tried to capture certain moments, and instead, we let so many moments slip right on by us. We essentially *killed* time. Whenever we try to capture what is gone or wish for things in the future, we kill what is present. We don't have to be high to kill time. To kill time today, all we must do is ignore what we need to do, or dream about how good something used to be or how good it's going to be. And what we gain is an entire dead day from the moments we failed to live.

When I kill time, there is no resurrection. Life is precious as my moments add up to a lifetime.

I am ready to experience the pain of awareness: that I was mistaken and stupid to waste so much precious time of my life doing drugs{...}.
~Chemically Dependent Anonymous P 171

October 17

Words can never hurt nor change us if we don't let them. And we won't let them if we are more concerned about what and how we are doing instead of what people are saying.
~Father John Doe

Even though we tried to hide it, we cared very much about what our using buddies thought of us. We did not want them to think that we weren't cool. Being nice was never cool, so any nice behavior was something we didn't get caught at. We pretended we cared nothing about what others thought, but really, we cared deeply. We still care, but soon learn that what others think of us is not our business—*it's theirs*! Our business is what *we do* and the words *we use*. Learning to be nice again in CDA is not a passive thing: We don't *have* nice days; we *make* nice days. We learn that although it's nice to be important, it's more important to be nice! We learn not to put too much stock into what others say about us and put a lot of stock into what we say about others. The only words that can really hurt us are the words *we use*.

For those weaker than me, I am kind to them.
For those stronger than me, I am kind to myself.

Even though living in reality was not my strong point, being victimized was a real fear.
~Chemically Dependent Anonymous P 332-333

October 18

Mood follows action. ~Ron R.

As practicing addicts and alcoholics, we tried to think our way out of emotional turmoil, uncomfortable situations, boredom, and endless scenarios in which we rehashed our problems like a broken record. Any insights we gathered never seemed to make it from our head to our feet. This kept us in a prison of confusion and indecision. We preferred the safety of the fantasy world where we could reside in the comfort zone skipping the hard task of taking responsibility for our lives. In recovery, we are presented with many opportunities to change the way we feel through some type of footwork. This footwork might mean getting to a meeting when we have no vehicle; taking a job we think is beneath us; working on a Step we've avoided; or taking a service commitment that is not the one we wanted. We learn to move our feet and the solutions follow.

**I recover, not with my head,
but with my feet.**

{We} have what it takes to move through the feelings and take action.
~Chemically Dependent Anonymous P 36

October 19

The only thing we ask of our members is that they have this desire. Without it they are doomed, but with it miracles will happen.
~Narcotics Anonymous P 62

Tradition Three: The only requirement for CDA membership is a desire to abstain from all mood-changing and mind-altering chemicals; including all street type drugs, alcohol, and unnecessary medication. In Chemically Dependent Anonymous, unlike other 12-step programs, we do not care what chemicals our members were addicted to. We do not care about their politics, religion, or sexual orientation. We do not care about race, age, or gender. We do not judge or limit our participation in other 12-step groups, nor do we censor the words members use to describe their addiction or recovery. In fact, all our meetings are open meetings. We are members when we saywe are members. Our desire to stop using is our own personal membership card and no one can take it from us.

**My desire to stop using is all that I need.
Nobody can revoke my membership.**

I started attending CDA meetings too and I now consider myself eligible for membership because of my chemical dependency to alcohol.
~Chemically Dependent Anonymous P XIII

October 20

The Program is as close as we'll get to gospel; the Fellowship is something else entirely, and it's good to know the difference. ~Anne Wayman

After being in the Program for a few twenty-four hours, we come to realize that there can be a significant difference between what's said at meetings and what's actually written in our basic texts. This goes for CDA as well as the other 12-step fellowships. What we hear in meetings, unless based on actual texts, is simply an opinion. Sometimes we think because our sponsor or a speaker at a convention said something, it must be gospel. For example, you'll hear people at meetings say things like "you can't date anyone for a year." This is not in our book. It is an opinion that might be sensible, but it certainly is not a Step and/or an official suggestion. The stories we tell at meetings are meant to help us identify and find solutions, but the ultimate solution for any of us is found in the CDA First Edition's first 136 pages and the A.A. Big Book's first 164 pages—not in opinions.

Even when I respect a speaker, I do not take their words as gospel, unless it's in our books.

What I want to share with you is my experience, my story and my own particular opinions.
~Chemically Dependent Anonymous P 339

October 21

Happiness too is inevitable. ~Albert Camus

When we first come into recovery, we are so beaten down by our addiction that our willingness to live is hanging on by a fragile string of hope. Yet the allure of drugs still beckons us to return with the false promise that *this* time we will be able to control our using and live a normal life. Oh, such good times when we were so unhappy! Although the power of the Program weakens the hold that drugs have on us, we are never entirely "safe" from the compulsions that sometimes drench us with unhealthy cravings. Old-timers with twenty or even thirty years speak of how complacency can turn off the recovery and turn on the cravings. So, it is not our amount of time abstinent, our new lives, our happiness, or even sheer time in the Program that can guarantee that we are safe. As they say in A.A., we have a "daily reprieve contingent on the maintenance of our spiritual condition." Our inevitable happiness is dependent on our spiritual condition, too.

Rather than seek happiness, I seek a strong spiritual program and happiness is inevitable.

And I decided that I would wait just one more day because it is true: If you work at this Program, happiness, too, is inevitable.
~Chemically Dependent Anonymous P 284

October 22

Practical experience shows that nothing will so much insure immunity from drinking as intensive work with other alcoholics.
~Alcoholics Anonymous P 89

Sponsorship has always been a two-way street. Not only do the sponsored benefit, but this service helps keep the sponsor chemical-free as well. There really isn't any exact science to sponsorship. The guidelines are simple: men sponsor men, women sponsor women, and we look for someone who has a darn strong program that we admire. We can look for someone with whom we feel comfortable or just someone who has what we want in recovery. We don't even have to like our sponsors—just listen to them! Our relationship with a sponsor, or with our sponsees, may grow as we grow, or maybe not. It's possible we may need to change sponsors as our needs evolve or fire sponsees as their needs change. That's okay because there is no proven formula. What works for us works.

I trust that my choice of a sponsor is the one that works for me.

A sponsor is someone who is willing to share his or her own experience, strength and hope with you on a personal level.
~Chemically Dependent Anonymous P 100

October 23

God has already forgiven us; when we work our Steps, we forgive ourselves. Anything else is not ours to bear. ~Young, Sober, & Free

Step Nine, the amends-making Step, is as much about forgiveness as it is about making things right. But this forgiveness is not *them* forgiving *us*. It is about us forgiving us. We cannot possibly learn to forgive ourselves for all the damage we have caused until we take responsibility for our past. In taking this responsibility, we do not anticipate getting pats on the back for our "goodness" by saying we are sorry or paying back the money we stole. Amends-making gets a lot easier when we stop trying to extract forgiveness from everyone to whom we make amends. What they choose to do with our attempts to make things right is up to them. We clean up our side of the street only. Amends is about how we see ourselves, not how others see us.

I do not make amends to hear what a good person I am. I do it to forgive myself.

We must be able to make amends where we can and forgive ourselves.
~Chemically Dependent Anonymous P 96

October 24

We ask ourselves, "Who am I to be brilliant, gorgeous, talented and fabulous?" Actually, who are you not to be? You are a child of GOD. Your playing small does not serve the world.
~Nelson Mandela

When good things happen for us, we can relax and enjoy them as they happen. Acting meek and undeserving gives a sour message to the newcomer. Recovery brings perks; we need to strut our stuff and let folks know that CDA works. We do not have to second guess the universe as to whether we are ready and deserving of all the perks. The Universe wants good things for us and wants us to demonstrateit to others. That is why we were brought to CDA We are brilliant enough to be coming to meetings, gorgeous enough to be admired by the newcomers, talented enough to work the Steps, and fabulous enough to be loved by members in CDA. By default, we know we *are deserving*. If we weren't ready, the situation would not have manifested itself in our lives.

I am prepared to see the fabulous me and allow others to see the fabulous me too.

There are still those days when I feel that I don't deserve it and I try to do something to ruin it.
~*Chemically Dependent Anonymous* P 284

October 25

I get up, I walk, I fall down. Meanwhile, I keep dancing. ~Rabbi Hillel

Falling down and failing are actually the building blocks to success when seen in the right perspective. We walk into the rooms of recovery feeling like failures—we have stumbled and fallen. It probably won't be the last time we fall either. What is important is that we never stop getting up and we never stop dancing. They say that failure isn't in falling down; it's in failing to get back up. And when we fall, we can learn from our experiences, which means we succeeded at something! Additionally, in our program it's the things we do *wrong*, our failings, that are often the bridge to other people. Seen in this light, our spiritual and emotional growth does not depend so much upon success as it does upon failures and setbacks. Because of this we learn to count failures as the rungs on the ladder of progress.

**I continue to dance
despite my falling down.**

He {my sponsor} used to tell me, "That's why they make erasers on pencils." What he did for me and for my program was to give me permission to make mistakes.
~Chemically Dependent Anonymous **P 234**

October 26

We are made to persist. That is how we find out who we are. ~Tobias Wolff

Persistence, discipline, determination, doggedness, and diligence were not our strong points in anything except in how we pursued our drug of choice. What Wolff says, "That is how we find out who we are" is so true. We were addicts of the nastiest kind. We proved as practicing addicts that nothing succeeds like persistence. We found our drugs in the most unlikely places and under the most stringent circumstances. We even found them when locked up! If we take that same persistence and apply it to staying chemical-free and working the Steps, how can we fail? What does persistence mean in recovery? It means going to meetings even when we don't want to, 12-stepping even in bad weather, sticking to a meditation schedule, and calling our sponsor on a regular basis. The same persistence that kept us addicted will keep us straight if we redirect the obsession and energy. It's still there, so why don't we use it to our benefit?

I am insistent, consistent, and persistent about my recovery.

I was determined to start a new life and it had to begin right back where I had fallen.
~Chemically Dependent Anonymous P 279-280

October 27

Faith is like a muscle: it grows with exercise. The more we see God accomplish in and through our lives, the more we are assured that He will accomplish.
~From Ron R.'s *Memorial Retreat 2005*

No one *has* to believe in God in order to work the Program of CDA, but like they say, "If you don't believe in God, we suggest you change your mind." It's understandable that many of us had problems withthe God concept. Some of us just flat out didn't believe in God, some of us were so angry at God that we couldn't see straight, and yet others felt that God had abandoned them. Yet, the truth is, *we had abandoned God*. As we come to understand our Higher Power, we realize that His unconditional love for us today, clean and sober, is no less than His love for us in the darkest depths of our addiction. When we don't believe, we learn to pretend. We pray even when we don't trust it, we turn it over even when we think it's hooey—basically, we act as if. Slowly, by exercising our muscle of willingness our faith steadily grows. It grows, quite simply, *because it works*.

Prayer works and God works, when I work.

{T}his adjustment in our spiritual attitudes is one of the characteristics or essentials of "getting" the Program.
~*Chemically Dependent Anonymous* P 15

October 28

I hated every minute of training, but I said, 'Don't quit. Suffer now and live the rest of your life as a champion.' ~Muhammad Ali

We have all been fighters to some degree or we wouldn't have made it to the rooms of CDA. But some of us come into recovery wanting all the trophies *yesterday*. We jump into recovery training and start the stopwatch. We get a sponsor, race through the Steps, take on three home groups—turning recovery into grueling training rather than a joyful new life. For those of us who can't step out of the ring when the trophies (job, money, or family) aren't happening in *our time frame*, we start feeling like throwing in the towel. We may cut back on our meetings, talk less to our sponsor, and do less service work because God has not given us a knockout win. But that is going backwards. God does not use a stopwatch. We need to slow down and trust in the process. We suffered before we got here—*that was our training*. Recovery is not hard-core training in order to win the championship—recovery is the championship.

I surrender to win, not suffer to win.

For some, surrender (the ultimate act of trust) comes in a single, overwhelming experience. The realization that this higher power loves us and is working in our lives fills us. For most, however, this is a gradual process.
~*Chemically Dependent Anonymous* P 32-33

October 29

As we awaken, we strive to start the day in a manner that stimulates our spiritual connection to our Higher Power. ~Dave G.

Every day, in our morning meditation and prayer, we remind ourselves that from our spirituality comes everything else we desire in our life. By doing so we give ourselves the best chance to enjoy today as we become closer to our Higher Power. There is no set formula for stimulating our spiritual connection. Prayer doesn't have to be formal and written out by sacred elders, but it certainly can be. Prayer can also be informal conversations with our Higher Power or our angels as we drive to work. It can be as simple as a few whispered words of gratitude before meals. Even when we cry out "Oh, my God," that is prayer, and our Spiritual Source listens. So, whether we pray, petition, plead, protest, implore, or praise our Spiritual Source on some issue, or whether we whisper words of gratitude or sing from the soul, this is prayer. And prayer is a spiritual connection.

**I acknowledge my every
good thought as a prayer.**

I'm now in contact with God as I pray on a daily basis.
~Chemically Dependent Anonymous **P 192**

October 30

I am not a has-been. I am a will-be.
~Helen Hayes

It is not unusual for us to feel we have wasted the better part of our lives on drugs and that we have little to offer ourselves or to anyone else. The older we are when we find recovery, the more likely we are to feel that we cheated ourselves and that our potential is over. Emily Dickinson wrote, "I dwell in possibility." We find that recovery is just that—dwelling in possibility. We learn that just sharing our experience, strength, and hope can support another person to get through one more day. What a great possibility—to help another. Occasionally we can touch many just by being ourselves, which is another wonder-filled possibility. The act of growing in sobriety allows others to bear witness to what is possible in their sobriety. It is a chain reaction of supporting our potential with each other. This ripple effect continues and increases the possibilities. We need not waste time on what has been lost; instead, we embrace the possibilities. With this attitude anything is possible!

**I don't waste time thinking
about what I can't change.**

We declare that the possibilities are endless. And as we say in every meeting: KEEP COMING BACK—IT WORKS!!
~Chemically Dependent Anonymous P 68

October 31

Humility Endless Is: you're never too old to make another big mistake. ~Yoda, *Star Wars*

As we progress in the journey of our program, we realize that we must humbly live each day with the understanding that our gift is living one day at a time. Although someone with twenty years statistically has a greater chance of being clean and sober tomorrow than someone with twenty days, we must remember that we are not statistics. Regardless of how much time we have, each of us is but one drink or drug from another *big mistake*. Anyone who has had a lot of years of abstinence, and then relapsed, will tell us that one of their problems was that they began counting the years and lost track of the days. To remain humble, we need to pay more attention to the days than the years; we focus more on our service work than our service title; we endeavor to obtain quality of sponsorship, not quantity. We do not have to humiliate ourselves with another big mistake before choosing to live with humility.

I find humility before it finds me.

Am I willing to give credit to my Higher Power for everything happening in my life {...}. If so, then I'm ready to receive the gift of true humility in the Seventh Step.
~Chemically Dependent Anonymous **P 46**

November 1

The turning point in the process of growing up is when you discover the core of strength within you that survives all hurt. ~Max Lerner

That core of strength for people in recovery from addiction to mind-altering and mood-changing chemicals is based on abstinence and learning to live by spiritual principles. In CDA we learn to prioritize. And through that process, we can leave our immaturity behind us and grasp the principles that grown-ups live by. One of the ways to find this core of strength is to take our recovery and put it above all else. We make the principles and abstinence the priorities upon which our lives are based. If we put our significant other ahead of our recovery, we are showing the immaturity of someone who cannot yet survive the ups and downs of sober life. Anything that we put ahead of recovery, such as a job or our reputation, is likely to be the very thing we lose first. We cannot survive the hurt of immaturity until our core of strength *is* our recovery. Once recovery is our priority, we can finally call ourselves maturing adults.

I find my recovery *Twelve Steps* past any lengths.

Today, my recovery comes first–above my husband, above everything else–because without sobriety, all of this would be gone.
~*Chemically Dependent Anonymous* P 227

November 2

When you get into a tight place and it seems that you can't go on, hold on—for that is just the place and the time that the tide will turn.
~Harriet Beecher Stowe

If we get to the end of our rope, CDA teaches us to tie a knot in it and hang on. All of us are stronger than we think, and we find we can keep going even when we think we can't. During our journey throughout sobriety there are moments that seem like the world is closing in around us. It might be when we lose a job, find out we are ill, are faced with a romantic break-up, or lose something precious to us like our child. God can do anything in twenty-four hours. When we allow our Higher Power to take care of things, rather than force our own solutions on events, the outcome can be miraculous. It seems that just as we come to a rough place in our recovery—the place where it all looks the bleakest—we discover that we can, and do, endure the storms that come along. We don't quit before the miracle happens. We know that God makes miracles happen every day—all twenty-four hours of the day!

**I keep going even when I think I can't.
I breathe in. I breathe out. I repeat.**

I've found a real joy in living and in sharing with others. It all goes to show, "Don't 'pick up' before the miracle happens."
~Chemically Dependent Anonymous P 134

November 3

Show due consideration as to how much ye owe the world, rather than as to how much the world owes you! ~Edgar Cayce

Before we came to 12-step recovery, we took and took and took. Our addiction told us what it wanted, and we complied. Feelings of entitlement ran deep. Others "owed" us a paycheck even when we did not do our work; the government "owed" us welfare even when we were capable of working; and certainly others "owed" us more consideration even when we didn't deserve it. We were *takers*, never understanding the other side as that of a *giver*. In recovery we still have to take from the Program, the Fellowship, and our Higher Power—every day. We never give up taking, but we do learn to balance it with giving. Slowly, beautifully, and gently, we are taught to give back what is so freely given to us. We are taught *balance*. Our spiritual recovery remains dependent on this principle: gaining the balance between giving and taking.

**I received without cost.
Now I give without charge.**

{T}he only way we were going to recover was by first admitting our lives had truly become unbalanced through addiction {...}.
~Chemically Dependent Anonymous P 89

November 4

Joy is what happens to us when we allow ourselves to recognize how good things really are.
~Marianne Williamson

Misery is an option. But, of course, gratitude does not come as standard equipment either. Yet we are told to live with an attitude of gratitude. How can we feel grateful when there is so much pain and suffering inside of us? It's easier than we think. What we need is a major change in our thought process. We have a choice to focus on good stuff or we can dwell on the misery. Everyone has pain, but misery is a choice. So, is it our intention to be grateful or to pick things apart? If our *intention* is to be thankful for the good stuff instead of hateful for bad breaks, then all we need to do is talk about what works in our life. Gratitude is not the word itself, but the *desire* to say the word. In fact, just the awareness of positive things can be energizing to our spirit. So, we make a choice. We talk about *how good things really are.* By talking about the good—declaring it to the world—we beginto recognize how good things really are in our world.

I speak of the good and energize my spirit.

Am I cultivating positive thinking?
~*Chemically Dependent Anonymous* P 40

November 5

> *Yet we teach ourselves to do the unnatural until the unnatural becomes itself second nature. Indeed, all self-discipline might be defined as teaching ourselves to do the unnatural.*
> ~M. Scott Peck

The natural state for any chemical dependent is to be loaded on drugs, whereas the unnatural thing is to be chemical-free. Therefore, getting clean and sober feels unnatural and uncomfortable. We are introduced to novel ideas. We are told to pray *every day* upon waking and at bedtime. We are told to take responsibility and not to blame others. How do these things help? We find that once we become willing to make the conscious effort to implement these ideas, they really do become more comfortable. In fact, our new habits become so natural that we find ourselves cringing when exposed to our old habits. Soon, our attitude changes so much that our new habits become our natural habits. The mere thought of usingbecomes the unnatural and uncomfortable thing. We come to see the benefit of the self-discipline that enables us to learn to do the unnatural.

Recovery is the natural order of my life.

{W}hen…things just weren't as hunky–dory as I wanted them to be, I did what is very natural for any alcoholic to do. I picked up a drink.
~Chemically Dependent Anonymous P 225

November 6

> *Our program will work for people who believe in God. Our program will work for people who don't believe in God. ~The Pocket Sponsor*

One of our biggest questions upon coming to CDA was, "Will their God work for me?" Even if we believed in God, we wondered if *their* God was for us. We were full of questions: "Do we *have* to believe in God? Will it work if we don't believe? Is this a religion and what are the rules?" We may have tried other recovery methods before like religion, going to jail, or becoming an exercise nut. But inevitably, we began using again more than before. So, we hit the doors of CDA with a lot of unanswered questions. When told that there were no rules, this was NOT a religion, or even a pseudo doctrine, the relief was tremendous. Because we didn't *have* to believe any particular way, it freed us up to explore a lot of ways. We pass that freedom on to newcomers every day. When they ask if it will work for them, even if they don't believe thus and such, we always say yes.

I tell the newcomer they don't have to believe anything; they just have to keep coming back.

{T}he things I heard when I first came in were an inspiration to me: to stay in the Program, to keep coming back {...}.
~Chemically Dependent Anonymous P 322-323

November 7

We are not born friends; we become friends. Friendship is a true virtue, a good habit we develop by giving of ourselves.
~Thomas Aquinas

We need fellowship. We need companionship. To live in isolation is truly hell for us chemically dependent people. Thank goodness CDA is about relationships, not accomplishments. So rather than run around and impress each other with our accomplishments in life, we practice a true equality—we are all just addicts trying to get well. When we say it's a "we" program, we mean just that. We are friends, we are family, and we are each other's helping hands. We feel most alive when we are actively using and sharing our God-given abilities in our friendships. God's love is, indeed, displayed in the context of our relationships in the Fellowship. We are His hands, and we are His mouth. But friendship is not a possession. It is an activity. We find it more important to occupy ourselves with friendships rather than accomplishments. As a friend, we need all the help we can give.

By working through me, God gets twice the result for the same amount of work, for both are helped.

But I have become physically, mentally and spiritually healthier. I have more friends who love me than I've ever had before in my life.
~*Chemically Dependent Anonymous* P 183

November 8

Our deepest fear is not that we are inadequate. Our deepest fear is that we are powerful beyond measure. It is our light, not our darkness that most frightens us. ~Timo Cruz

The foundation of our work in recovery is to turn our will and our lives over to God, identify our character defects, share them with someone we trust, and then ask God to remove these defects of character. Once that process is in place, nothing stands between us and the path of service. Through the rest of the Twelve Steps, we are released from the fear of our dark side, embarking upon an incredible and powerful journey. What can possibly hold us back, except the fear of our powerful light side? Like the fear of success, we know that our new self is powerful. We now have influence over others, they listen to us, and that can be frightening. Are we truly able to handle it? We are no longer afraid of the dark...now we fear where the light may lead. Let us remember, though, that God doesn't lead us to anything we can't handle.

**My inner light is Higher Powered.
I have no need to fear what God generates.**

I pray that he can find the light that I have, and that he will be able to overcome his difficulties.
~Chemically Dependent Anonymous P 209

November 9

We were not that good at being bad. ~Patti W.

Even though we become entirely ready in Step Six to have God remove all our defects of character, and then ask for them to be removed in Step Seven, the way it works can remain mysterious. In our practicing days, we may have known we weren't very "good" people, and so we might have tried to be really good "bad" people. But, none of us were very good at being bad. We were too sick and conflicted for that. But we find that some of the traits we considered bad have a wonderful way of turning into virtues under God's direction. For instance, maybe our Higher Power redirected our greed for power, lust, and acquiring money and turned that same energy into greed for recovery, lust for service work, and acquiring benefits for newcomers. Another example might be our over-sensitivity to the slightest criticism. God can turn that into being sensitive to other people's needs, a trait we call empathy. Nothing is all good and nothing is all bad, including us!

The best of me is not all *that* good and the worst of me is probably not all that bad. I get over it.

...{I} couldn't wait to get up there and tell you what a bad-ass I was–how much alcohol and how many drugs I had used. I was really going to impress everybody with my story.
~*Chemically Dependent Anonymous* P 340

November 10

It's not easy being grateful all the time. But it's when you feel the least thankful that you are most in need of what gratitude can give you.
~Oprah Winfrey

One of the things we receive from the Program is a sense of profound gratitude and thankfulness. This comes only as a result of working the Twelve Steps. Our blessings include simple things that were once beyond our grasp. We have enough food, a warm place to spend the night, friends to associate with, and a safe place to share our lives with people just like us. Although we might want more, we consider the addict living on the street, the hungry addict, the bone-weary addict, the addict with HIV, or the one who has lost their kids and family. They would give anything to have what, today, we take for granted. We start out thankful for the small things and these become big things. The more we give thanks, the more our blessings increase. This is because what we focus on increases. So, gratitude becomes a daily prayer.

**I have everything in life, this day,
that is necessary to meet my needs.**

Am I grateful for recovery?
~Chemically Dependent Anonymous P 38

November 11

You've got to love like you'll never get hurt. You've got to dance like there's nobody watching. You've got to come from the heart if you want it to work.
~Susanna Clarke

Matt Talbot of Dublin drank for sixteen years, then found sobriety in his last forty. His life of sacrifice, prayer, and sobriety may have gone unnoticed except for the marks and chains found under his robes when he died. Some attributed the chains to his repentance for drunkenness. Thank God we are not required to grovel to find recovery. We are quite sure that God wants us to be happy, not self-flagellating and wrapped in chains! Fortunately, we have many opportunities in CDA to experience the joy of living and just plain old non-chemical induced fun. We have dances, conventions, ski trips, dinners, sports games, and sober excursions. And to think, once we thought we weren't going to have any fun without drugs! We start the process of having fun by signing up for the next fun activity planned by CDA.

**I look in the bulletin and sign up
for a clean and sober activity today.**

Yet when it comes to thinking about what life might be like in sobriety, you may be wondering if there is a life after addiction. CDA offers a wide range of activities for all its members.
~Chemically Dependent Anonymous P 117

November 12

Life's most persistent and urgent question is:
What are you doing for others?
~Martin Luther King, Jr.

Without others carrying the message to us, we wouldn't be clean and sober today. So important is this concept to our recovery that in Alcoholics Anonymous, our parent program, it is written, "For if an alcoholic failed to perfect and enlarge his spiritual life through work and self-sacrifice for others, he could not survive the certain trials and low spots ahead."

A.A. also tells us, "Practical experience shows that nothing will so much ensure immunity from drinking as intensive work with other alcoholics. It works when other activities fail." It is essential that we grasp this concept of service and self-sacrifice in order to stay clean and sober, and in turn, reap all the benefits of recovery. It is a sense of responsibility and spiritual maturity to help others who have also suffered as we have. The longer we help others in the Program and do all that we can in service work, we will continue to grow stronger in our resolve for recovery.

My service work can save a life. Mine!

Today, I still make it a habit to do whatever I have to do to grow in my Program. I sponsor many people. I go to retreats. I even do things that I don't want to do. And that seems to be what makes it work.
~Chemically Dependent Anonymous P 271

November 13

If I take five minutes out of each day to remember to treat people the same way I want to be treated, we could accomplish wonderful things together.
~Bob Fishel

Who among us has not heard of the Golden Rule? "Do unto others as you would have others do unto you." Yet it is not the lavish gifts but the little things in life that make the difference. When people offer us a cup of coffee, listen to what we say, show interest in something we are working on, bring a bone for our dog—those are the gestures that put a smile on our face. Is giving a compliment, opening a door, or greeting with a hug the way we want others to treat us? What do we want? We want respect, sympathy, perhaps someone to ask us about our kids, or maybe bring us a plate of cookies. Whatever it is we want for ourselves, we begin the process by doing that very thing for others. Miraculously, the universal law of like-begets-like kicks in and soon we are receiving the very things we give to others.

I find peace and happiness as I remember to treat others the way I want to be treated.

How am I growing in CARING?
~Chemically Dependent Anonymous **P 38**

November 14

God doesn't do anything to us, but always through us. ~Emmet Fox

Among the many things that our disease taught us was that no matter how far or how fast we ran, we couldn't outrun our addiction. The wonderful news is that the same truism applies to the God of our understanding. When we were using, we tried to run from any obstacles in our path. We pitied ourselves for any tribulation we had to go through. We were like little toddlers stomping our feet and yelling at life. But our Higher Power was fast on the heels of addiction. He took every situation we ran from and turned it to our highest good. Eventually, we found we didn't have to run from addiction. Nor did we have to run to God. We could relax and stay put because God still makes house calls. Wherever we find ourselves, when we allow God to work through us, instead of letting life beat us down, we come out stronger. Once we stop using, we find that God never does anything *to us*, but instead, works *through us*.

**Since I can't run from God,
I'll let God run me.**

Faced with this reality, we learned, grudgingly at times, to trust that God offers us guidance and strength that we could never have on our own.
~Chemically Dependent Anonymous P 59

November 15

For where your treasure is, there will your heart be also. ~Matthew 6:21

What is it we treasure in this life? The answer is always simple and obvious. What we treasure is determined by where we spend our time and energy. In our using days, we treasured the high, the drugs, the excitement, and the risk. That is where we "spent" ourselves. In recovery we get the message that spirituality means we "should" be treasuring serenity, gratitude, forgiveness, service, and love. Again, the answers are as simple as they are obvious. Do we spend more time getting our chopper decked out to impress people when we roar up to the meeting or more time helping newcomers get their vehicles up and running? Do we spend as much time getting ready for the meeting as we do at the meeting itself? Although there is no judgment about this in CDA, what good is it to be sober if we are still chasing the same empty treasures? We learn in recovery that a fulfilling life is of more value than good living.

I consider where my energy is spent to evaluate what treasures I am seeking.

We will frequently act in ways that are not consistent with our spiritual values, and we will need help in recommitting to those values.
~Chemically Dependent Anonymous P 67

November 16

We either make ourselves miserable, or we make ourselves strong. The amount of work is the same.
~Carlos Castaneda

Not only in Shaman teachings, but also in Eastern philosophies, we are told that in all affairs of life, at every moment, we have a choice. During active addiction, of course, mind-altering chemicals hijacked our ability to choose. But today, one of our greatest blessings is that we are once again free to choose. We get up in the morning and choose whether to eat a Twinkie or have a high protein meal. We choose whether to speed, taking the chance of getting a ticket, or to stay calm, arriving to work in peace. Each day we choose whether to pick up or stay clean and sober. We choose to do the right or wrong thing. We choose to either do God's will or our own. The amount of work in choosing is the same, but the result is very different. So, what do we choose today?

**Today I choose to give up the old lie,
"I had no choice."**

God gives people the freedom of choice and we must choose at some point to say, "I have had enough of this pain," or we will perish.
~Chemically Dependent Anonymous P 90

November 17

There are two ways to acquire power: On the outside or from the inside. God offers power from the inside. ~Keeping God in the Small Stuff

Usually, when people want to acquire power, they go at it from the outside. They beef up their body, make lots of money, or buy a gun. In CDA, we learn to power up from the *inside* by putting God's Power to work for us. This process of powering up begins with Step Three: We made a decision to turn *our will* and *our lives* over to the care of God. We don't need to have fame, fortune, or weapons for God to be a powerful influence in our lives. We don't have to have special qualities—just be willing to allow our Higher Power to run the show. We become a channel for the work of God. That makes us mighty powerful indeed. We are like a vehicle. Our cars by themselves are nothing. But when we get in, turn them on, and drive, the car seems pretty powerful. Yet, without us in the driver's seat the vehicle can't do much. When we want to power up, we put God in the driver's seat.

In order to be powerful, I don't need this world's power, I have a world of power inside.

However, we now have something in our lives that is much more powerful—a God of our understanding and the decision we made to turn our will and our lives over to the care of that God.
~Chemically Dependent Anonymous P 36

November 18

If you are patient in one moment of anger, you will escape a hundred days of sorrow.
~Chinese Proverb

The time to deal with anger is the moment we feel it, not later. It's of no use to just say, "I don't want to get angry, so I won't," because emotions do not work that way. But we can say, "I don't want to express my anger destructively, so I won't," and that is a promise we can keep. When we feel anger welling up, our first step is to DO NOTHING. We hold back our reaction until we assess the circumstances and decide how we want to handle it. What we need is a plan that we have created ahead of time so that anger doesn't catch us off guard. If we decide not to confront the source of our anger when it flares up, we will still need to let go of it. Getting our anger out doesn't necessarily mean yelling, throwing things, or setting ultimatums. Letting our anger go means letting it be felt and then releasing it. Holding anger in or hurting others with it makes us sick; anger felt and dealt with appropriately keeps us sane and healthy.

**I call my sponsor today and create
a plan to deal with my angry moments.**

Where does my misdirected ANGER hurt others and me? Do I rage, subjecting others or myself to physical, emotional, sexual or verbal violence?
~*Chemically Dependent Anonymous* P 39

November 19

I am not bound to win, but I am bound to be true. I am not bound to succeed, but I am to live up to the light I have. ~Abraham Lincoln

Who among us has not, at one time or another, been preoccupied by our overemphasis on outcomes? We wanted to win at all costs, be right so everyone would know how smart we were and stand out from the crowd. We wanted to be the prettiest, the strongest, the first, or if not those then we tried to be the best at being the worst. We are reminded of the guy who tries to "impress" the ladies with his laundry list of felonies, or the blonde who tells us in a little girl voice that she just "can't" remember directions. The way we play the game doesn't seem to matter, only that we stand out by coming in dead first or dead last. As our integrity grows, our emphasis in life changes. We learn that it isn't crucial to be the best or the worst, and instead we learn to play as a team member. We do not have to be winners or high achievers so much as we must be real human beings. This is what we call "livingup to the light" in CDA.

I stand up, not out, as a light in the Fellowship.

If I can't impress these people with how bad I am, maybe if I take all that energy, try to use it in apositive way, try to do well and work this Program the right way, that will impress them.
~Chemically Dependent Anonymous P 340

November 20

Denial is not a river in Egypt, but you can drown in it. ~Walk Softly & Carry a Big Book

Chemical dependency is a disease of denial. In active addiction we spent an inordinate amount of time trying to convince others that we were not using, that we could handle it, or that it was not a problem. Often, from the repetition, we believed these untruths to be facts. Denial can be a very hard habit to break, but it is one that affects our recovery at its core. Newcomers often secretly believe that they can eventually get to the point where meetings, service work, fellowship, and a sponsor are not needed. It is not uncommon for newcomers to harbor beliefs that they weren't *that* bad, not as bad as the rest of us. This type of belief will affect the way they work the Steps and how they prioritize their actions. It is our job to expose denial as something that can sabotage recovery. We bring denial into the open at meetings, and with our sponsees, so no one views the world through those "old denying eyes."

If "denial" hasn't been a topic in my home group lately, I will suggest it at the next meeting.

Even the professionals now tell us that it is in this return to denial that we set ourselves up to relapse.
~Chemically Dependent Anonymous P 42

November 21

I learned not to be led aside by anything;{…} and a just admixture in the moral character of sweetness and dignity, and to do what was set before me without complaining. ~Marcus Aurelius

Anything taken to an extreme cannot be good for us chemical dependents. Thus, one aspect of our program is the business of restoring balance to our lopsided selves. In relating to others, it seems we either resorted to people-pleasing—always submitting to the whims of others—or we became warriors—taking umbrage with anything anyone else wanted. And, although remaining clean and sober is our number one priority, we do not pursue recovery with such a vengeance that would exclude civility. We learn to temper our pursuit of recovery with a sense of self-worth, which we can extend to others. We maintain graciousness in our thoughts and deeds. We *can* make a difference in our lives and the lives of others, with a hug—not a hammer, compliance—not complaint, and with a grin—not gritted teeth.

I find a way today to take care of my needs without people-pleasing or people-pushing.

A new sense of self-worth is born in us and, along with it, a sense of responsibility to those around us.
~Chemically Dependent Anonymous P 76

November 22

Have we "bought the lie" that getting high is the solution? ~John F-B.

Relapse behavior is nurtured when we buy into the lie that chemical substances can help us deal with every situation. We might envy the "normie" because when things get tough, they have the optionof taking any drug they want, while we must explore other alternatives before considering a chemical one. Maybe we are pissed off because others get to take a pillfor chronic pain, and we are told to use biofeedback. Maybe we want to say, "Screw it. I've been sober X number of years and I still have problems so why not get high?" Yet, we know in our gut that if we have a problem *and* use drugs, then we will have *two problems*. If we relapse, we will lose the ability to process feelings and emotions with any wisdom. We have then put ourselves in charge of the solution. And *that* becomes a problem without a *healthy* solution. Unnecessary drugs are *not* an option in recovery. To think they are is a lie.

If I entertain the thought that a drug is my solution, I will notify my sponsor at once.

We of CDA do not make distinctions in the recovery process based on a particular substance. The basis of our program is abstinence from all mood-changingand mind-altering chemicals{…}.
~Chemically Dependent Anonymous P 3

November 23

Confused, fearful, mistrusting, arrogant, proud, vain, empty, he frantically avoids even looking within himself. ~Father John Doe

We were arrogant and fearful when using. Taking our own inventory never crossed our minds. We could see others as bad examples, but we never looked at the bad example we were. We were afraid to look within because of what we'd find. By pointing to the flaws of others, it was, and still is, easy to skip over our own. Carl Jung believed that our vision would become clear only when we looked inside ourselves. Working through Steps Four and Five, we begin the process of self-introspection. We are required to do it without pointing fingers at others. In Steps Ten and Eleven, we continue the self-introspection, adding prayer and meditation to look within. This allows us to identify the enemy, and it is us! Only the enemy is not the only entity we find within, we also find our own best friend! And that is us too!

**I work on developing a healthy
relationship with my own best friend, me!**

I was spiritually dead but had no desire to stay that way. I was finally ready to look inside and find the stranger I never knew.
~Chemically Dependent Anonymous P 197

November 24

Stopping the negative behavior is true willingness. The defect may still be there eating us up, but we act willing and then progress to Step Seven.
~Young, Sober, & Free

In Step Six, it is not sufficient to merely pray for the removal of a temptation. We must do our part to remove ourselves from the temptation and stop our negative behavior. We all want things to work in a kind of magical way, but Step Six is not passive. We must *not* do the behavior if we are to show our willingness to give it up. Praying for the willingness is not enough. For instance, if we want revenge on someone, we do not take such revenge by sending a nasty email, slashing tires, or poisoning their dog. By *not acting* out in a vengeful manner, we demonstrate our willingness to give up the character defect. We cannot expect God to remove our anger if we want to hold on to resentments. God will not remove our lust if we go to strip clubs. We must cooperate with God by doing the things that let God know we are willing.

**I do not expect God to do for me
what I can do for myself.**

If the readiness IS there, Step Six is completed. Give the image in the mirror a smile. It's time for Step Seven.
~Chemically Dependent Anonymous P 46

November 25

Treachery don't come natural to beaming youth; but trust and pity, love and constancy, they do, thank God.
~Charles Dickens, *Mrs. Lirripers Legacy*

There was once a beaming child in us that expected and dreamed of all the wonderful things of adulthood. Then addiction hijacked our dreams. Yes, we did become treacherous as our addiction took us further and further away from the kids we once were. However, everything that addiction took away, 12-step recovery has given us back tenfold! Active addiction stole our dreams, our morals, our careers, our families, and our ability to feel. In CDA, each one of these things is restored to us as we practice the principles of the Program in all our affairs. We do find within ourselves all the wonderful things we dreamed of as children. Respect, trust, love, and constancy *area* part of our makeup, once again. It is never too late to find and nurture that beaming child within.

I treat my beaming inner child to something special right now: an ice cream cone, a swing in the park, or something I adore.

There's this big kid inside me who still likes to have fun.
~*Chemically Dependent Anonymous* P 348

November 26

Those having religious affiliations will find here nothing disturbing to their beliefs or ceremonies. There is no friction among us over such matters.
~Alcoholics Anonymous P 28

Although some religious bodies may have had trouble accepting 12-step programs, Chemically Dependent Anonymous is an organization that has no trouble accepting them. Some religious organizations, in reaction to 12-step groups working with their drunks, began support groups of their own. We say kudos to them and encourage those groups to assist any addict. We support whatever works and cherish such diversity. Our diversity is found in the chemicals we used, the way we work the Twelve Steps, how we liveour daily lives, and most importantly, our ownunderstanding of God. Honoring this diversity is our greatest strength. CDA is an inclusive 12-step program. We refuse to separate ourselves from each other for reasons of politics, lifestyle, drug histories, and especially religion.

I applaud each person's right to be true to their own understanding of God.

The essentials for belonging are simply these {...}: reaching our own "bottoms" and the eventual grasping of a spiritual understanding that fits our individual needs.
~Chemically Dependent Anonymous P 15

November 27

There is a Law that is called the Law of Attraction. Like attracts Like. Thoughts attract thoughts of their own kind.
~Wally (Vladimir) Kuskoff

We need to act like a winner to attract the winners into our lives. As a practicing addict, we attracted losers, boozers, and users into our life. We didn't want some goody two-shoes around who might question our usage, ethics, behaviors, or even our very selves. No, we wanted people around *like us*. The ones who used like us, lied like us, and got into trouble like us. By being a loser, we attracted losers. Today we wish to attract those worth knowing; so today we must be somebody worth knowing. If we want honesty, we must be honest. If we want respect, we must be respectful. If we want healthy, positive relationships, we must first be a healthy, positive person. We attract what we are, not what we like.

> **I become the kind of person
> I want to attract into my life.**

I was attracted to the people in the Fellowship and found I could relate to many of them. I also liked the very comfortable atmosphere in the group.
~Chemically Dependent Anonymous P 283

November 28

The wise leave aside fleeting pleasures, looking instead to far-reaching happiness. ~Shakyamnni

"I want what I want when I want it" could easily be the chant for our addictive, self-centered, selfish selves. It's not that we didn't work for our pleasures—sometimes it was darn hard work—such as gettingthat trip to Las Vegas, a pair of designer jeans, or a line of coke. But those things never lasted, they were fleeting pleasures. Once we start growing up in the Program, we learn to delay pleasure for our higher good and for the deeper, long-lasting gratifications. But we grow up slowly, letting go of the transitory "highs" like sex, shopping, or chaos a little slower thanwe let go of the chemicals. These quick thrills act like a diversion keeping us from working on the things thatbring lasting happiness like wisdom, serenity, charity, and love. Lasting happiness comes from thinking further into the future than the here and now. Happiness is earned. It is a state of mind rather than something we can just pick up and buy.

I work to become, not to acquire.

I became more dedicated to work but also more dedicated to drugs and alcohol. And I was more sexually active {...}. The candle was definitely burning at both ends.
~Chemically Dependent Anonymous P 331

November 29

> *It is a spiritual axiom that every time we are disturbed, no matter what the cause, there is something wrong with us. If somebody hurts us and we are sore, we are in the wrong also.*
> *~Twelve Steps and Twelve Traditions*

Oh, how we hated this spiritual axiom! *We* are the ones being hurt; *they* are doing the harm; *we* are right; *they* are wrong. All of this may be true; however, we do not have to be sore. It is time for us to own our own feelings. No one can *make* us feel anything. If someone called us a "self-absorbed pissy littlebastard," we might feel quite upset. We say, "I can't control my reactions." But if someone said, "I'll pay you one hundred dollars not to be upset at what I say," and then they call us the same bad names, or worse, and we would *not be upset*. So, given the right circumstances, we *can* control our reactions. Truly, it is up to us to create those circumstances. We know that whatever people call us, it doesn't define us. *We define us*. We own our feelings.

**What I feel is a direct result of what I think.
If it doesn't feel good, I'm not thinking it right.**

I believe that when I depended on that person tomake me feel good, I also gave that person the ability to hurt me.
~Chemically Dependent Anonymous P 184

November 30

The best remedy for those who are afraid, lonely or unhappy is to go outside, somewhere where they can be quiet, alone with the heavens, nature and God. Because only then does one feel that all is as it should be. ~Anne Frank

It is not our Higher Power that leads us into a more stress-filled life. We do that quite well on our own. We pile on the stress by working longer hours to make more money to buy more things. We buy stuff that requires supplies and maintenance, so we need to make even more money. We want to impress people, so we spend a lot of time fussing with our looks and clothes. We make sure that our vehicle is detailed so we look hot while driving up to the meeting. We might make promises to our kids *and* to our group, creating conflicting schedules. This increases our stress because someone is let down. God doesn't clutter up our lives, *we do*. The busier we get, the more important it is to go to the beach, the park, a rooftop, or just sit by ourselves and absorb some peace.

The next time I am too busy to go outside and relax, I go outside and relax *at once*.

After approximately half a year, the busy period was over; the work was done. But I didn't start going back to meetings as I had always done before. And I don't know why.
~Chemically Dependent Anonymous P 224

December

December 1

There is nothing to writing. All you do is sit down at a typewriter and open a vein. ~Walter Smith

One of the most difficult Steps to take is sitting down with that 600-pound pencil and trying to write the Fourth Step. Many a sponsee has offered excuses to their sponsor for not writing this Step. "I already covered this in my journal," or "I can do it in my head," or "I already know I'm a jerk, so I don't need to make myself feel worse." The sponsors in CDA have heard it all. But the Steps don't work themselves. There is a reason for the stipulation that each Step is to be worked a certain way. With the guidance of a caring sponsor, we set about the healing process of *writing* our Fourth Step. Some of us pray to the God of our understanding before we begin writing. We ask for guidance, direction, and the ability to be rigorously honest. It is not easy to list that which we have done wrong while ignoring what *they* have done wrong. By doing so, we face our darkest selves. Step Four places us at the threshold of true change.

I take stock of who I am in Step Four, not just a history of ugly incidents.

If we are making excuses or otherwise avoiding Step Four, we are forgetting Step Three and falling back into self-centered fear.
~*Chemically Dependent Anonymous* P 35-36

December 2

I'm always relieved when someone delivers a eulogy and I realize I'm listening to it. ~George Carlin

Old-timers often say, "Any day above ground is a good day." We might laugh, but there is a deep sentiment here. Our disease is a fatal one. Many of us have known fellow addicts that did not make it into the rooms of CDA before succumbing to one of the numerous fatal aspects of our disease. As we continue throughout the years, we will surely meet others who do not make it. Many of us will have the grim duty of attending funerals and providing support to loved ones left behind. Sometimes they just stop attending meetings, sometimes a medical problem opens the door to unnecessary medications, and sometimes tragedy strikes and rather than use us, they use drugs to get through it. Let today be a reminder that, through the grace of God, we beat the odds. Each day clean and sober is a humongous victory for those suffering from the disease of chemical dependence.

I am grateful to know that my recovery isn't a death sentence—it's a life sentence.

And if I continued to use, I would die. I had a friend who had died from an overdose, and I had seen other friends locked up in jail.
~Chemically Dependent Anonymous P 129

December 3

Know the first principles: There is good in all that is alive. ~Edgar Cayce

There is so much good in the worst of us and so much bad in the best of us that it doesn't behoove any of us to judge another. Putting another down does not raise us up. In fact, to belittle another is to belittle ourselves. So, if we are going to focus on something about another person, it should be on what's good about them—not what's wrong. It should include what's working for them, and what they do that makes life better for their family, the Fellowship, and the world. Even when we don't really like someone, if we work at it, we can find some bit of good in them. Our business is neither to take another's inventory nor to engage in finding fault. To do so would not add a whit to the betterment of our lives. Fault-finding and inventory-taking behaviors *are not* spiritual gifts. That is unless we are taking our own inventories and examining our own faults.

I think of one person that really bothers me, and then I list at least three virtues that person has to offer.

As sick as I am, I've no idea what she can possibly see in me. K. is an angel; she only looks for the good in people and focuses on that.
~*Chemically Dependent Anonymous* P 105

December 4

Feeling right is a strong drug. Some people sacrifice a lot to be right. Ever hear the expression "dead right"? ~John Roger and Peter McWilliams

Everything we do does not have to be competitive. There are many situations that don't call for "winning." Being "right" doesn't make us better than the other guy. As said in A.A., "We ceased fighting anybody or anything." Let us be mindful that fighting includes the need to win and the need to be right. We do not say we are better than this group or that group. We don't claim dominion over addicts with regard to spirituality, literature, or organizational structure. In CDA, we practice Tradition Six by cooperating with other organizations—not competing. We first learn to cooperate with fellow chemical dependents in our home group and then those in other 12-step fellowships. Even though we do not affiliate with other programs, we respect their accomplishments. We continually express gratitude for all those in recovery regardless of which fellowship they attend.

The fastest way I can end an argument and foster cooperation is to give up being right.

A CDA group can cooperate with anyone but never to the point of connecting itself to or sanctioning any of these facilities or enterprises in any manner.
~Chemically Dependent Anonymous P 76

December 5

Remember this, the choices you make in life, make you. ~John Wooden

Sometimes our choices in life boil down to this very basic question: Am I going to give my power to the disease or to my Creator? The answer to this question will determine our willingness to confront our character defects. Whether we fly off the handle screaming in rage rather than pausing to ask God for guidance is evidence of our answer. Giving up our power to the disease could be as serious as deciding to pick up again. We've heard people say, "It was so bad that I either had to pick up or kill myself." How sad it is when our disease has progressed to the point that we believe we are limited to two such choices. By allowing the addict in our head to take over, we have chosen to give our power away. We learn in CDA, that at these moments, rather than give in to the inner addict, we could keep our personal power by making healthier choices such as taking a walk, reading recovery literature, praying, or calling a sober buddy.

I always have two choices in recovery: Take it or leave it. If I leave it, I leave myself no choices.

The choice of whether or not to use will always be there. After staying straight over several 24-hour periods, we have found that we choose not to use rather than return to the misery which brought us here.
~Chemically Dependent Anonymous P 98-99

December 6

Now is the time to do deeper self-care. ~Perry G.

Newcomers often find that managing to abstain from mood-changing and mind-altering chemicals is a mighty tall order. But once our bodies are free of chemicals, and we have worked the Steps, it is time to consider what other areas of our lives may need to be cleansed. Maybe we find that our new spiritual selves are better reflected in different clothes. Maybe we now feel the need to get tattoos removed or perhaps even added! How about a better hair style? What about exercise and an improved diet for our healthier, chemical-free body? Our exterior world may also need cleaning. Keeping our house in order and cleaning our car are forms of respect and deeper care for ourselves. Perhaps we need to go to a dentist. Do we need to visit a doctor about that old injury in need of care? Have we made that appointment? Inrecovery, cleaning up the outside—our exterior world—is as important as cleaning up the inside. This recovery thing is a total package.

**I take care of my body and my space.
This is where I live.**

I care about what I'm doing for the first time. I'm interested in what happens with my life and other people's lives.
~Chemically Dependent Anonymous P 283

December 7

The teacher of God is anyone who chooses to be one. His qualifications consist solely in this; somehow, somewhere he has made a deliberate choice in which he did not see his interest as apart from someone else's.
~A Course in Miracles

The organization of CDA is a perfect set up for all of us to become teachers of God. We have no actual leaders; instead, we are but trusted servants. Our parent organization, A.A., taught us that our "job now is to be at the place where {we} may be of maximum helpfulness to others." Keeping the good of others at the forefront of what we do, we learn to serve. Maybe we don't see ourselves as teachers of God or spiritual guides. Our whole foundation of recovery is based on this important principle: We carry the message to the still suffering chemical dependent. That message is abstinence built on spiritual principles. Recovery *is* a spiritual path. Our whole way of life is based on not seeing our interest as apart from our brothers and sisters both in and out of recovery.

**I am a teacher of God. I am also a student.
I go to a meeting today to listen to my teachers.**

With the help of my Higher Power, my sponsor, co-sponsors, spiritual advisors, and the newcomers, I'm here, one day at a time, for the rest of my life.
~Chemically Dependent Anonymous **P 213**

December 8

In this period of change, you owe it to yourself to remove from your path all obstacles which might prevent you from realizing the new goals you have set for yourself. ~Carlino Giampolo

As the holidays approach, there is a tendency to see them as obstacles to recovery. Holidays can become a catalyst for some of our worst behaviors, cloaked under society's general acceptance of drinking to celebrate. If new to recovery, we might have mixed feelings as to how to celebrate clean and sober. If we have been around a few twenty-four hours, it is our responsibility to make sure that the newcomers do not do holidays alone. We don't just set out flyers and make announcements at meetings about clean and sober events. This is not enough. We reach out to newcomers and discuss their plans, offering suggestions. We need to remember how lost we felt during our first sober holidays. By sharing those memories with newcomers, they become confident in our assurances that they are not alone.

I don't let the Holidays become Helladays for anyone.

What did I ever do with my time before I came into the Program? My life was never full the way it is now.
~Chemically Dependent Anonymous P 114

December 9

Teaching without words is understood by very few. ~Lao Tzu

We are a program of attraction rather than promotion; we do not *sell* sobriety to the newcomer. Throughout our addiction, we had to constantly sell ourselves because our behavior was predictably unacceptable. Now that we are in recovery, however, we must live by the power of example. We can suggest that people go to meetings, read the First Edition, call their sponsor, and seek conscious contact through prayer. The problem is, unless we follow these suggestions ourselves, our words are empty. If someone wants what we have, then they will do what we do. What a great responsibility--as well as an honor! If questioned by a newcomer as to how the Program works, we would not consciously lie. However, if our actions do not match our instructions, lying is exactly what we are doing. We must give up the "do as I say, not as I do" routine. We need always to remember that our actions carry far greater weight than our words.

I behave today as if my sponsees have a video camera in my home, in my car, and at my job.

By setting a good example through actions taken in our sober lives, we are the Program's best public relations representatives.
~Chemically Dependent Anonymous P 83

December 10

I always wanted to be somebody, but I should have been more specific. ~Lily Tomlin

In early recovery, we suddenly realized that we had the rest of our lives ahead of us. Some of us felt compelled to try and make up for "lost time." So, we rushed headlong into a frenzy of activity designed to catch up with the "normal" world. Our sponsors responded by suggesting that we *relax*. They assured us that God has a plan for our lives, and he has not brought us this far simply to let us go. We need only show up for life, report for duty, and do the best we can on a daily basis. Of course, there may be regrets about the past. We may sometimes feel overwhelmed by our current situation. But we remember that every event leading up to today has helped us become the clean and sober person that God wants us to be. So, there is no "lost time" in reality because it is part and parcel of the real us.

I can't go back and make a brand-new start, but I can start now and make a brand new ending.

I'm here to live day by day and to learn who I am {…}. Because of CDA, I have a chance to start my life over{…}.
~Chemically Dependent Anonymous P 199

December 11

There is only one proof for the presence of love: The depth of the relationship; and the aliveness and strength in each person concerned; this is the fruit by which love is recognized.
~Erich Fromm

Genuine personal relationships of depth were almost non-existent when we were using. At the close of our active addiction, if any family remained, it was because of *their* genuineness, not ours. We may have had a hostage that we labeled "a relationship." We may have had people who fed our ego or supplied our drugs that we labeled "relationships." Truthfully, the authentic relationship was seldom authentic from our side of the street. To claim any depth in our relationships would have meant they would have to *really* see us, and then they would be able to prove our insane behaviors to be delusional. Consequently, our first healthy adult relationship probably was the sponsor-sponsee bond. The love our sponsors give to us is the beginning of the process of learning to love another person unconditionally.

I send loving energy to everyone I meet today, *especially* when they don't deserve it.

As Tradition Two tells us, we realize that our God is a loving God. We find that this is not the limited and conditional thing that we sometimes call love. Rather, it is unconditional and beyond our imagination.
~Chemically Dependent Anonymous P 33

December 12

Our public relations policy is based on attraction rather than promotion; we need always maintain personal anonymity at the level of press, radio, and films. ~CDA's Tradition Eleven

We have found that our policy of attraction, not promotion, is entirely effective. This does not mean, however, that we keep our addiction and recovery a secret. When we go before the media, we can say that we are addicts. We can state that today we are clean and sober, but we refrain from saying we are in CDA. Why? Under no circumstances do we want people to think we speak for CDA. That would be playing the big shot. We cannot stay clean and sober *and* play the big shot. In addition, if we kept recovery a secret, there would be nothing for people to be attracted to! So, we let people know that recovery works by our example. We just don't jeopardize CDA, or our recovery, by placing our ego or CDA's reputation on the line. We only break our anonymity with those we would help – friends, acquaintances, co-workers, and any who might need what we have to offer.

I speak *about* CDA, but never *for* CDA.

Furthermore, it would be far too easy for well-intentioned members to put forth their personal beliefs and experiences as a model for sobriety.
~Chemically Dependent Anonymous P 83

December 13

If we can't stop the battles in our minds, how can we expect to stop the battles in the world? We need to begin with ourselves and understand first our own personal conflicts. ~Ruth Fishel

Are we at war with our food, weight, drugs, or alcohol? Do we spend more than we can afford? Are we going back and forth between should I or shouldn't I? Do we struggle with fear versus faith, selfishness versus generosity, and so forth? It is helpful to acknowledge whatever it is with which we struggle. This is no different than the struggle between two people, two families, two communities, or two nations. As we become willing to resolve our own inner struggles, outside issues often resolve themselves. Each time we are willing to look at our own issues, we come to a greater understanding of the conflicts others have. Conflict cannot survive without our participation. When we work on our own inner struggles, these outside conflicts have a wonderful way of disappearing without our participation in them.

I work on stopping my own internal wars before attempting to solve the wars of the world.

Now {my soul} speaks strongly (though not all the time) but my head is still trying to convince me that my soul is wrong. All my life I searched for the truth outside of myself.
~Chemically Dependent Anonymous P 198

December 14

When a woman tells the truth she is creating the possibility for more truth around her.
~Adrienne Rich

Even though we hear repeatedly in CDA that we must practice rigorous honesty, there are many instances in life when telling the truth seems irrelevant. How many times have we told ourselves that to be honest would hurt their feelings? How many times have we thought that it's simply none of their business? We cannot allow ourselves to rationalize the suppression of truth based upon our assumptions of how a person will respond to the truth. We all know the difference between the truth and a lie. So, why do we so often grant ourselves the authority to bend or change the facts according to our own will? We rationalize to ourselves that we know "what is and is not important, and which facts ought to be lied about." Thank God our sponsors' ears are finely tuned to the channel of truth. As we strive, according to Step Twelve, to "practice these principles in all our affairs," truthfulness becomes more than just a concept.

I feel a new freedom toward life, love, and God when I am honest.

After we enter the Program, we come to understand that honesty is still the single most important ingredient in our recovery.
~Chemically Dependent Anonymous P 90

December 15

I can choose peace, rather than this.
~Wayne Dyer

It seems that we need only a moment of adversity to allow our "ism" to take over and create chaos. When something doesn't go our way, we quickly forget our spiritual base and yield to our egoism. Suddenly, a minor oversight becomes a major injustice. Our spouse neglected to compliment our efforts in preparing dinner, so we fume and quickly decide that we won't compliment them on anything! One red light too many, and now we're late for the meeting. It's the city engineer's fault, of course. After all, they control the traffic lights! We know that swearing under our breath for the light to change is useless, but we fuel our frustration anyway by swearing at the light. After moments like these, it is wise to start our day over. By guiding our thoughts back to our morning meditation, we return to our spiritual base and thank God for waking us up clean and sober. Choose peace for this day, not an "ism."

**When an "ism" attacks,
I start over and choose peace.
Now God and I can work together.**

Today I feel at peace with myself in my recovery with my recovery tools. I know what to do to stay clean and sober.
~Chemically Dependent Anonymous P 296

December 16

A man's conscience, like a warning line on the highway, tells him what he shouldn't do - but it does not keep him from doing it. ~Frank A. Clark

Often in our travels we see many signs: Warning! Caution! Do Not Enter! Beware! These signs are posted for our safety. We cannot ignore the warning signs. Our inattention could cause us to take a detour and exit onto Harm's Way. In treating the disease of addiction, it's crucial that we remain alert. Fortunately, those who traveled on the road of recovery before us posted warning signs to guide our journey. Thesesigns can rightfully be called "Warning Slogans:"

- You won't slip if you don't go to slippery places.
- One is too many and a thousand not enough.
- Let go of old ideas.
- Easy does it but DO it.

If we are mindful, these "Warning Slogans" will prevent us from getting lost throughout our day. Otherwarnings consist of what we hear in meetings, from our sponsor, and from our conscience.

Remember, I have a disease that tells me it is okay to ignore the warning signs.

When this happens, we need to see it as a warning sign. Our guides in CDA tell us that whenever we are disturbed or upset, no matter what the situation, WE have a problem.
~Chemically Dependent Anonymous P 58

December 17

The whole problem with people is that they know what matters, but they don't choose it.
~Sue Mond Kidd

We, as addicts, know that gratitude is an essential aspect of recovery. It is often the topic at both meetings and conventions, as well as it is the basis for many of our slogans. But too often, we forget to "keep it green." For many of us, after our initial burst of appreciation for sobriety, gratitude tends to whither. It's not that we don't have the tools to practice gratitude; we just choose not to use them. The choice is ours. Are we addicts that express *gratitude* in our daily lives, or are we addicts that express *attitude* in our daily lives? Here are tools of the Program that we can use today: 1) Make a list of what we are grateful for; 2) Carry the list with us and review it; 3) Recite to newcomers what that list contains; 4) Recite the list to God and say "Thanks."

Just as we use gardening tools to keep our garden green, we use recovery tools to nourish our gratitude, keeping our recovery green, too.

I choose to nourish Gratitude, not Attitude today.

We in CDA believe that gratitude is an action word and that being a trusted servant is a positive way of expressing gratitude and passing on what has been so freely given to us.
***~Chemically Dependent Anonymous* P 72**

December 18

I may be changed by what has happened to me, but I refuse to be reduced by it. ~Maya Angelou

It is an old adage that to grow emotionally and spiritually, one must experience pain. We've all heard the slogan, "no pain, no gain." But seasoned members of CDA have come to understand that the "pain" requirement just isn't so. All growth does not have to be painful, but all pain *can* be used as an experience for growth. It is up to us. Just as we can change our socks and shoes, we can change our attitude and behavior. What is painful is *the resistance to change*, not the change itself. If we never change our socks and shoes, holes will wear in them, we'll get blisters, our feet will smell, and it will be painful. Changing our socks and shoes and changing our attitude and behavior is the same—it keeps us fresh, clean, and able to take steps, painlessly.

**I commit to making one change today
that my sponsor suggests.
I will call and ask now.**

It is said that if we stay the same, we will use again. Recovery is about change and growth.
~*Chemically Dependent Anonymous* P 93

December 19

I must not fear. Fear is the mind killer. Fear is the little death that brings total obliteration. I will face my fear. I will permit it to pass over me and through me. ~The Notebook of Dune

Fear is the mother of all character defects. It is about either not getting what we think we want or losing what we already have. Being afraid is what keeps us from God's plan for us. This is because, in our fear, we take over and try to control the outcome. In the past, we allowed fear to keep us using. Fear has stopped us from being successful in our work lives. We have given into fear in our personal relationships. We have let fear keep us from doing our part in Steps Six and Seven, which keeps God from removing our character defects. Perhaps the worst thing fear has done is lead us to relapse when we don't turn things over to our Higher Power. We cannot wait until we are "fearless," or we'll never do anything. So, we learn to face our fear with the faith of the Fellowship and our Higher Power. Fear faced is fear erased.

I do not let fear fool me. There is nothing God and I can't do together.

The desire to control, like most aspects of the disease, is based on fear. It may show itself as rage, immaturity, manipulation or a hundred other "defects of character," but it is about fear.
~Chemically Dependent Anonymous P 46-47

December 20

Learn to pause ... or nothing worthwhile will catch up to you. ~Doug King

One of the easiest things we can do to lead a more serene life is to simply "pause" before making any major decision or taking any instinctive action. *Stop. Breathe. Ask for guidance.* Making hasty decisions or reacting to situations in a haphazard manner has been a failing for many of us. How many of us have spoken when angry and made the best darn speech that we ever regretted? Who among us has not written a nasty email, clicked before thinking, and caused a lot of embarrassment for ourselves and hurt to others? In the A.A. Big Book they tell us to "pause, when agitated or doubtful, and ask for the right thought or action." When we react hastily and without direction, we sabotage ourselves. This destructive behavior doesn't allow the good things in our new life to catch up with us.

I learn to pause, so something worthwhile can catch up to me.

What will help us get through most situations is to pause, pray, meditate about what the proper action might be and then do it.
~*Chemically Dependent Anonymous* P 90

December 21

It is not a special vocation, it is a universal vocation to all mankind—to be the saints, to be perfect. What does this really mean? It means first and foremost that we must accept ourselves as we are today. ~Father John Doe

Just because we know we will never be perfect doesn't mean that we don't work at it. It is a delicate balancing act—working for perfection *and* accepting ourselves as we are. We may or may not have been seeking a spiritual life when we were using drugs— but the very fact that we were using drugs meant we could not accept who we were at the time. Recovery now means we have a vocation—to strive for perfection, to become a saint, as Father John Doe claims. We know we will not attain perfection but working for it is the most fantastic journey. Accepting our imperfection is part of this journey! We believe that striving for perfection is as perfect as we will ever get on this plane of existence. So, we accept our new vocation of working for that perfection, and we accept the imperfection along the way.

I strive for perfection, and I accept progress.

We have come too far to accept the old ways any longer. However, as we are often reminded, we are not perfect.
~Chemically Dependent Anonymous P 56

December 22

Today I am open to making small changes in my life that lead me, a step at a time, on my spiritual path to recovery. ~Ruth Fishel

We have a fabulous resource in which to know what small changes to put into action on our spiritual path. Our fellowship is a treasure trove of life lessons made available to us through the relationships we build in the rooms. These lessons come from many sources: experiences shared during meetings, our sponsor, our spiritual advisor, and casual conversation with other members before and after the meeting. The important thing is not *who the messenger is*, but that we *listen to their message* and *honestly* give their suggestions a chance to work in our lives. Too often we decide "that won't work for me," without ever trying. Growth comes through change. Change comes by seeing patterns in ourselves *and in the lives of those around us and* being open to the lessons. Are we open to making the small changes? Are we open to hearing the lessons made available through the Fellowship?

I trust I will intuitively know when the time is right to take the suggestions of those around me.

{T}he valuable lessons on the importance of fellowship, keeping honest, open-minded and willingto try, along with the Twelve Steps were slowly absorbed as I began to work the Program.
~*Chemically Dependent Anonymous* P 244

December 23

Feel it; Reveal it; Release it.
~ Brian McLaren, Ron R. *Memorial Retreat 2005*

How do we really turn anything over to our Higher Power? We are asked in Step Three to turn our will and our life over to the care of God. Yet, our will is not something we can see or grasp or send in a package to the great beyond. Because of this, practicing the Third Step can be difficult. We learn that our will and our life can be described as our emotions and thoughts. This is what we really struggle with. Our emotions and thoughts are what we tried to anesthetize with our drinking and drugging. In thepractice of Step Three, we focus on a strong emotion that is bothering us. We let ourselves truly feel this emotion without reservation. We then put a name to the emotion so we can clearly and deeply surrenderto its reality. With time, we ultimately release this strong emotion to God...a God who really cares aboutus and wants us to be at peace.

**Today, I choose one strong emotion
to truly feel. I give it a name, and
then release it to God.**

How surprised and delighted we are to discover that Step Three means strength rather than weakness!
~*Chemically Dependent Anonymous* P 33

December 24

It does not matter how slowly you go as long as you do not stop. ~Confucius

Just as addiction and alcoholism are progressive, so is recovery. Sometimes it doesn't feel good. We feel as if we're moving backwards or downwards, despite how hard we work the Steps. We need to remember that recovery is a process and bit by bit we set our lives in order. It can be likened to cleaning a messy closet. Each piece of clothing that has been shoved into the closet must be separated into piles: some things go back into the closet, some are thrown out, some go into a box to be taken to the thrift store, and some go to other rooms because they didn't belong there in the first place. Little by little the area around and within the closet becomes cleared-up. In the end, the closet itself is finally in order. Although the middle of the process looked messy and felt uncomfortable, if we had stopped there, we would've ended up with an even bigger mess! It's a lot like working the Steps. Keep going ... trust the process. Let it unfold.

I didn't get sick overnight, and I don't expect recovery overnight. I am slow and sure.

Slowly, I started to feel more a part of the world. When I first came into CDA, I was told it had taken me 16 years to get there so I wasn't going to be able to change overnight.
~Chemically Dependent Anonymous P 236

December 25

Often, we let ourselves be limited by the thought that only when we give money and expensive gifts can we do good. If anyone takes a quick inventory of himself, or herself, they will find that they have much to give.
~Reverend Christopher Ian Chenoweth

What can we give during this holiday season that comes from our heart and soul and not our wallets?
Our time: provide a ride to a meeting on Christmas Day; help set-up for a sober holiday event; call a CDA shut-in and listen for as long as they want *on Christmas Eve*.
Our creativity: send homemade recovery cards to institutionalized CDA members; bake cookies with CDA page numbers on them for our next meeting.
Our concern: stop a chain of gossip or hurtful rumor; tell a newcomer we believe in them; give the gift of non-criticism—refuse to say anything bad all day.
Our charity: pass out CDA pamphlets containing a meal coupon on skid-row; give our old meditation books that we no longer use to newcomers.

I will volunteer to lead the meeting on Christmas Eve or Christmas Day.

But if we work for them, the Program promises that we will receive even more important gifts: happiness, freedom, peace, selflessness, wisdom, security, and a sense of God's plan for our lives.
~*Chemically Dependent Anonymous* P 157

December 26

It ain't no disgrace for a man to fall, but to lie there and grunt is. ~Josh Billings

We don't have to worry about other people "dissing" us when we do a pretty good job of it ourselves. To fall is no disgrace. Neither is making a mistake nor failing to succeed at something right away. If we don't get up after the fall, however, to admit and correct a mistake, or if we give up because we didn't succeed the first time, then we invite *dis*grace. How do we "dis" ourselves? We *dis*grace ourselves by becoming *dis*honest. Maybe we rationalize away our defects. We *dis*grace ourselves by becoming *dis*tant from the principles. This is when we fail to recognize they apply to us today. We *dis*grace ourselves when we are filled with *dis*harmony because our focus is on personalities and not the principles. Finally, we *dis*grace ourselves when we are *dis*respectful of our new way of life. We don't lie there and grunt; we get up and apply the principles.

By practicing the principles in all my affairs, I don't allow the *dis*ease to win.

Part of practicing the principles is knowing that we can begin the Steps again at any time.
~Chemically Dependent Anonymous P 68

December 27

Darkness has a hunger that is insatiable and lightness has a call that is hard to hear.
~Indigo Girls

The outside world beckons us to pleasure while sentencing us to pain and darkness. Commercials show booze as being the mother of all aphrodisiacs. Sitcoms depict put-downs and one-liners as a legitimate, hip way to treat others. Radio stations and TV play music that glorifies drugs and denigrates authority. Their lyrics tell us to seek immediate gratification at the expense of anything that gets in our way. It is so easy to slip into the dark side. We need the help of a Divine Source of our understanding to hear the call to something higher. We ask our Higher Power to help us hear the call of that small, still voice within. Asking, however, is only part of the equation. We also must follow our prayer *with action*. That means that we mute the commercials, turn off the sitcom, and refuse to listen to songs that go against our values. We learn not to allow the world's hedonistic background noise to drown out the calls we *want to hear*.

I take the right action and I get the right results.

These actions are utterly contrary to our using behaviors; they express and affirm our recovery work. In short, they declare that we are not who we were and open the door to the person we are meant to be.
~Chemically Dependent Anonymous P 44

December 28

Never step on the same river twice can you, each time the river hurries on, each time he that steps has changed. ~Yoda, *Star Wars*

As the river of time continues to flow, we slowly notice the magnificent changes in ourselves directly due to this new way of life. We become aware of the vast world around us. We see that we can no more return to our troubled past than we can step in the same river twice. Moreover, we cannot return to the *wonderful* past either. Each day that we arise, some of the world has changed and something in us has changed. It is impossible *not* to change. So, when they say that each day is a new beginning, we recognize the truth in this. The river rushes on and the one who steps in it is different today then he or she was yesterday. Change is never painful, but *resisting* change is. So, when we accept that we *can't stop change*, we accept the flow and rejoice in the renewal.

I learn to wear life as a loose garment.

We saw ourselves and our lives change. While this change would occasionally manifest as a dramatic shift, it usually showed up in a gradual way.
~*Chemically Dependent Anonymous* P 64

December 29

The only Zen you find on the tops of mountains is the Zen you bring up there. ~Robert M. Pirsig

A sincere spiritual life begins with a sincerity practiced in our daily life. Most of us understand that being a Christian is not a matter of kneeling by the bed saying, "Now I lay me down to sleep." Likewise, we know that to practice Buddhism is not a matter of standing on a mountain with outstretched arms staring at the heavens. Who of us hasn't seen the weekend warrior attend a sweat lodge and claim to be embracing Native American spirituality? We can posture all we want, but it fools no one—especially not our Higher Power. Spirituality involves effort; and it's not the kind of effort it takes to climb a mountain! It is the effort to go out of our way to pick up someone for a meeting. True spirituality is the effort it takes to open a meeting on a holiday, to hug a drunk that reeks, or to get up at three in the morning to make a 12-step call. It is the effort that it takes to look at the details of what goes on around us and ask, "What would my Higher Power have me do?"

Today I practice some random acts of spirituality.

If I'm not continuously paying attention to my spiritual health and trying to further develop my relationship with God, all the material things in the world aren't going to matter.
***~Chemically Dependent Anonymous* P 227**

December 30

Yes, you can be a dreamer and a doer too, if you will remove one word from your vocabulary: impossible. ~Robert Schuller

Recovery teaches us many things, not the least of which is that *nothing* is impossible in God's world. Once we work our way through the Twelve Steps, we find that our Higher Power has much more in mind than simply stopping the use of mind-affecting chemicals. What God has in mind for us is what we *have in our minds*. God's intentions are reflected inour dreams and in our desires. Our dreams are God's opportunity to demonstrate the power of our way of life. And what a power it is! We have seen convicts whose lives so changed they ended up in charge of the prisons. We have seen high school drops-outs go on to get their PhDs. We have seen former drug pushers reach the top of huge corporations. The big promise of the Twelve Steps is that with clean and sober recovery, anything and everything is possible.

**I rely on God to deliver
the impossible after I've done
what is possible.**

I never could have dreamed, in my using days, that I would be sitting here in a home with my family back together, with a two-week-old son born of the same mother as my first two children.
~*Chemically Dependent Anonymous* P 147

December 31

An optimist stays up until midnight to see the New Year in. A pessimist stays up to make sure the old year leaves. ~Bill Vaughan

This coming year we have an opportunity to choose to look on the bright side of things. On New Year's Eve we can utilize Step Ten and do a review of the past year. Did we keep up with our promises? Were we negative or positive? Were we helpful or contrary? We can also use the Fourth Step questions on pages 37-40 in our CDA First Edition as a basis for a review of our past year. If we are optimistic to begin with, we might choose to help others find our same level of enthusiasm for life. If we find that we have been more on the negative side, we ask our sponsor what actions we can take to lift our spirits. Usually this involves a gratitude list and giving hope to a newcomer. We stay positive by magnifying the good and minimizing the not-so-good. Our New Year can begin on an optimistic note by celebrating all the good we've accomplished.

This coming year, I choose to see my coffee cup as half full rather than half empty.

The clock strikes Midnight. The kisses and hugs begin as we say goodbye to the old and welcome in the new year.
~Chemically Dependent Anonymous P 119

The Twelve Steps

1. We admitted we were powerless over mood-changing and mind-altering chemicals, and that our lives had become unmanageable.
2. We came to believe that a power greater than ourselves could restore us to sanity.
3. We made a decision to turn our will and our lives over to the care of God as we understood Him.
4. We made a searching and fearless moral inventory of ourselves.
5. We admitted to God, to ourselves, and to another human being the exact nature of our wrongs.
6. We were entirely ready to have God remove all these defects of character.
7. We humbly asked Him to remove our shortcomings.
8. We made a list of all persons we had harmed and became willing to make amends to them all.
9. We made direct amends to such people wherever possible except when to do so would injure them or others.
10. We continued to take personal inventory and when we were wrong promptly admitted it.
11. We sought through prayer and meditation to improve our conscious contact with God as we understood Him, praying only for knowledge of His will for us and the power to carry that out.
12. Having had a spiritual awakening as the result of these Steps, we tried to carry this message to other chemically dependent persons and to practice these principles in all our affairs.

The Twelve Traditions

1. Our common welfare should come first; personal recovery depends upon CDA unity.
2. For our group purpose, there is but one ultimate authority—a loving God as he may express Himself in our group conscience. Our leaders are but trusted servants; they do not govern.
3. The only requirement for CDA membership is a desire to abstain from all mood-changing and mind-altering chemicals; including all street type drugs, alcohol, and unnecessary medication.
4. Each group should be autonomous except in matters affecting other groups or CDA as a whole.
5. Each group has but one primary purpose—to carry its message to the chemically dependent person who still suffers.
6. A CDA group ought never endorse, finance, or lend the CDA name to any related facility or outside enterprise, lest problems of money, property, and prestige divert us from our primary purpose.
7. Every CDA group ought to be fully self-supporting, declining outside contributions.
8. CDA should remain forever nonprofessional, but our service centers may employ special workers.
9. CDA, as such, ought never be organized; but we may create service boards or committees directly responsible to those they serve.
10. CDA has no opinion on outside issues; hence the CDA name ought never be drawn into public controversy.
11. Our public relations policy is based on attraction rather than promotion; we need always maintain personal anonymity at the level of press, radio, and films.
12. Anonymity is the spiritual foundation of all our traditions, ever reminding us to place principles before personalities.

The CDA Gifts

As we work the CDA Program of Recovery, our old ideas are replaced with new ways of thinking and new attitudes. We believe these are gifts of a spiritual nature from our Higher Power. When we follow this path, we become healthy, responsible people and live a life of peace, healing and serenity.

1. We live one day at a time with dignity and self-respect.
2. We replace fear and self-pity with courage and gratitude.
3. We accept the changes in our life with optimism and hope.
4. We learn how to lighten up, laugh often and have fun again.
5. We find that challenges and setbacks become the touchstones of spiritual growth.
6. We discover our talents and gifts and unlock their full potential.
7. We experience freedom as we forgive ourselves and others.
8. We are willing to take risks as we choose growth over fear.
9. We develop healthy relationships as we learn how to communicate with respect and love.
10. We believe that love and service are the foundation of a lifetime of happiness.

As we continue on our journey, the possibilities are endless. Remember, "The Sky's the Limit!"

INDEX

A

Abstinence—March 25, April 17, July 10, July 22, Oct. 12, Oct. 31, Nov. 1
Acceptance—March 8, May 20, June 10
Acceptance of Self—Feb. 8, April 5
Action—March 24, April 1, May 5, June 20, July 31, Aug. 9, Oct. 18
Action Steps—March 6, April 29, Sep. 3
Action Words—Jan.12, April 9, April 18, Dec. 9, Dec. 17
Anger—April 13, May 13, July 5, Nov. 18
Attitude—Jan. 7, May 5, Aug. 11
Attitude of Gratitude—April 4, May 5, Aug. 30, Nov. 4, Dec. 17

B

Balance—Jan. 19, April 2, May 25, Sept. 20, Oct. 4, Nov. 3
Belief—Jan. 6, Feb. 25, Nov. 26
Blame—Jan. 3, April 29, June 15, Aug. 2
Blessings—Feb. 21, May 30, Aug. 5, Aug. 21, Sept. 26

C

Carrying the Message—March 5, March 21, Aug. 17, Nov. 12
Challenge—Feb. 29, March 29
Change—Jan. 9, June 28, July 20, Aug. 13, Dec. 22
Change (Resisting)—Aug. 25, Dec. 18
Change (Self)—Feb. 18, March 12, April 27
Character Defects—Jan. 14, Oct. 13, Dec. 19
Choice—Jan. 6, April 1, May 30, Sept. 15, Nov. 16, Dec. 5

Commitment—Jan. 1
Conscious Contact—Jan. 16, March 27, June 9
Control—March 8, May 5, Nov. 29, Dec. 19
Courage—March 2, July 23
Criticism—Sept. 11

D
Denial—Nov. 20

E
Ego—Jan. 28, May 9, July 11, Sept. 9
Emotions—March 2, May 31, June 19, July 8, Oct. 19, Dec. 23
Expectations—April 17, June 6, July 22, Sept. 1

F
Failure—May 30, Oct. 25
Faith—April 30, June 4, Sept. 8, Oct. 27
Fear—Jan 26, Feb. 6, April 27, July 23, Aug. 26, Oct. 11, Nov. 8, Dec. 19
Fellowship—Feb. 1 Feb. 9, March 11, March 20, July 26, Sept. 8, Oct. 20
Forgiveness—Feb. 14, May 13, July 2, Oct. 23
Freedom—April 15, Aug. 28, Sept. 7, Oct. 8
Friendship—Feb. 19, April 11, June 25, Nov. 7, Nov. 23

G
Geographical Cure—May 15, July 16, July 22
Giving it Away—Sept. 5
Goals—Feb. 23, Aug. 9
God's Will—Feb. 17, Feb. 28, March 8, Aug. 7
Gossip—March 14, June 5, Aug. 4, Oct. 17

Gratitude—(*See also Attitude of Gratitude*) Feb. 29,
  April 7, April 18, May 14, Nov. 10
Grief—March 11, April 18, May 1
Guilt—Sept. 16

H
Happiness—Jan. 19, Jan. 24, March 5, March 30,
  June 22, Oct. 21
Happiness Earned—Jan. 7, May 4, Nov. 28
Hate—Jan 14
Helping Others—March 14, April 21, May 11, July 29,
  Aug. 29, Nov. 7
Honesty—Feb. 8, April 6, June 8, Oct. 14, Dec. 14
Hope—June 28, July 1, Sept. 8
HOW—Jan. 2, Oct. 14, Dec. 22
Humbleness—June 6, Sept. 4, Sept. 20, Oct. 31
Humor—Oct. 2

I
Integrity—Feb. 8, Feb. 11, June 1
Inventory—March 28, Nov. 23, Dec. 25
Inventory (Taking other's)—Feb. 22, May 25, Dec. 3
'Ism'—April 24, Dec. 15

J
Joy—March 11, May 14, May 15, Nov. 4
Judge—Jan. 2, Jan. 29, Feb. 7, April 29, July 17,
  Aug. 12
Judgment—April 15, Nov. 15

K
Keeping it Simple—Jan. 23, Feb. 20, June 18, Aug. 3
Kindness—March 25, April 5, Sept. 6, Sept. 21, Oct. 7

L

Laughter—Feb. 1, Aug. 30, Oct. 2
Learning to Live—Jan. 13, Aug. 30, Dec. 10
Lessons—April 13, Dec. 22
Letting Go—April 25, May 21, June 19, July 15, Aug. 25
Life on Life's Terms—May 17, Aug. 3
Listening—Feb 19, June 12, June 23, July 6, July 7, Dec. 7, Dec 22
Listening to Our Heart—Jan 8, March 4, Aug. 4, Aug. 30
Listening to God—April 10, June 9, July 21, Aug. 22, Sept. 24
Listening to Ourselves—July 27
Live and Let Live—Feb. 22, March 17
Living in the Now—Jan. 11, April 13, April 28
Living New Lives—Jan. 9, July 10
Living the Program—Jan. 1, July 30
Lonely—Feb. 2, May 23
Love—Feb. 6, Feb 8, March 9, March 17, April 9, Dec. 11
Love (Accepting)—Feb. 14, March 15
Love (God's)—May 2, May 17, June 19, Oct. 27
Love (Romantic)—July 15
Loving Others—Jan. 29, Feb. 3, April 19, Sept. 5, Sept. 14, Sept. 18, Oct. 7
Lying—April 6, June 3, June 8, Oct. 14

M

Making Amends—July 28, Oct 23
Meditation (See also Prayer/Meditation)—Aug. 16, Sept. 12
Meetings—April 23, June 6, June 27, July 2, Aug. 12, Aug. 15, Aug. 22, Dec. 7

Miracles—May 6, May 18, Nov. 2
Mistakes—July 11, Oct. 9, Oct. 31, Dec. 26
Morality—Feb. 11, Feb. 21, June 3, Oct. 3

N

New Ideas—Aug. 15, Sept. 28
Negative Messages—July 1, Oct. 10
Negativity—Jan 6, May 25, July 17, Aug. 21

O

One Day at a Time—April 13, Sept. 27
Opportunity—Feb. 15, April 18, Aug. 21

P

Pain—Jan. 31, march 29, April 22, July 23, July 29,
 Dec. 18, Dec. 28
Partnership with God—April 10, May 2
Past—Jan 19, Jan 22, April 8, July 31, Sept. 3,
 Sept. 17
Past and Present—Jan 11, Jan. 25, Feb. 29
Patience—May 12, Sept. 1, Sept. 20
Peace—Aug. 18, Aug. 20, Nov. 13, Dec. 15
Perfectionism—May 28
Perseverance—July 22, Oct. 26
Plans—April 28, Aug. 14, Sept. 2, Sept 27, Nov. 18
Plans (God's)—Jan. 26, Feb. 26, March 3, July 4,
 Dec. 19
Positive Thought—March 10, May 25, July 17,
 Sept. 29, Nov. 4, Dec. 31
Powerlessness—Jan. 3, Feb. 12, May 5, June 20,
 Aug. 13
Prayer/Meditation— May 24, June 7, June 9, Oct. 29
Pride—Feb. 24, May 7, July 11

Problems—Jan. 31, March 2, March 10, March 11, April 11, April 18, June 11, Aug. 21, Sept. 12, Nov. 22

Procrastination—April 1

Program of Action—Oct. 13

Progress, not Perfection—May 6, July 11, Sept. 20, Oct. 9, Dec. 21

R

Relationships—Feb. 10, June 7, Sept. 16, Nov. 7, Nov. 23, Nov. 27, Dec. 11

Relationships (Romantic)—March 15, July 15

Resentments—Feb. 7, May 1, June 5, June 17, Oct. 1

Respect—April 6, Aug. 16, Sept. 23, Oct. 6

Responsibility—Jan 3, June 15, July 20, July 28, Aug. 2

Responsibility to the Newcomer—Feb. 3, Feb. 15, April 19, May 19, Nov. 12, Dec. 8

Right Action—Jan. 7, Feb. 21, March 18, July 7, Dec. 20, Dec. 27

S

Secrets—May 31, Dec. 12

Self-esteem—July 9

Self-pity—Feb. 26

Self-will—Jan. 12, March 8, May 4

Serenity—June 10, Aug. 30, Oct. 2

Serenity Prayer—April 16, May 3, May 24, June 5, June 19

Sharing—April 1, April 8, Oct. 9, Nov. 7

Slogans—Jan. 23, April 16, April 28, Dec. 16

Solutions—Jan. 31, March 2, April 1, April 14, July 14, Sept 13, Oct. 20, Nov. 22

Spiritual Awakening—Jan 9, Feb. 22
Spiritual Progress—March 1, July 12
Sponsorship—Feb. 3, March 19, April 21, July 6, July 21, Oct. 22, Dec. 9
Success—Jan. 19, March 23
Surrender—Jan 23, Feb. 17, June 26, Sept. 22, Oct. 28

T
Temper—May 31, July 5
Tolerance—Sept. 20
Turning it Over—June 26, July 13, July 26

U
Uniqueness—Jan 10, June 11
Unmanageability—Jan 3

V
Victim—Jan 6, April 1, April 29, Aug. 2, Oct. 17

W
Wholeness—April 24, June 1, July 18, Aug. 27, Oct. 4
Willingness—Jan. 9, March 8, April 21, Sept. 14, Nov. 24
Wisdom—Jan. 23, March 2, April 16, June 29, Oct. 18
Wonder—Jan 16, Oct. 15
Working the Steps—Jan 5, May 16, Dec. 24

Y
Yesterday, Today, and Tomorrow—March 31, June 20, July 1, Sept. 3

CDA Outreach Program

The purpose of the CDA Outreach Program is to distribute CDA literature to institutions that carry the message of recovery to those who still suffer from chemical dependency. The Outreach Program is also able to help jump-start new CDA meetings.

If you or your organization would like to start a CDA meeting in your area, or would like information on how to obtain CDA literature for your institution, contact us at 1-888-CDA-HOPE or outreach@cdawebsitedev.com.

CHEMICALLY DEPENDENT ANONYMOUS
General Service Office
P.O. Box 423
Severna Park, MD 21146

www.cdaweb.org